Urban Memory and Visual Culture in Berlin

Cities and Cultures is an interdisciplinary humanities book series addressing the interrelations between contemporary cities and the cultures they produce. The series takes a special interest in the impact of globalization on urban space and cultural production, but remains concerned with all forms of cultural expression and transformation associated with contemporary cities.

Series editor: Christoph Lindner, University of Amsterdam

Urban Memory and Visual Culture in Berlin

Framing the Asynchronous City, 1957-2012

Simon Ward

Amsterdam University Press

Cover illustration: Bauwochen exhibition tour of the urban motorway between the Funkturm and Jakob-Kaiser-Platz, at the 'Nordwestbogen' bridge in Charlottenburg. 9 September 1962. Photograph: Karl-Heinz Schubert. Courtesy of Berlin Landesarchiv

Cover design: Coördesign, Leiden
Lay-out: Crius Group, Hulshout
Printed and bound by CPI Group (UK) Ltd, Croydon, CR0 4YY

Amsterdam University Press English-language titles are distributed in the US and Canada by the University of Chicago Press.

ISBN	978 90 8964 853 2
e-ISBN	978 90 4852 704 5
DOI	10.5117/9789089648532
NUR	670

The cathedral leaves its locale to be received in the studio of a lover of art
– Walter Benjamin

Berlin has a lot of empty spaces... I like the city for its wounds.
They show its history better than any history book or document. [...]
[The] empty spaces allow the visitor and the people of Berlin to see through the
cityscape [...], through these gaps in a sense they can see through time.
– Wim Wenders

ERAP 718116

Table of Contents

Acknowledgements

This book has its origins in the paths I walked across the open space between the Potsdamer Platz S-Bahn station and the Staatsbibliothek in the winter of 1992, during a year I spent in Berlin as a part of my doctoral studies. I did not possess a camera at the time, so I do not possess what would now be a rich repository of photographs of that strange, liminal wasteland in the middle of the former divided city. Of course, I can always search Flickr.

Ten years later I returned to Berlin on a scholarship from the Berlin Parliament (the Studienstiftung des Abgeordnetenhauses von Berlin), to begin work on a tentative project on the ruins of Berlin. Potsdamer Platz was certainly different, but more crucial was the renewing of the intellectual friendships I had made during that first visit, as I sought to think through some of the conundrums with which the cityscape confronted me. More than another ten years on, and thanks in large part to the support of AHRC Research Leave Scheme from September 2009 to January 2010, regular research assistance from the Carnegie Trust for the Universities of Scotland and the British Academy, and research leave periods granted by my former employer, the University of Aberdeen, this book has finally found a form.

My thanks are due, primarily, to all those editors who read and commented so carefully on my ideas as they crystallized over the years. Thanks are also owed to the many friends and colleagues in Berlin, Aberdeen, Durham, and elsewhere, who have given of their time in indulging, and questioning, my obsession with the ruins of this city. A non-exhaustive list must include David Barnett, Martin Dammann, Paul Flaig, Katherine Groo, Uta Kornmeier, Karen Leeder, Christoph Lindner, Jonathan Long, Nikolaj Lubecker, Arwed Messmer, Bill Niven, Dora Osborne, Joachim Seinfeld and Geoff Westgate.

My greatest thanks go to my enthusiastic children, Verity and Dominic, who provided great company on recent tours of Berlin, and above all to my acutest editor and least melancholic reader, my wife, Janet Stewart, without whose unwavering support and belief this work would not have seen the light of day.

As is the nature of such a long-term project, fragments of it have been previously published in different forms and contexts, none of which specifically addressed the book's central question of urban memory. Material that is reused here in Chapter Two first appeared with Wiley in a special issue of *German Life and Letters* in 2010 dealing with 'Cityscapes of the GDR', and more recently in *Edinburgh German Yearbook 2016* (Camden House). Some of the writing in Chapter Three previously appeared in Peter McIsaac and Gabriele Mueller's 'Exhibiting the German Past' (University of Toronto Press, 2015). Some material in Chapter Four previously appeared in Christoph Lindner's volume *Globalization, Violence and the Visual Culture of Cities* (Routledge, 2009) and *Berlin: Kultur und Metropole in den zwanziger und seit den neunziger Jahren* (iudicium, 2007), and other parts more recently in Karen Leeder's special edition of *New German Critique* (Duke University Press, 2015) on 'Figuring Lateness in Modern German Culture'. I am grateful to all these publishers for allowing me to reuse this material as part of a coherent whole.

Introduction

Berlin and the Question of 'Urban Memory'

Contemporary Berlin, a city scarred by the twentieth century, displays its past on almost every street corner, it would seem. The upheavals it has experienced have not just been political, but have also been accompanied by a series of radical physical transformations in the built environment. A large body of literature has been produced on the sophisticated memory work that has been undertaken in Germany, and Berlin in particular. One of those authors, Aleida Assmann, asserts that German places of memory cannot be adequately understood through Pierre Nora's model of *lieux de mémoire*, in which modernity's process of accelerated renewal and obsolescence generates, in a compensatory reaction, the proliferation of museums and sites of memory. Assmann ascribes this to the fact that the traumatic sites are the locations of acts of atrocity that surpass human understanding.[1] Contemporary Berlin's memory landscape has been read almost exclusively through its expression of Germany's troubled national past, be it National Socialism or the German Democratic Republic. This book is not primarily concerned with the narrative elaborations of identity that take place around sites of National Socialist atrocity in Berlin. That work has been done, by amongst others, Brian Ladd and Rudy Koshar, as well as Andrew Webber, who takes a psycho-topographical approach to the city in *Berlin. City of the Twentieth Century*, Karen Till, who focuses on the politics of contemporary place-making in *The New Berlin*, Jennifer Jordan, who investigates processes of place-making in *Structures of Memory* in relation to the demands of 'real estate', and Janet Ward, who devotes a section to Holocaust memorial architecture in her study of *Post-Wall Berlin*. The validity of this earlier work is assured. This engagement with the material past has in earlier work generally been framed in terms of 'remembering well'.[2] What might it mean to remember well, beyond the frame of national trauma?

This book evolved at the same time as a spatial turn in Berlin urban studies that is less tied to narratives of the national past. This has much to do with the desire to see the post-unification period as something radically different from what came before. This turn has produced work that explicitly deals with the politics of urban redevelopment in post-unification Berlin (Colomb, 2011), as well as Barbara Mennel and Jaimey Fisher's 2011 heterogeneous edited collection, *Space, Place, and Mobility in German Literary and Visual Culture*. While I endorse Colomb's shift from identity politics

1. Photograph: Axel Mauruszat.

to the politics of space, this book offers a historical trajectory that suggests a
continuity in forms of urban memory that cross the ostensible caesura of the
fall of the Wall that determines studies such as Colomb's and Janet Ward's.
Similarly, Colomb examines the discourses of place marketing beyond
the merely architectural production of place, while this book moves in a
different, if related direction, towards a close reading of how the encounter

with place has been framed over the past fifty years, and of the aesthetic practices that have emerged in that context.

To address this question, the book's focus is on Berlin as a generic city (both a polemical exaggeration and a necessity, in order to move away from the specificity of the 'traumatic' city), and its theoretical frameworks are taken from thinkers who have thought about place and the city in more abstract terms. Berlin's places of memory are, however, not solely traumatic sites. The Anhalter Bahnhof, the site photographed in figure 1, is a useful example to start with as an ambivalent location of various urban pasts. This book focuses not on what happened 'here', in the past, but what happened *to* the site, in terms of demolition, reconstruction, and remediation, tracing how the remembrance of place has been constructed in the city in reaction to radical material upheavals in the city, both in East and West. Both halves in the city become paradigmatic experiments in modernist urban reconstruction in the post-war era, albeit at slightly different paces. While the east of the city was initially dominated by Stalinist architectural dictates, by the mid-1960s urban planning practices were fundamentally in line with those which had dominated in the western half of the city since the end of the war (in theory), and from the mid-1950s (in practice). Responding to this radical reconstruction, many interventions in, and framings of, urban sites in the built environment in both East and West Berlin over the past fifty years have sought to recover an experience of place in the city. Berlin's varied *lieux de mémoire*, some of which are of course sites of traumatic past experience, have not merely had constructed narratives around them, but have also been explorations of the dynamics of place memory in the city. This 'place memory work' responds to what has been experienced as a loss of place in two related forms; the (re)construction of urban milieux, and the curation of the 'wounds' or 'empty spaces' of the city which enable a critical perception of time in the city.

Over the course of the past fifty years, Berlin has become an increasingly internationally inflected city, not so much in political and economic terms but in the sense of being an international cultural hub, where architects, artists and tourists have gathered. This particular city can provide key insights into how the mechanisms of urban memory – a term that will be elaborated in this introductory chapter – have developed more generally in an era of globalization, migration, and the concomitant effects of gentrification, tourism and the acceleration and synchronization of experience. The development of urban memory is not simply a phenomenon of the two decades since unification, but has been central to the development of Berlin's memory culture since the late 1950s. As we shall see, the question

of how to shape attention to place applies to all sites of an urban past that
are threatened by urban transformation. 'Remembering well' ultimately
involves remembering how to attend to place, so that, following Maurice
Halbwachs, one might *first of all* remember how to remember in the city.

This introductory chapter begins by building a framework for approaching
urban memory as a form of place memory in the city. Place memory is taken
up through the work of Maurice Halbwachs and Paul Connerton, both of
whom juxtapose the abstractions of modernity with an authentic experience
of place. Halbwachs's conception of 'place memory' as a spatial image opens
up questions of visualization and the role that visual culture and its technologies of place-making play in 'remembering well'. The visuality implied in
the spatial image is primarily theorized through Andreas Huyssen's concept
of the 'museal gaze' which is modified in order to incorporate theoretical
perspectives on the dynamics of place memory in modernity as well as the
urban subject, attention, and the 'memory value' of the built environment.
This book's history of place memory, and the history of theorizations of place
memory, in Berlin since 1957 is structured around the way that this 'museal
urban gaze' emerges in response to the synchronic modernist city. The
introduction then takes a specific example of urban memory work (Hans
Hoheisel's installation at the Brandeburg Gate in 1997) as a way of illustrating
the method of interrogating the museal urban gaze. The chapter concludes
with an outline of the book's structure and description of its content.

After 'place memory'

In many discussions of the topic, place memory is invoked after the fact,
after its disappearance, as something authentic and spontaneous in contrast
to an inauthentic modernity that has forgotten how to remember place
'well'. In Pierre Nora's work, this opposition is presented as a contrast
between 'true memory [...] which has taken refuge in gestures and habits,
in skills passed down by unspoken traditions, in the body's inherent self-
knowledge', and 'memory transformed by its passage through history, which
is nearly the opposite: voluntary and deliberate, experienced as a duty, no
longer spontaneous.'[3] Another version of this melancholy lament can be
found in Paul Connerton's 2009 book on *How Modernity Forgets*. Although
Connerton does not refer to Nora, and understands modernity's effects
quite differently, they both juxtapose the abstractions of modernity with
an authentic experience of place.

For Connerton, modernity's erosion of place memory through those 'processes that separate social life from locality and from human dimensions',[4] is ascribed to 'the repeated intentional destruction of the built environment', removing the 'architectonic props' necessary for the production of place memory. For Connerton, 'modern space' destroys place memory because it is 'space wiped clean'.[5] This account of modern space echoes Henri Lefebvre's conception of 'abstract space' – space conceived as a commodity with 'exchange value', where 'the tendency to homogenization exercises its pressure and its repression with the means at its disposal: a semantic void abolishes former meanings.'[6]

Crucially, abstract space *tends* towards homogeneity, but what, then, of the surviving remnants and their 'former meanings', as well as the mode of encountering them? This book offers Berlin as a counter-example to Connerton's over-dramatization of the effects of modernity, by analysing two ways in which the dynamics of place memory are generated within the city as 'urban memory': first, how the repair of urban environments has sought to revivify processes that connect social life to locality; and second, how the encounter with material remnants left behind by the successive reconstructions of the urban environment since the end of the Second World War have been subject to technologies of urban memory production. To be sure, neither of these is entirely 'authentic', but neither are they simply to be dismissed as 'mere' artifice.

Neither of the Assmanns's conventional terms of 'communicative' or 'cultural' memory adequately capture the meaning of 'urban memory', which contains elements of both, and indeed spans the conceptual division between the two, as will be discussed below and throughout.[7] Urban memory describes a mode of encounter that has its roots in Maurice Halbwachs's work on collective memory and in particular a close reading of his analysis of the relationship between place and social memory.[8] In his essay on 'Space and the Collective Memory', Halbwachs offers a subtle way of thinking about how the rupture of modernity affects the working of place memory. He begins by sketching how collective memory is present in the built environment: 'the forms of surrounding objects [... stand] about us a mute and motionless society. While they do not speak, we nevertheless understand them because they have a meaning easily interpreted.'[9]

'Interpretation' is not here the work of allegorical deciphering: each detail of these places has a meaning intelligent only to members of a particular group, for 'each portion of its space corresponds to various and different aspects of the structure and life of the society' and 'each object appropriately placed in the whole recalls a way of life common to many men. The meaning is thus self-evident to the group whose spatial practices are imprinted upon that particular environment.'[10] Not only this, but the relationship is recipro-cal: 'place and groups have received the imprint of the other', or, in the words of Henri Lefebvre, such physical surroundings are a 'faithful mirror' of the collective.[11] This kind of environment facilitates a collective experience and it is this kind of 'communicative' relationship between society and space that has been envisaged by those who have sought to restore a memory of collective experience of the built environment to Berlin over the past fifty years.[12] In Berlin, this is a form of urban memory after the fact that emerges as a resistance to the radical transformations in the Berlin cityscape since the end of the Second World War, which saw large parts of the city being restructured to construct a modern urban environment configured around the automobile and the automobilization of experience.

'Place memory' and the 'spatial image'

Unlike Connerton, Halbwachs addresses how local tradition responds to urban transformation, investigating how 'habits related to a specific physi-cal setting resist the forces tending to change them. [...] This resistance best indicates to what extent the collective memory of those groups is based on spatial images.'[13] For Halbwachs, such resistance, 'the force of local tradition', 'manifests itself in physical objects, which serve as its image.'[14] Collective memory only becomes visible at the moment of its threatened oblivion; these physical objects at that moment are framed as 'spatial images'.[15]

The term 'spatial image' implies that the embeddedness of the object in a spatial framework is central to its function as a site of resistance to the wiping clean of modern space. Local tradition calls attention to the site as having a connection to its collective past and frames it as a 'spatial image' that is read against the (otherwise anonymous) abstracting forces of urban transformation. The 'framing' is crucial, for it must not simply preserve the object, but also the mode of encounter.[16] The 'spatial image' thus retains not only physical traces of the location, but also the traces of the mode of encountering that place; 'image' in this sense implies a network of relations rather than simply a visual object. In unpacking the spatial images of the past fifty years in Berlin, a visual culture approach which understands the image in this way is crucial to interrogating how a spatial image functions as place memory in a 'memory contest'. This is not a contest in the conventional sense, where there is a contest over the meanings and narratives to be attributed to a particular location. Rather it is a contest over *whether* a physical location has any memory value and how it is to be encountered. The mode of encounter ultimately determines the production of place.

Connerton and Halbwachs describe the dynamics of place memory in ways that help us understand what kind of encounter is imagined. The key to these descriptions is that they describe a *former* mode of encounter. While Connerton apparently describes an 'existing state', his argument for the forgetfulness of modernity is predicated on its disappearance.

Connerton:

> We experience a locus *inattentively*, in a state of distraction. If we are aware of thinking of it at all, we think of it not so much as a set of objects that are available for us to look at or listen to, rather as something which is inconspicuously familiar to us. It is there for us to live in, to move about in, even while in a sense we ignore it. We just accept it as a fact of life, a regular aspect of how things are.[17]

Halbwachs:

> Nowadays, in an old church or convent, we *inattentively* walk on flag-stones marking the location of tombs and don't even try to decipher the inscriptions engraved in the stones on the sanctuary floor or walls. Such inscriptions were continually before the eyes of those who worshipped in this church or belonged to this convent. The space that surrounded the faithful was permeated with religious meaning by means of funeral stones, as well as altars, statues, and pictures of the saints. We fashion a well-nigh inaccurate conception of the way their memory arranged remembrances of ceremonies and prayers, of all the actions and thoughts that make up the devout life, if we are ignorant of the fact that each found its place in a specific location.[18]

Connerton and Halbwachs both use the term 'inattentively'. For Connerton, the relationship to place has the connotations of a 'tactile', unmediated experience of the built environment, as Walter Benjamin formulates it in his 'Work of Art' essay. For Halbwachs it indicates a modern 'lack of attention'. Connerton's collective is still intimately connected to its place; Halbwachs's collective is unable to perceive how the collective memory of place works, because it has forgotten. There are two tasks which Halbwachs sets this 'inattentive' visitor (or tourist): first, to recall how earlier societies remembered spatially, but second, implicitly, to begin to relate to space as they did. The recovery of the place's former 'meaning' is not important; more significant is the attempt *to recover how place is remembered*:

> Space is a reality that endures: since our impressions rush by, one after another, and leave nothing behind in the mind, we can understand how we recapture the past only by understanding how it is, in effect, preserved by our physical surroundings. It is to space – the space we occupy, traverse, have continual access to, or can at any time reconstruct in thought and imagination – that we must turn our attention. Our thought must focus on it if this or that category of remembrances is to reappear.[19]

There are three key points to be made in relation to the above passages in terms of the dynamics of place memory. The first is the sense of collectivity: that the mode of encounter is not predicated on an atomized 'modern' individual whose cognitive engagement with the site is the determining factor, but on a body that is part of the collective body of the city. In these passages, Halbwachs has moved beyond Connerton's collective 'we' that experiences the built environment as lived memory, to a belated collective 'we' that is being asked to recover the past experience of collective space.

The second key dynamic of place memory involves the recovery of a particular mode of attention to space. Here again, Halbwachs's position is subtler than Connerton's, as it recognizes that the past is no longer self-evidently present in conditions that constrain attention to the built environment. For Halbwachs, it would appear, we don't attend to space anymore.

The third aspect is the encounter with the authentic, surviving material environment. The material object is accorded an auratic power. This question of the authenticity of place is central to the work of Halbwachs and Connerton, where place is attributed natural qualities in terms of how it evolves. A cityscape is, however, also an artificial intervention into landscape. In his essay on the 'Work of Art in the Age of Its Mechanical Reproduction', Walter Benjamin argues that the authenticity of the art object is 'interfered with' when it is removed from its unique site by the means of mechanical reproduction. Although he claims that 'no natural object is vulnerable on that score', he also, in the same paragraph, argues that the authenticity of a landscape is depreciated when it 'passes in review before the spectator in a movie.'[20] A landscape or indeed a cityscape is the product of an encounter between the viewer and an environment, so that an environment is not in and of itself a 'unique sight', as the position of the viewer is not the same each time. That encounter is also dependent on the position of the viewer *vis-à-vis* the object. For Benjamin, implicitly, film provides a reproduction that alters the duration of the encounter. As Benjamin noted in his 'Work of Art' essay, 'historical testimony rests on the authenticity, [of the object], and [authenticity], too, is jeopardized by reproduction when substantive duration ceases to matter. And what is really jeopardized when the historical testimony is affected is the authority of the object.'[21] A key question for this study is the relation between the material object and the idea of its testimony of substantive duration, a duration grounded not just in the longevity of the object, but in the duration of the encounter in the generation of the auratic effect. This is a question we shall address through the concept of the 'museal gaze', as outlined below.

Halbwachs proposes his model of place memory (which is predicated, like all theories of place memory, on a stable built environment) from a point after which it has ceased to be the dominant mode of relating to space. It is not, like Connerton's, a model steeped in nostalgia, but a call for a revitalization of a particular attention to material space. It is a call that comes *after* the traditional coordinates of place memory have been undone by the forces of homogenization and distraction in the city.

The spatial image of the synchronic city

How do these forces of homogenization work in the city? If place memory is generated not only by the physical site, but also through the mode of encounter with it, and the concomitant production of 'spatial images', then whatever threatens or attenuates place memory must also be related to the organization of the perception of the built environment. The role played by homogenization lies not just in the demolition of places, but also in the structuring of a way of encountering the city.

In Michel de Certeau's essay on 'Walking in the City', the 'concept-city [...] provides a way of constructing space on the basis of a finite number of stable, isolatable and interconnectable properties.'[22] This concept-city, a synonym for modernist urban planning of the post-war era, sees the 'substitution of a nowhen, or of a synchronic system for the indeterminable and stubborn resistances offered by traditions.' This is not just the organization of the gaze upon the city (in the 'exaltation of the scopic drive' which gazes down on New York from the top of the World Trade Center), but of the perception of time in urban space.

By contrast, Aleida Assmann's discussion of 'places of memory' is underpinned by a distinction between abstract space and meaningful place:

> 'Space' is a neutralized, de-semiotized category of fungibility and dispos-
> ability; attention directs itself [richtet sich] towards the 'place' with its
> enigmatic, unspecified significance [Bedeutsamkeit].[23]

Attention plays a key, if rather unacknowledged role in her construction
of this distinction. The implication of Assmann's assertion is that while
'place' involves attentiveness, 'space' does not. The perception of space
does however involve a mode of attention. For Assmann, 'the concept of
space contains a potential for planning that points to the future', whereas
De Certeau points to a 'nowhen' in the concept-city, a time without past
or future. The concept-city, and its designers, imagine space without historical time; the concept-city is a disciplinary framework that constructs
a synchronic experience of an interchangeable space, in which time is
activity. This shapes a mode of encounter with the city in modernity that
is instrumentalized towards systemic functioning, is goal-oriented and
result-driven. Walter Benjamin in his 1932 essay on 'Experience and Poverty'
discusses the concomitant loss of experience (*Erfahrung*), when, according to Benjamin, the city is experienced (*erlebt*) in the mode of attention
required by the synchronic rhythms of factory conveyor-belt production.[24]
Attention is organized as a functional, calculable capacity driven by the
sensory-motor requirements of a synchronically organized, interchangeable
environment.

'Place' is not just the product of attentiveness in itself – one can be
attentive to the traffic infrastructure, after all – but a different kind of
attention grounded in experience, and frequently defined in opposition
to a synchronic gaze that privileges the visual over other senses, following what Lefebvre terms the 'logic of visualization'. The synchronic gaze
produces a form of 'civic seeing', in Tony Bennett's terms, which models
the 'good citizen' understood as one who 'maintains perceptual synthesis'
by learning 'how to isolate sentiments in the sensory field at the expense
of others',[25] and is thus best adapted to the most efficient circulation of
goods and consumers.

The synchronic urban gaze produces a particular 'regime of attention'
which emerges from 'the civic lessons embodied in [these] arrangements'
which 'are to be seen, understood, and performed' by the citizens, as Bennett describes the organization of attention in the modern museum at the
beginning of the twentieth century.[26]

David Frisby suggests a way out of this perception of a determinist cityscape:

> If our experience of modernity is to be any more than the endless affirmation of the ever-new that is presented to us on the surface of everyday modern life, then it must access the contradictions and differentiations of modernity that exist within it.[27]

For Frisby, the subjective activity of flânerie 'seeks to make sense of the fragmentary experiences and images of the metropolis, to search for the traces of origin, [...] following traces, including memory traces, in order to reconstruct the past.' Frisby focuses on the 'making sense'; the focus in this book is how this access to the temporal contradictions and differentiations of modernity is facilitated. A more differentiated perception of time as layered, as including past and perhaps even future, rather than simply a synchronic present, would be what De Certeau describes as an 'obstacle' to efficient urban circulation, as it forms a resistance to the synchronic rhythms of the modernized urban environment. The 'obstacle' in this study is the 'spatial image' of place memory, both a material site and a mode of perception, a network of relations. How does the encounter with that obstacle come about?

The spatial image of the asynchronous city

'Memories often cleave to the physical settings of events', asserts Brian Ladd at the beginning of *Ghosts of Berlin*, but it is precisely how this 'cleaving' *takes place* that is at stake here, how it is done?[28]

> Berlin has a lot of empty spaces... I like the city for its wounds. They show its history better than any history book or document. [...] [The] empty spaces allow the visitor and the people of Berlin to see through the cityscape [...], through these gaps in a sense they can see through time.[29]

How does the asynchronous city become visible to the body moving through the city? The position of Wim Wenders in the quotation above is echoed by Karen Till's observation that 'open wounds create an irritation in everyday space through which past collides with present.'[30] Such ambiguous encounter with the material remnant in the urban environment can be described through Andreas Huyssen's term, the 'museal gaze'. In his 1994 collection of essays, *Twilight Memories*, Huyssen observed that the boundaries of the contemporary museum were becoming ever less distinct. Huyssen embraced this development, arguing that it undid the traditional mission of the museum as the purveyor of an exclusionary, conservative narrative of nation.[31] In this, Huyssen was in line with Tony Bennett, who, in his essay 'Civic Seeing: Museums and the Organization of Vision', charts the shifting 'regimes of vision' in museums, whereby 'the directed forms of vision that have dominated Western museum practices since the Enlightenment' have 'given way to more dialogic practices of seeing which, in enabling a greater degree of visual give-and-take between different perspectives, might prove more conducive to the requirements of "civic seeing" in culturally diverse societies.'[32]

Beyond this embracing of diversity, there was another positive element that Huyssen identified, a 'newfound strength of the museum and the monument in the public sphere.'[33] This strength has, on the surface, little to do with Huyssen's celebration of the post-national museum. Rather, Huyssen surmised that it might have 'something to do with the fact that [the museum and the monument] offer something that television denies: the material quality of the object.'[34] Huyssen designated this, rather cursorily as 'the museal gaze'.[35]

Huyssen privileged this particular aspect of the museum experience in reaction to postmodern critiques of the museum in the 1980s, and in particular in response to Baudrillard's assertion that musealization is 'the pathological attempt of contemporary culture to preserve, to control [and] to dominate the real.'[36] Musealization, in this critique, 'simulates the real'. For Huyssen, the 'museal gaze' redeems the idea of a 'museal' that enables a connection to the real. In the case of both the museum and the monument, there is a 'live gaze' that interacts with the object.[37] For Huyssen, the auratic power of the object is produced by this live gaze:

> Objects of the past have always been pulled into the present via the gaze that hit them, and the irritation, the seduction, the secret they may hold is never only on the side of the object in some state of purity, as it were; it is always and intensely located on the side of the viewer and the present as well.[38]

It is the live gaze that endows the object with its aura, much as Pierre Nora argues of *lieux de memoire* that 'even an apparently purely material site becomes a *lieu de memoire* only if the imagination invests it with a symbolic aura.'[39] For Huyssen, however, the museal gaze is dependent on the live presence both of the observer and of an object, whose key qualities are its materiality and its opacity, and the fact that:

> the more mummified an object is, the more intense its ability to yield experience, a sense of the authentic. No matter how fragile or dim the relation between museum object and the reality it documents may be, either in the way it is exhibited or in the mind of the spectator, as object it carries the register of reality which even the live television broadcast cannot match.[40]

Distancing himself from the postmodern critique of the museum, Huyssen was clearly still invested in the ideal of the rational, attentive, well-ordered museum-going public, an ideal which, as Bennett suggests, was originally founded on the rejection of 'the clouding, diverting, hynoptic, dazzling, numbing, or shock effects of more popular visual technologies' of urban life at the end of the nineteenth century.[41] At the end of the twentieth century, Huyssen's museal gaze is a counterpoint to the 'television gaze'; its encounter with the 'register of reality' defines the anamnestic dimension of the material object. This anamnestic dimension, which Huyssen terms 'memory value', needs to be distinguished from the transmission of critical historical knowledge and understanding. Rather, the museal gaze 'may be said to [...] reclaim a sense of non-synchronicity and of the past.[42] This aligns Huyssen's conception of the 'spatial image' of the object with De Certeau's in the appreciation of the asynchronous. Not only does Huyssen value asynchronicity, but in the process he alludes to a form of attentiveness:

> The older an object, the more presence it can command, the more distinct it is from current-and-soon-to-be obsolete as well as recent-and-already obsolete objects. That also may be enough to lend them an aura, to reenchant them beyond any instrumental functions they may have had at an earlier time. It may be precisely the isolation of the object from its genealogical context that permits the experience via the museal glance of reenchantment.[43]

Not only does Huyssen use the term 'glance' here, to suggest an almost involuntary, indirect encounter with the object, but, in elaborating the 'memory value' of the material object, he is also close to Alois Riegl's definition of the contingent 'age value' of the unintended monument.[44] The 'age value' of the material object bears testimony to the passing of time, rendering time visible where it would otherwise be invisible.

Huyssen's museal gaze produces, in the interaction between live spectator and opaque material object, an awareness of past time that is at odds
with a synchronous, televisual present. Riegl's unintended monuments were
implicitly situated in public space and, crucially, Huyssen sees the museal
gaze as operating both in conventional museums and in the museum in an
expanded, amorphous sense, in relation to monuments in 'reclaimed public
space, in pedestrian zones, in restored urban centres, or in pre-existing
memorial spaces.'[45]

An important caveat must however also be applied to Huyssen's museal
gaze, and that is his use of it as an academic practice when confronted with
the built environment of Berlin. At one point in his seminal essay 'The
Voids of Berlin', Huyssen recalls his encounter with the empty space of
post-unification Potsdamer Platz. As he walks across this space, he writes
that he *could not help* remembering' [my italics – SW] that this had been
the site of the Imperial Chancellery and of Speer's plans for Germania.
Huyssen relies upon the assumption that the built environment can give
unmediated access to history: the transmission of historical knowledge
is validated through an apparently unmediated, spontaneous, indeed
involuntary memory.[46]

This is a key aspect of the dynamics of place memory, poised between the
immediacy of communicative memory and the musealizations of cultural
memory. Crucial in the above example was that Huyssen was actually
moving across the space. The 'live'-ness of Huyssen's gaze is central to
overcoming the negative connotations of the site's musealized presence.
Huyssen does not investigate how this gaze might be organized, or even
how, as Hilde Hein writes in her brief consideration of Huyssen's concept,
'the aura-conferring gaze rests upon an object's musealized presence.'[47] Most
of the locations under consideration in this book are not 'musealized' in
the conventional sense. They are 'unintended monuments' in the terms of
Alois Riegl, not subject to a regime of preservation. Where does their aura
come from?

The remnant as ghost

The non-musealized remnant is often metaphorically described in terms
of the 'ghost', a clear trope of asynchronicity. As Steve Pile suggests, 'ghosts
haunt the places where cities are out of joint; out of joint in terms of both
time and space.'[48] As Pile notes of Derrida's invocation of ghosts, they are
not fixed in history. While the presence of the ghost is taken for granted

as a trigger that confirms a pre-existing 'will to remember', it is often used to approach the past through a pre-determined lens in order to write a *counter*-history, a *different* elaboration of the past that nevertheless still fixes the ghost in its historical place. Christine Boyer, writing in the context of the gentrification process of the 1980s in New York, rejects the reified commemorations of the city of collective memory in favour of a different set of narratives that tell other histories embedded in the city. Influenced by Pile, Karen Till's discussion of 'open wounds' slips directly from the encounter to a defined (traumatic, national) meaning of the wound:

> These commemorative sites are 'out of place' in the contemporary urban setting, for they are defined by (re)surfacing and repressed memories of violent pasts. The open wound asks visitors to confront their feelings of being haunted or not by valid national histories that remain present, yet invisible, in the city.[49]

Till papers over the fracturing of urban time with the invocation of national histories, reducing an ambiguity that was evident in Wenders's reading of the wounded cityscape.

Ghosts are much more ambiguous in Michel de Certeau's essay, 'Ghosts in the City'. This essay revises the arguments of the aforementioned 'Walking in the City' in light of the reconstruction of the Marais quarter in Paris in the 1980s (though it does not name this specifically). De Certeau writes that 'the technicians [of the 'concept-city'] were supposed to make a tabula rasa of the opacities that disrupted the plans for a city of glass', but in fact the 'strategy that, yesterday, aimed at a development of new urban spaces has been little by little transformed into a rehabilitation of national heritage.'[50] De Certeau identifies a logic of conservation, where the dissemination of objects from the past 'works yet again at extending the museum out of its walls, at museifying the city.'[51] De Certeau contrasts this form of spatial image with the image that emerges from the encounter with obsolete remains, 'the opaque ambivalence' of these 'seemingly sleepy, old-fashioned things', 'these inanimate objects', which, 'by eluding the law of the present, [...] acquire a certain autonomy.' This autonomy is framed in terms of language:

> These [...] defaced houses, closed-down factories, the debris of ship-wrecked histories still today raise up the ruins of an unknown, strange city. They burst forth within the modernist, massive, homogeneous city like slips of the tongue from an unknown, perhaps unconscious, language.[52]

Against the musealizing ennoblement of objects in the city, which 'see themselves recognized with a place and a sort of insurance on life,' these remains 'actually [...] function as history.'[53] This is not history in the sense of Nora's critical historiography, for it consists in opening 'a certain depth within the present, but [the objects] no longer have the contents that tame the strangeness of the past with meaning. Their histories cease to be pedagogical; they are no longer "pacified" or colonized with semantics – as if returned to their existence, wild, delinquent.'[54]

This is a much more radically contingent sense of the presence, and indeed visibility, of the past than that suggested by other writers on the ghost in the city. While Nora suggests that *lieux de memoire* were remnants, 'fundamentally remains, the ultimate embodiment of a memorial consciousness', they were nevertheless 'created by a play of memory and history. [...] To begin with, there must be a will to remember.'[55] In Nora, there is the reassertion of intentionality by a remembering subject. In De Certeau's account, these opaque objects have autonomy and the subject who perceives the depth within the present is not identified and is certainly not an active agent.[56] Rather, s/he seems to be part of the collective consciousness of the city. De Certeau secures the involuntary spontaneity of a memory which 'bursts forth' but the result is opacity and, as Nora would see it, arbitrariness. For De Certeau, however, the remnant from a forgotten past is always already valorized for its capacity to disrupt the city's synchronic organization through its asynchronic presence, prior to any narrativization it experiences.[57]

This arbitrary remnant has a tradition in discussions of obsolescent material. Alois Riegl, writing at the beginning of the twentieth century, claimed that the value of an 'unintended monument' (*ungewolltes Denkmal*) was its 'age value' (*Alterswert*), which expressed a contingent but material relationship to past time.[58] Victor Burgin described such remnants as unresolved 'monuments of melancholia', in contrast to official 'monuments of mourning'. Burgin proposes thinking of the material remnant as a mnemic trace, 'an element in a narrative that is nevertheless independent.' Burgin significantly focuses on the spontaneous, involuntary encounter with the obsolescent material object: 'if the past is really to touch us then it is more likely to be when we least expect it, as when some of its litter blows across our path.'[59] The encounter with the past comes as a surprise interruption of a purposeful movement through space. In his discussion of detritus in the city, Michael Sheringham focuses on the arbitrary nature of the encounter with the trace, echoing De Certeau's essay on 'Ghosts in the City', with the difference that Sheringham problematizes the status of the subject in this encounter. Sheringham is actually investigating the process by which the material remnant becomes translated from the repository to the archive (at which point it is pacified by semantics). Sheringham formulates the encounter with the past in the city as '[losing] the outlines of one's own familiar identity and gaining access to a hidden dimension of urban reality',[60] '[experiencing a defamiliarization of] the city we thought we knew, and [wrenching] us out the present, into an intermediate zone of overlapping timescales.'[61] Sheringham argues for a voluntary surrender of the self to the material of the city, so that we may 'find ways of being [the city's] amanuensis, by consenting to let go of our familiar reference points in personal and collective space and time.' Sheringham implies that accessing the past means surrendering a secure subject position, but also the emergence of a new urban subject, 'a kind of philologist, *attentive* to shifts and slides, bifurcations and compressions' [my italics]. This mode of attention supposes a merging between subject and object to the point where 'it is the city that walks the walker, making the archivist part of its ever-expanding archive.'[62] Ironically, this is a reiteration of Halbwachs's account of memory and social space: 'not only homes and walls persist through the centuries, but also that whole portion of the group in continuous contact with them, its life merged with things', although Sheringham has reduced this to an individual encounter. Sheringham, like Halbwachs and Connerton, is de/prescribing a return to a former mode of attending to space, theorizing a memory of how the place memory of a collective works, of how a spatial image emerges through the encounter with the remnant.

The unmusealized object has qualities which precede any instrumentalization and which make themselves evident in the moment of encounter. This shifts our focus from the informational content of a monument's framing – the commemoration of a specific place or event – to understand the act of remembrance as, first and foremost, a mode of encounter with a contingent past, in which 'historical transmission' is not the communication of a specific history, but the moment at which we remember how to remember place.

De Certeau describes a 'pacification' of the object, which is explained by Aleida Assmann's distinction between 'repository memory' – a storehouse of unsorted fragments – and 'functional memory' – the selective functionalization of those fragments within a particular culture. Assmann, however, implies that the only value a remnant can have is in its refunctionalization within a founding narrative:

this pre-history which can only be grasped in traces can be of great
significance if [a] later time recognizes/acknowledges [the German here
is ambiguous – SW] a normative foundation of its own era. Ruins and
relics that have become unnoticed and invisible can suddenly become
visible again when this beam of attention falls upon them.[63]

Assmann's account of how the past is collected and curated usefully
theorizes two different forms of collection of the past: 'storage memory'
in an expansive, potentially limitless repository, and 'functional memory'
in the archive, but she does not provide an account of the mode in which
the repository is accessed and activated by this 'beam of attention', failing to consider the dynamics of urban memory, the acts of evocation and
reminiscence, as technologies in themselves. Assmann writes of 'places of
memory' that they are 'exploded fragments of a lost or destroyed lifeworld
(*Lebenszusammenhang*)':

With the surrender and destruction of a place, its history is not over,
it retains material relics that become elements in narratives and thus
points of reference for a new cultural memory. These places are however
in need of explanation: their significance has to be secured through
verbal transmission.[64]

In contrast to Assmann's final assertion here, Dolores Hayden suggests
that 'the urban landscape is not a text to be read, but a repository of
environmental memory far richer than any verbal codes.'[65] This poses a
challenge to traditional readings of cultural memory work which analyse the construction of narrative (and counter-narratives), and offers a
corrective in line with Lutz Koepnick's assertion that German Studies
scholars dealing with Berlin's built environment 'should develop conceptual means to distinguish between and evaluate different strategies of
negotiating history and memory', rather than assuming that architectural
structures themselves can index historical events and embody memory,
which is nothing other than a 'conflation of remembrance and history'.[66]
Assmann falls into this trap, as, in her work, Nora's 'will to remember' is
reformulated as a 'beam of attention' directed towards the establishing
of identity and the reappropriation of the remnant within an ordered
archive of the past. For Assmann, the remnant only has value if its
meaning is secured within a narrative framework. As we saw, for De
Certeau the remnant only has value if it 'bursts forth' and is encountered
spontaneously.

There are three aspects that we can draw from the foregoing discussion, in order to theorize the nature of the encounter with the remnant. First: the contingency of the past is a central aspect of this encounter with the material trace. It is not a specific or communal past that is being recalled, but a sense of the past itself, which is collective in the very broad sense implied by Victor Burgin's collective noun when he suggests that 'we may be touched by a past we have not actually lived in ways that go beyond the affectless observation of a ritual' [my italics – SW]. Burgin here moves beyond one of the key precepts of place memory (that is connected to the lifeworld of a community), and yet maintains the dynamic encounter of place memory.

Second: the curator of the remnant is not a collective agent, but an individual Benjaminian flâneur, something which has implications for the (generally unreflected) position of the scholar writing about this kind of activity.[67]

Third, this encounter is founded on a rhythm that is in consonance with the environment and on a loss of control that enables the activation of the archive. As Henri Lefebvre suggests, 'to grasp a rhythm it is necessary to have been grasped by it; one must let oneself go, give oneself over, abandon oneself to its duration.'[68] The capacity for attending to the past involves some kind of surrender of a secure subject position. It will be possible to construct out a narrative on the basis of the remnant, to create, as Burgin sees it, 'a monument of mourning', and an official site that makes the case for the remembrance of a specific event.

This was the position taken up by Georg Dehio in the still-telling debate about 'monumental preservation' at the beginning of the twentieth century in the German-speaking area between Alois Riegl and Georg Dehio; it is precisely attention that is at stake.

Dehio was attempting to establish the institution and discipline of monument preservation as a response to the pessimistic diagnosis of a new era imbued with the spirit of liberalism, which expresses itself in the impositions of both the legal system and the economic system, in the growth of private ownership, of the increasing importance of traffic and circulation and 'individual utilitarian motives in general'. This diagnosis of the 'new era' has much in common with Connerton's assertion that modernity 'separates social life from locality and human dimensions' and with the analysis of modernity provided by Georg Simmel in his 1903 essay on 'The Metropolis and Mental Life', which also analysed the increasing dominance of abstract, contractual relations in the modern city, even if Dehio approaches this new era from a much more judgemental perspective.

Dehio insisted on the imposition of a narrative of cultural identity, a 'national optic', which would guide the authorized curator in the collecting, archiving and exhibiting of the substance of the nation. This would require restrictions upon the aforementioned phenomena of modernization, but would also have to combat the threat of material destruction (the rapid turnover of buildings in the city, as bemoaned a century later by Connerton) and the 'loss of the capacity for reception' (*Verlust der Aufnahmefähigkeit*), which echoes the diminished modern urban attention span identified by Simmel in his essay. For Dehio, this is to be combated by the imposition of a different form of attention to the material built environment: *pious devotion*.[69]

The capacity to impose and secure a narrative is dependent on the mode of the initial encounter. Dehio's pious devotion echoes Halbwachs's formulation of how place memory works (his model was, after all, a cathedral), and implies not only an unmediated form of attention to the built environment, but also reformulates a mode for the investment of symbolic aura. The value of the preserved monument resides in the historical continuity of the nation that, through its material presence, it can be brought to symbolize. For that reason, Dehio rejects the idea of leaving a building to decay 'naturally', as this would obviously imply the instability of the idea of nation.[70]

We can contrast Dehio's attempt to curate sites of memory as 'official' sites of national identity-formation (in a text-book illustration of Aleida Assmann's theory of the production of sites of cultural memory), with Riegl's recognition, and indeed celebration, of the democratic contingency and materiality of the site. Riegl and Dehio are both responding to modernity, something that is expressed through their conception of attention. For Riegl, the modern built environment shapes the 'beam of attention' that is directed towards the building with 'age value'. Dehio demands a mode of attention, a form of 'civic seeing' that is organized as a counterweight to modern distraction and which is not detachable from the meaning that is transferred from the object to the viewing subject. Dehio's demands remains dependent on the mode of encounter with the monument. It is not primarily the (historical) meaning of the sites that is at stake, but the mode of encounter – the 'museal urban gaze'.

Rather than assuming that a specific past is transparently expressed through the object, we need to think through the technologies of transmission that facilitate the production of 'spatial images'. The cityscape is not simply a medium in itself, but it requires a framing and construction as a 'spatial image'. There are fundamentally three major technologies: musealization, site-specific installation, and exhibition. These are technologies that engage with attention, embodied experience, and the experience of time in the city.[71] The synchronic and museal gazes are not only present in visual culture, such as photography, film and site-specific installation, but is implicit in many kinds of text (in the broadest sense) that formulate an encounter with the city. For that reason, the material under consideration in this book is quite heterogeneous: it involves institutional exhibitions, theoretical reflections, newspaper articles as well as film, photography and installations. It should go without saying that it is in the nature of such a project about elusive remnants that the material dealt with can make no claim to being exhaustive. It has been selected and curated to frame the argument of the book.

Materials, method: pausing at the gate of the Germans

To offer an insight into the kind of materials and the strategy of close reading in which this book will engage, I look here at a case of memorialization drawn from the introduction to Aleida Assmann's 2006 book *The Long Shadow of the Past: Memory Culture and the Politics of History*. Here, Assmann discusses an art installation. Or rather, she discusses a photograph of an art installation, Hans Hoheisel's 1997 work, 'The Gate of the Germans', in which, for a few brief moments, an image of the infamous gates to Auschwitz concentration camp, with the slogan, 'Arbeit Macht Frei', was projected on to the Brandenburg Gate.

    The slogan functions as a perverse form of memorial plaque, one of the key technologies of memory transmission. Attention needs to be paid to how varying forms of 'plaque' organize attention and time, from the solid bronze adornments on the Kaiser William Memorial Church (discussed in Chapter One), through the provisional placards at the Topography of the Terror (Chapter Two) to the kind of 'temporary' signage as in this kind of installation.

    Assmann writes of this installation (Fig. 2):

> In the photograph the unique and fleeting performance, which like an involuntary flash of memory was only perceptible for a brief moment for few people on that cold January night, was mothballed (*stillgelegt*) and preserved, through which it can be made available to others at a temporal and spatial distance.[72]

Photography is on one level a musealizing activity that obviously involves a pause, yet, with Mike Crang, we have to be wary of attributing 'to the moving

2. Hans Hoheisel, 'The Gate of the Germans', Berlin, 1997. Photograph taken by the studio of Hans Hoheisel. Courtesy of the artist.

body the immobility of the point through which it passes', something which will be significant in our discussion of photography's museal gaze in this book.[73] Assmann appropriates the photographic representation of Hoheisel's installation and translates into a fixed, isolated image, which she later terms a 'Denkbild', presumably an allusion to 'Denkmal', the German for monument. This translation is based on her own theory of memory transmission, by which objects, once their initial function has been exhausted, can be taken from the repository and refunctionalized within the framework of cultural memory which operates at temporal and spatial distance. The now reified 'Denkbild' is open to Assmann to decipher, which she does by effectively providing a historical supplement to the image, performing the same kind of activity engaged in by Brian Ladd, in *Ghosts of Berlin*, in outlining the meanings which have been attributed to the monument, which was built in the 1790s, from then to 1989. She supplies not only historical depth to the image, but also situates it in the media context of the early twentieth century, as she notes how the Gate was used for commercial advertising projection purposes during its renovation between 2000 and 2002. The third context through which she draws meaning from the photograph is through its invocation of the Holocaust: according to Assmann, Hoheisel's work is able to make the problematic of German national memory 'in unmittelbarer Evidenz deutlich' (immediately and clearly evident). This is an interesting claim, since it is founded on a reading of a photograph of the installation. Yet this reading, in its effort to delimit the significance of the installation to the 'studium' of the photograph (to use Roland Barthes' classic term for the intended subject of the image), and the lens through which Assmann chooses to read it (since her book is about the dynamic of individual and collective remembrance in the 'long shadow' of a traumatic past), actually misses one curious aspect of that photograph, which reminds us of other dimensions of works of visual culture such as Hoheisel's that become invisible once, in the peace and quiet of our academic study, we contemplate a 'Denkbild'.

If we look at the photograph again, we might notice that the photograph is clearly not of an 'instant', but that the shutter's exposure time has been lengthened, with the result that a moving object (presumably a bus, given the yellow traces in the bottom left-hand corner) has left a trace of light that passes through the gate and veers to the left (following the required traffic regulation). Assmann's analysis can do nothing with this particular aspect of the photograph (let us call it, continuing to follow Barthes' terminology, the 'punctum'). It is one aspect that exceeds her framing of the photograph. One could also interrogate the location of the camera, set to one side of the Gate, since presumably a conventional frontal position was rendered inadmissible by the same traffic regulations that shaped the movement of the bus.

By considering the photograph a transparent document of an art installation, Assmann misses the fact that the photograph (with its extended exposure time) is itself a 'spatial image' in which the environment of the encounter plays a significant role: the photograph temporalizes space, rather than spatializing time, as the 'Denkbild' does, much as the original installation temporalized space through its interruption of the apparently static structure that is the Brandenburg Gate.

This suggests that the photograph, and certainly the installation, cannot simply be used to abstract, and explicate allegorical significance. Rather the spatial image, including the transient encounter with the installation itself, was not only an engagement with Germany's traumatic past, but also an engagement with the spatial and indeed the temporal structure of an urban space, and how one attends to it.

In the motion of the bus we have spatial practices that are shaped by the synchronic organization of space and time that is embodied by the bus timetable and the city street network. That bus, of course, would be the 100 that ran from Zoologischer Garten through the Brandenburg Gate from 1990 until 2000, when the Gate was closed to motorized traffic once more. The itinerary was marketed as a 'tourist route', another set of spatial practices that produce a certain perception structured by what John Urry terms the 'tourist gaze', so that the passengers may well have had their attention drawn to the Gate's presence at the moment of the projection. If this was a 'memory event', in the manner of Christo's 'Wrapped Reichstag' (discussed in Chapter 4), then, given the time of its intervention, it is probably an ironic commentary on that phenomenon.

The Brandenburg Gate is an odd place to start, given that this book is primarily concerned with the (in)visibility of marginal(ized) urban sites, which are brought together under the conceptual umbrella of 'unintended monuments'. There can be few Berlin landmarks as remediated as this Gate. Hoheisel said that, in the course of his preparation for the installation, the Gate had become 'ever more of a simple projection surface'.[74] Yet, as Assmann's history of the monument demonstrates, precisely this function of the Gate as a projection surface, a *lieu de memoire* to be invested with symbolic aura, means that it shares many qualities with those sites. Its original function as a celebration of military victory has long since given way to a variety of transient projections, be they the Nazi celebration of 1933, or the post-Wende, pre-unification euphoria of New Year 1990. In that sense, the Brandenburg Gate can also qualify as an unintended monument, in that, free from any fixed function, it can always be reinvested with meaning. Assmann claims of the Gate that it 'announces (*verkündet*) and embodies history', but this assertion is grounded in what Jonathan Long critiques as the 'expressive' view of the built environment.[75] Assmann herself, through her detailed explication of the Gate's complex historical layers has already placed this self-evident expressive dimension in question. Yet this claim, along with her earlier assertion that Hoheisel's installation was 'clear and immediate evidence' of the problem of German national memory, is founded not only on the expressive fallacy that the material object embodies history (as we also saw with the example from Huyssen) but also the fallacy identified by James Elkins, who has argued that 'images, in visual studies, are too often either immediately self-interpreting or stand-ins for information that is non-visual.'[76] The power of these fallacies is undeniable, but how they are produced can be productively interrogated in order to get a clearer understanding of the dynamics of place memory.

Visual/memory/event culture

As suggested, Hoheisel's installation can also be read as a commentary on a contemporary memory 'event culture' that is prevalent in Berlin. Examples of this are discussed in Chapter Four, and their prehistory traced in the first three chapters of this book. These events directed towards 'the past' in the city in a collective fashion through a Debordian 'spectacle' that, in Lutz Koepnick's terms, contains 'possible anxieties about the mutability of meaning and identity in modern society' and redefines 'a shared sense of stability and orientation amid the frenzy of progress'.[77] For Koepnick, the only break in the spectacle comes with the technological breakdown of the event screen, and with that the emergence of a rare opportunity to 'question how our own present ever more forcefully expands into, reframes and gobbles up the rest of the time'.[78] This book is similarly focused on moments of breakdown in the synchronic order of the city, but in particular how these breakdowns can also be engineered, as by Hoheisel, through a critical visual culture.

As this book shows, visual culture engagements with Berlin's cityscape have often served as barometers of the emergence of more general processes, as well as reflections on contemporary technologies of visualization and reproduction. What is then the relationship between artistic practices of remembrance, such as Hoheisel, and everyday practices of memory? As Assmann observes elsewhere in her by now extensive oeuvre on memorial practices, art is not only a means of representing memories, but is a 'hand-maiden' to communication about memory', a 'social trigger for the liberation of blocked memories'.[79] Yet this trigger does not just happen at the level of content. If this were the case, 'remember Auschwitz' would then be one of the messages of Hoheisel's installation as a straightforward reversal of other, earlier triumphant uses of the Gate. The form of the spatial image is also significant, however, precisely in the absence of uniformly organized bodies or flags. As Assmann herself admits in another volume, artists 'prefer to approach the less-remarkable and invisible things' and transform them into a 'spur to thought about that which does not have any value as a monument and does not have the status of a recognized historical place.' For Assmann, artists make an important contribution to 'the perpetually open question as to what we recognize at any time as history in the present'[80] and focus on 'the mechanisms for the production and dissolution of attention'. Indeed many of the artists at work in this book investigate what might constitute the mechanisms of a relatively invisible everyday 'memory culture' on the margins of official commemoration, and yet influence in the longer term how that official policy works (as the examples of Boltanski and Garazaibal in Chapter Four illustrate). There remains the question of the artwork itself, and particularly a site-specific installation such as Hoheisel's in this installation a reworking of how we attend to urban space and time in the production of a (fleetingly) aestheticized space. Hoheisel's installation can be read as the production of place memory, after its disappearance, through the *technological* construction of a spatial image.[81]

Image technologies and the museal gaze

Spatial images need not only be site-specific installations, but can be produced in other forms of visual culture that involve an encounter with, and carrying over of, an indexical image of a particular site.

Photography and film are clearly significant here; painting will play less of a role given its indirect relation to the 'register of reality' (Huyssen) that is so central to the museal gaze. The photography at stake here is not 'rubble photography' in the conventional sense understood by scholars whose studies of such images focus on the iconicity of the ruin and the significance of bearing witness to wartime trauma.[82] The remnants does not possess the 'shock value' of an intact world demolished, but actually function as a remnant of a disavowed past. Eugène Atget is a crucial reference point here, not only because his work was also rescued from obscurity, but because his procedure of producing a 'spatial image' of a world under threat due to the radical transformation of the modern cityscape resonates with the photographic production from the 1960s to the 1980s which similarly sought to record the vanishing landscape threatened by postwar reconstruction. The construction of a photographic archive of the rubble-strewn cityscape could lead us to read the photographer as a 'camera-bearing conservationist', as Stefan Gronert describes the work of Bernd and Hilda Becher.[83] The photographic archive can *also* be an archive of urban sites. Yet, as a *photographic* archive, it is more mobile and easily reproducible than material objects in the city – the transplanted Hotel Esplanade at Potsdamer Platz being the exception that proves the rule, as discussed in Chapter Four. Photography is also more susceptible to an interventionist curatorial and exhibition practice, which has implications for the discussion in Chapter Three of how photographs of the immediate post-war era have been used.

In the age of technological reproduction, cinema's indexical relationship to a pro-filmic world has been constantly invoked as a form of encounter with reality by the likes of Siegfried Kracauer and Andre Bazin. Emma Wilson brought Huyssen's 'museal gaze' into her discussion of Alain Resnais's use of tracking shots in *Night and Fog* (1955). For Wilson, these produce 'a more mobile, three-dimensional, even haptic encounter with history and its material relics than the conventional museum provides', which 'might be aligned with Andreas Huyssen's reflections on the new possibilities of the museal gaze'.[84] Such extended tracking shots, as well as powerfully haptic close-ups, are also a striking feature of Resnais's next film, *Hiroshima Mon Amour* (1959). This latter film can be read as a prime example of cinematic scepticism towards 'conventional' museum practice, for which the Hiroshima museum stands in, despite, or perhaps precisely because of the way in which Resnais's camera encounters it, in fluid sweeps that undermine 'the singular and fixed spectatorial position that museums sought to arrange as the ideal vantage point from which to see and understand the logic underlying the exhibition arrangements.'[85]

Such haptic encounters in cinema undo, in Laura Marks's terms, 'visual mastery' but also the mastery of the past as a discrete object. They run counter to clarified historical seeing as comprehension, which is constructed in *Hiroshima Mon Amour* as the museum's mission and ultimate failing. Through his refusal to frame the object, Resnais's tracking shots point not only to the limits of historical understanding, but also to the necessity of the encounter for any beginning of understanding. The extended tracking shot draws our attention to the duration of the encounter with the object, the material extent of the object, and frames, or rather, constantly reframes our gaze upon the object, in contrast to the conventional museum's static framing, which compels the visitor's body to halt in order to gaze upon the framed object. As Julie Ng describes it in her discussion of Daniel Libeskind's post-unification models for Berlin, 'the museum-goer [...] encounters artefacts that contain affective significance because of the vast quantitative distances in time between the viewer and the viewed that, none the less, are closed by what seems to be the immediacy of the object.'[86] The camera, by contrast mimics a mobile gaze, imitating the way in which 'the museum-goer is being moved both by the [museum] design and the object.' Ng expands her discussion through reference to Gilles Deleuze, whose film theory is also useful for a discussion of the representation of the encounter with the abandoned remnant. In *Cinema 2*, Deleuze discusses the kind of image that emerges from the cinematic engagement with the 'any-space-whatever',[87] a disconnected space that provokes the breakdown of the conventional sensory-motor schemata of habit that conventionally dictate the stimulus- and-response-driven logic of the urban environment, leaving the subject a mere 'spectator' rather than agent. For Deleuze, the model for this kind of disconnected space was, tellingly, the ruined post-war European city framed in neo-realist cinema. For Ng, such a space produces 'paralysis' in the subject, but this can also be read as the 'loss of subjecthood', that, following Sheringham, is a central element in the dynamics of place memory. For Deleuze, this immobility can also be read as opportunity for thought. This book will examine how this is enabled by the construction of a spatial image, a recovery of 'attentiveness' through the technology of a museal gaze, which connects 'age value' with the undoing of the synchronic rhythms of the city. This production of place memory is at the same time a moment of discovery and a moment of preservation, but is also a technological production (as Ng underlines in her discussion of Libeskind's designs). An awareness of the technological form of transmission is crucial in understanding how urban memory works as a hybrid form of communicative and cultural memory.

This work will be traced throughout this book's history of the production of spatial images in Berlin, elucidating the longer history of the urban memory culture in which Hoheisel's installation took place.

Overview

Chapter One, 'Remembering the "Murdered City": Berlin 1957-1974' traces the gradual emergence of local place memory work from the late 1950s through to the mid-1970s. The chapter begins in 1957, the hegemonic moment for the *autogerechten Stadt* (the 'automobile city', which we might also translate as the 'concept-city') in the west of the city. This was the year of the Hauptstadt Berlin international building exhibition, which shows how the synchronic urban gaze of the planners was exhibited in the attempt to construct a form of civic behaviour that was adapted to the new planned urban environment. At this moment, in the local resistance, for example, to the planned demolition of the Kaiser William Memorial Church, we can begin to see the production of 'spatial images' of resistance, the tentative emergence of a museal gaze in response to the 'murdered city', as the post-war environment in West Berlin was polemically described by the journalist Wolf-Jobst Siedler. Siedler sees post-war urban planning as the 'second destruction' of the city, following on from the effects of the air war. The chapter focuses on public debates about urban reconstruction, and the accompanying critique of the synchronic gaze, both in the writings of Siedler and of the social psychologist Alexander Mitscherlich and the photography of Elizabeth Niggemeyer. Other technologies discussed involve the musealization of urban façades, enshrined in the rather limited official policy of *Stadtbildpflege* (preservation of the city image). This musealization process becomes visible in both halves of the city in the late 1960s. While urban planning policy in West and East seeks to respond to, and to some extent, regulate that emergent museal gaze, the practice of critical visual culture was slower to respond. Wim Wenders's early film, *Summer in the City* (1970) is an investigation of movement through urban spaces that links to our discussion of a Deleuzian 'any-space-whatever' in its foregrounding of the rhythms of space and time in the encounter of the city under threat of demolition.

Chapter Two, 'Place Memory Work in East and West Berlin 1975-1983', traces how 'place memory work' develops across forms of visual culture from the mid-1970s through to the early 1980s. This period sees the emergence of curators, as representatives of a generational shift in historical and urban consciousness in which the absence of 'place' is keenly felt in tandem with a rejection of the regime of attention shaped by the dominant synchronic urban gaze. For these curators, the need to respond to the presence of traces of the historical process (both before and after 1945) leads them to theorize how to 'work with place' in the production of spatial images in architecture, site-specific intervention as well as photography and film. This chapter illustrates how place can be produced through the direct encounter with the material remnant, but also through the indexical recording forms of the photograph and film, whose strategies for exhibiting the cityscape dovetail with the display strategies of spatial interventions.

Architecture and urban renovation is addressed in the analysis of the International Building Exhibition from the late 1970s. In its two sections, IBA-Neu and IBA-Alt, it focused on the production of spatial images in the Southern Friedrichstadt, an area that had been neglected in the post-war era and was rediscovered, curated and exhibited in the 1970s. These two sections developed related, but importantly distinctive forms of urban memory in 'activating the silent reserves of place'.[88] The first, IBA-Neu, was founded on the Senate's demand that the 'genetic structure' of the city was to be the basis of future urban development, whereas IBA-Alt criticized the IBA-Neu as an aesthetic programme and saw its own task as the recovery of forgotten social histories, including everyday experience under National Socialism, in Kreuzberg. The IBA-Alt's museal urban gaze sets itself against the synchronic gaze as a form of 'social amnesia', exemplified by the memory work at the former SS-headquarters, now the Topography of the Terror. The IBA-Alt promoted the production of 'memory value' within the cityscape through encounters with remnants that generate critical depth and an awareness of the discontinuities of the history process.

Critical visual culture takes up this work at other, less prominent sites in Berlin (Hotel Esplanade, Anhalter Bahnhof, the former Embassy Quarter in West Berlin) in projects that precisely interrogate the interaction between the memory of place and the narrativizations of cultural memory. We also see this in the field of photography, the curation of previously neglected photography from the immediate post-war period (e.g. Fritz Eschen and Friedrich Seidenstücker) and the emergence of photographers in West and East who critically dissect the synchronic urban gaze and at the same generate a museal urban gaze upon neglected, obsolescent spaces of the city. This process is also evident in a series of films in East and West from this period.

Chapter Three, 'The Remembered City on Display 1983-1994', examines how this 'place memory work' becomes codified in forms of display that establish the paradigm of the city itself as a museal space between 1984 and the early 1990s, spanning the fall of the Wall. This is illustrated with reference to the public outcomes of the IBA-Neu and -Alt projects, and then to a series of projects related to the 750th anniversary of the city's founding in 1987, which establishes a new technological dimension to the dynamics of place memory: the installation as 'collective' event. The 1986 Mythos Berlin exhibition on the site of the Anhalter Bahnhof illustrates site-specific urban memory production ('the city as museum') as a specific technology in the evocation of past time and experience, but also as an embryonic form of event culture. An extended analysis of Wim Wenders's *Wings of Desire* (1986) focuses especially on how the film shapes the viewer's encounter with the 'wounds' of the southern Friedrichstadt and Potsdamer Platz. Wenders curates the city in such a way as to (re) formulate the viewer's experience of the cityscape through the undoing of the sensory-motor habits of the urban environment. The Nikolaiviertel reconstruction in East Berlin allows for a broader consideration of the positions of monument preservation and reconstruction in the period, especially in comparison with the aims of the West Berlin IBA-Neu. Its construction of urban memory is read against the late GDR film, *The Architects* (1989/1990) which revisits the themes of critical visual culture, the synchronic city and obsolescence, that were also visible in the films discussed in Chapter Two. *The Architects* was begun before and completed after the fall of the Berlin Wall, and expresses a continuity that is to be found in the immediate post-wall era. Jürgen Bottcher's documentary film *Die Mauer* (1991), about the fall of the Wall and its aftermath. This film works with the visual language of obsolescence familiar to the GDR – not however now as a tacit form of state dissidence, but as a form of resistance to the synchronic time regime of the new post-unification order with its associated historical narratives. A similar continuity is evident in Christian Boltanski's *Missing House* and Shimon Attie's *Writing on the Wall*, both of which are explicit interventions in the urban fabric shape encounters that foregrounds the city as simultaneously repository, archive and display museum.

Chapter Four, 'In Search of a City? Urban Memory in Unified Berlin', looks at how Berlin's memory culture has responded to what Paul Virilio diagnoses as the increasingly porous condition of the city in a globalizing world. The focus of this chapter is less on specific 'wounds' in the cityscape and more on the large 'obsolescent' spaces left behind by the collapse of the GDR regime and which need to be integrated into the working conception of a historic city: the Potsdamer Platz, which had been criss-crossed by the Wall, and the 'Schlossplatz' which housed the Palace of the Republic from 1973 onwards. These spaces are too large and too central to be 'invisible' or 'marginal', but the memory culture that emerges from them remains intelligible in terms of a museal urban gaze that (re)produces the dynamics of place memory. One key form is the IBA-Neu's architectural model of urban memory, which became established as a paradigmatic form in the so-called 'critical reconstruction' of the city in the 1990s. With particular focus on the (re)construction of Potsdamer Platz as 'the memory of place', the chapter illustrates how Kleihues' original concept of the built environment as collage is adapted to the construction of a 'new urbanist' environment to ensure the appropriation of fragments of the past into a carefully bounded conception of the 'city'. The automatization of movement through the city is less directly associated with automobiles and becomes more implicitly a pedestrian form of consumption of the Wall, the Hotel Esplanade and other remnants of the past at Potsdamer Platz, where the palimpsests of past time are one of many commodities to be consumed. At the same time, other projects at Potsdamer Platz continue to produce a critical museal gaze, such as the photographic work of Arwed Messmer that interrogates substantive duration in the built environment. This section concludes with an analysis of Thomas Schadt's 2002 film, *Berlin. Sinfonie einer Grossstadt*, a museal invocation of Walter Ruttmann's 1927 celebration of the synchronic machine city. Schadt's film is situated *after* the city as synchronic machine and interrogates how the image of the city serves to transmit the past. The film not only frames a musealized city, but also questions as to the nature of the city *per se* in the contemporary 'postmodern' moment.

With the 'completion' of Potsdamer Platz in 1998, Berlin-Mitte became the new paradigmatic site of 'unintended monuments' in the city, due both to the obsolescence of the Palace of the Republic, and also to the 'emptiness' of the spaces produced by the synchronic urban gaze of the GDR's planning institutions. While the Palace of the Republic was a site of local and national memory contestation in the 1990s,[89] it becomes increasingly a site for international artists to engage with a more general, contemporary concern with obsolescence and modernization, as is seen in projects such as Tacita Dean's film *Palast* (2004) and Lars Ramberg's installation *Zweifel* (2005), which are documents of an obsolescent building that invite the viewer to experience the passage of past time in a medium-specific context.

International artists also reflect on this tension between a marketable urban memory and processes of obsolescence. We see this in Allora and Calzadilla's piece about the Palace of the Republic, 'How to Appear Invisible', and Lars Ramberg's revivification of his Zweifel project in digital form on the internet. This is memory produced and consumed from an almost infinitely expanded urbanized (hyper)space.

The conclusion takes up Paul Virilio's idea of the 'overexposed' city and Rem Koolhaas's rejection of urban nostalgia to analyse the practices of the 775th city anniversary in Berlin in 2012. It constrasts these with Juan Ga-razaibal's installation, *Memoria Urbana* (2012), which recreates the skeleton and floorplan of a disappeared church at an anonymous crossroads in the Mitte district. This installation also speaks to the dematerialization of, and yet ongoing value of urban memory in a context beyond the conventional linguistic and geographical borders of the city, in an era of global migration. Above all, it addresses a collective that is neither local or global, but allows us to recuperate the word 'denizen' in its historical sense, to denote those who are accorded civil rights without belonging to the place.

In an era where the urbanization of space, and spatial experience, seem-ingly know no bounds, it is crucial to understand the mechanisms by which a relationship to the past is fostered. By observing how asynchronous spaces are archived and exhibited, it is possible to see how a critical recalibration of urban attention is attempted so that, following Halbwachs, one might remember how to remember place.

We are able to see the continuities in conceptions of place memory that follow through from the late 1970s as discussed in Chapters One and Two into the post-unification period. This reframing of urban memory in Berlin coincides then with the need to reconceptualize the city in the era of the global and the virtual. It is in this post-urban and post-GDR context that the paradigm of remembering National Socialism 'well' collapses not only into a more diffuse content (the remembrance of different pasts), but also ever more complex forms of museal gaze, imbricated with technologies which show how artists are interested, beyond the material remnant and its past, in attention, but also, importantly, in technologies that organize attention to space. The ostensible unimportance of the local does not diminish the production of forms of place memory and indeed the embodied encounter with the built environment in Berlin. The critical practice of urban memory, divested of a nostalgic longing for authentic place, can be a tool for continuing to generate vigilance towards the cityscape as an indirect object, and towards the discontinuities and asynchronicities of urban time and space.

An academic book about the cityscape – not a coffee table picture book – is obviously formally constrained in how much visual material it can present. For that reason, I have created a web site – asynchronouscity-berlin.wordpress.com – which hosts further visual material that can be read alongside this publication, as well as links to other sites with relevant visual material.

1.   Remembering the 'Murdered City'

Berlin 1957-1974

This chapter traces the tentative emergence of post-war urban memory from the late 1950s through to the mid-1970s. The chapter begins in 1957, the year of the Hauptstadt Berlin International Building Exhibition, an event that illustrates how the synchronic urban gaze of the planners was displayed in constructing a form of civic perception adapted to the new urban infrastructure. At this moment, in local resistance to the planned demolition of the Kaiser William Memorial Church, for example, we can begin to see the production of spatial images of resistance. Other technologies examined include the musealization of vernacular 'islands of tradition', in the form of urban façades, in the rather limited official policy of *Stadtbildpflege* (preservation of the city image). This musealization process becomes visible in both halves of the city in the late 1960s.

This points to the tentative emergence of a museal gaze in response to the 'murdered city', as post-war West Berlin was polemically described by Wolf-Jobst Siedler. The chapter focuses on how urban reconstruction is exhibited and debated in city space, and the accompanying critique of the synchronic gaze in the writings of Siedler and of the social psychologist Alexander Mitscherlich, the photography of Elizabeth Niggemeyer and in Wim Wenders's early film, *Summer in the City* (1970), which investigates movement through urban spaces in its foregrounding of the rhythms of space and time within the encounter with the city under threat of demolition.

Designing and displaying the synchronic city

1957 can be seen as the high point of the hegemony of the post-war concept-city in West Berlin. This year sees the culmination in the western half of Berlin of the initial planning that had begun in the immediate post-war period to conceive a reconstructed city amidst the rubble of 1945 as a *Stadt von morgen* (city of tomorrow). This was visible in the utopian plans submitted to the Hauptstadt Berlin architectural competition, and in material form in the construction of the Hansa quarter, which was the central exhibit of the Interbau (International Building Exhibition) of that year.

The connection between these two visualizations was made by Berlin's Senator for Building and Housing, Rolf Schwedler, in two related speeches he gave in 1957, firstly at the 102nd Schinkel festival in Berlin on 13 March, and then at the conference of the International Association for Housing and Urban Construction and Planning, and its German counterpart, on 26 August. Common to both the Hauptstadt exhibition and the Hansa Quarter projects was their (dis)regard for the existing building stock. Schwedler framed it as follows:

> The war produced such a level of destruction, that in 1945 many experts believed that one should develop a completely new conception for a new Berlin – perhaps even at a different location. [...] All people of insight soon recognized that one could only consider a new urban order, whereby of course interventions into the remaining building stock were and are not to be avoided. [...] In this regard, the demands and requirements of modern man are to be taken fully into consideration.[1]

According to Schwedler, in a paradigmatic statement of the synchronic urban gaze, this intervention was to take the form of a 'structural purification' of 'ugly mixed-usage neighbourhoods'; such work was an essential precondition for the ends of 'traffic planning.' This process of 'gutting' (*Entkernung*) would be facilitated by the fact [sic] that the inner city had already been 'destroyed'. For Schwedler, traffic infrastructure formed the 'arteries of economic life', and their presence was the precondition for the 'frictionless functioning of the capital'.[2] This philosophy also shaped the guidelines for the Hauptstadt competition, where the prescriptions for the plans focused almost completely on traffic infrastructure: primarily the road network, where, beyond the roads that would encircle the city centre and the Strasse des 17. Juni and Friedrichstrasse, 'all other roads may be altered, if it appears to be necessary for the completion of the task.'

The Hauptstadt plans pay little or no attention to what the West Berlin Senate had wished to retain as monumental landmarks (*Festpunkte*). These have no role to play in the envisioning of the cityscape. According to the plans, they would be translated into true 'islands', disconnected from the spatial practices and the milieu of the new city dwellers. The vernacular 'old' was simply disregarded:

> The so-called 'Hansaviertel', whose total destruction offered the space for a uniform solution [...], belongs to those parts of the rapidly expanding young Imperial Capital [of the late nineteenth century – SW] that contained literally no buildings of artistic merit, or even of only local-historical interest.[3]

Harald Bodenschatz later underlined that, in the area of the Hansaviertel on which the planning focuses, there were still 20 buildings (out of originally 160), containing 283 apartments and 22 businesses.[4] The cellar foundations of the destroyed buildings were still intact, the streets and the underground infrastructure were largely untouched, while the ownership of the land itself was overwhelmingly in private hands. The refusal to perceive this ongoing presence of the 'former' Hansaviertel is of a piece with the more abstract perspectives of the Hauptstadt Berlin competition. The gaze that meets the vernacular ruins sees only space at its disposal.

This gaze also seeks to shape a particular form of interaction with the built environment. It is a city without pedestrian interaction, as is somewhat exaggeratedly described in the literary-textual accompaniment to Otto Hagemann's photobook of contemporary Berlin in 1957:

> If, one morning, suspecting nothing, one wants to set one's foot out on the street – it's gone. A little later the suspicious eye notices a new, much broader, much straighter, much longer street. Somewhere or other, it opens its jaws, spits out a tunnel and swallows cars like shooting stars. And the pedestrians? Our new streets cannot deal with such incorrigible Neanderthals. If you want to get somewhere, sit in a car, and if you don't have one, then you are merely going for an idle stroll and would be best placed as swiftly as possible in the nearest park.[5]

Hagemann's celebration of the new city contrasted the 'over-intricate façades' [of the few buildings that had not been demolished] on the edge of the Hansaviertel with 'the new', which was 'more healthy and honest'.[6] The old was thus also associated with the decadent (in an echo of the rhetoric of the moral obsolescence of the 'old' which we will see in the GDR).

As Bodenschatz later described it, the aim of this new urban planning, of which the Hansaviertel was the first manifestation, was the production of the 'new human' as individualized house-occupant, as automobile driver, as a member of a classless society.[7] This implies not just a different form of living and another form of city, but also a new rhythmic form, one that emerges in dialogue with the technologically defined environment. The city is organized around circulation, the circulation of goods, but also the circulation of bodies, with almost complete disregard for the existing infrastructure (and the spatial practices associated with it).

Hagemann's photobook is typical of a form through which the synchronic gaze's disregard for former structures was transmitted; another paradigmatic example is H.C. Artus's *Zehn Jahre Danach* (Ten Years After), which juxtaposes photographs of the ruined German cities (including Berlin) with images of the reconstructed urban environments ten years on in 1955. Socio-psychological amnesia may be at work (as it would be diagnosed by Alexander Mitscherlich ten years further on), but such a diagnosis fails to take into account Berlin's place in a wider context of European post-war urban reconstruction.[8] Other visual media were also employed to communicate the vision of the synchronic urban gaze, such as *Verliebt in Berlin* (1957), a film made to 'sell' Berlin as a consumer success story to a West German audience. The film is also strikingly attuned to the synchronic rhythms of the city that exceed the conventional tourist-consumer gaze; at one point, our female tourist-protagonist visits a *Verkehrsschule* (traffic school) in West Berlin, where the children are learning the rules of the road (not just crossing the road, but how to navigate a car round the city). The 'traffic school', a phenomenon born of the 1950s – the Steglitz school in the film was in fact established in 1957 – is of course an explicit training for the synchronic experience of the city.

City officials employed a variety of technologies to manage public awareness of the transforming city, including the decision to build on the success of the Interbau by having a bi-annual exhibition of building projects in West Berlin, entitled the 'Berliner Bauwochen' (the Berlin Construction Weeks). The importance of the Hansaviertel was underlined by its ongoing presence in the visual material advertising the first Berliner Bauwochen, which ran, within the frame of the German Industrial Exhibition, from 15 September to 2 October 1960. The cover of the brochure showed one of the high-rise towers from the Hansaviertel and the foreword, by Rolf Schwedler, reinforced this continuity:

> In recent years – triggered by the International Building Exhibition in 1957 – the construction of Berlin has been followed with attention and participation by the citizens of the city and its friends around the world.[9]

It would be a mistake, however, to think that the Bauwochen themselves were entirely devoted to the new synchronic city; there were two lectures on 'Monument Preservation and New Building',[10] one on 'Urbanity and Neighbourhood', as well as, less surprisingly, sessions on 'Traffic Planning', the experiences of the Hansaviertel project and the opening of the second section of the urban motorway (between Hohenzollerndamm and Schmargendorf).[11] Of these topics, the first was illustrated in the brochure by the reconstruction of the 'Deutsche Oper' in Charlottenburg – exemplifying, once more, how 'monument preservation' was less focused on the urban

3. Bauwochen exhibition tour of the urban motorway between the Funkturm and Jakob-Kaiser-Platz, at the 'Nordwestbogen' bridge in Charlottenburg. 9 September 1962. Photograph: Karl-Heinz Schubert. Courtesy of Berlin Landesarchiv.

milieu, ensemble or vernacular, and more on the unique object. The question of motorized traffic in the city came up in two articles in the brochure. First, the opening of the North-West bridge on the Fürstbrünner Weg over the Spree in Charlottenburg was addressed by Rolf Schwedler. Schwedler thanked those who had understood the need for the construction of broad, open roads, and he praised the bridge, in particular for the fact that it provided a lovely view over the 'landscape', though precisely how this view was to be appreciated remained unclear (Fig. 3). The second article related to this was a piece by the Senator's building director, Erwin Klotz, outlining the principles of the urban motorways in Berlin. The article was illustrated by four images: two diagrams – an arterial map that reiterates the plan for the Hauptstadt competition and a cross-section of the roadscape – and two photographs, one illustrating traffic accessing and leaving the motorway at Halensee, and one demonstrating the signage at the Hohenzollerndamm exit. The sparse, technical functionality of these images mirrored the dry, technical prose that explained the function of the motorway, pausing only briefly to remark on the 'interesting' bridges. The didactic tone of the prose was underlined in an article on the Hansaviertel buildings that discussed how inhabitants were using the new residences 'in the wrong way', a useful reminder that the training intentions of the synchronic gaze may not always be seamlessly translated at ground level.

Overall, in terms of display, the past had no place at the Bauwochen of 1960. Citizens were invited to a series of 'tours' of sites of new construction; these were either of new transport infrastructure developments (underground stations, the aforementioned bridges, the motorway openings), new public structures (schools, swimming pools) and, strikingly, a 'view of the city' from the (then) tallest structure in Berlin, the Telefunken-house on Ernst-Reuter Platz. These tours familiarized the citizens with the new way of seeing the city, and the exhibitions of the Bauwochen were similarly interested in the display of the new and coming urban infrastructure ('Streets of Today and Tomorrow', '10 years of construction in Berlin').[12]

The cityscape and history

1957, the year of the Hauptstadt competition, was also the year in which the public discussion of the fate of the Kaiser William Memorial Church reached its peak. Dating back to the 1910s, the Wilhelmine church had been long considered an obstacle to frictionless circulation in the city and in its post-war ruined condition seemed ripe for demolition, especially as it belonged architecturally to the neo-historicist phase for which monument preservation had little time. The public response expressed dissatisfaction with the wholesale restructuring of the urban environment under the synchronic urban gaze and this led to the concomitant production of 'spatial images' of the site, particularly in the media.[13] With the case of the Kaiser William Memorial Church, former spatial practices and images and encounters with the cityscape become discursively present for the first time since the war. This perhaps explains why 'the past' was more explicitly visible in the Bauwochen programme of 1962, the centrepiece of which was a 'discussion event about "Cityscape and History"' (*Stadtbild und Geschichte*).

This event can be understood as an attempt to regulate the emergence of the museal urban gaze. It was led by cultural figures such as the German architectural historian, Julius Posener. Conceptions of time in the city were presented here by experts who shared a set of common assumptions and fears about a technologized society that was most visible in the modern city. The debate reiterated a traditional concern in German culture, between a profound and rooted *Kultur* (cultural tradition) and a technologized (mass) civilization. In that context, Heinrich Gremmels, Director of Town Planning in Königslutter in Lower Saxony, gave a helpful summary of this position:

> The fundamental rift in the structure of the modern world between domestic urbanity and machine civilization can be brought back to the fundamental opposition between house and machine. The house was always on the side of tradition, but [this has] long since been surpassed by the mechanical organism that storms without consideration into the pure future.[14]

The mismatch between the technology of modernity and the means for discussing it, effectively traditional public speaking to an interested cultural elite in a privileged corner of the city (the Academy of the Arts), does not apply so straightforwardly to Julius Posener's talk, which did not take up these questions of 'culture' that so obsessed the other contributors. Rather, Posener addressed the question of the cityscape, and the tension between the idea and the practice of an urban gaze. 'We have grown accustomed', he suggested, 'to recognizing images when we look landscapes – but we are looking at cities', which, he argues, are something different. For Posener, 'planned' cityscapes are 'empty'; what is needed is not 'the monumental' or 'the image', but a view of the city as a vernacular structure from which life is generated. Emptiness for Posener is both the absence of life and the absence of history, a cityscape without history.

An important irony is that Posener constrasts the 'empty' landscape not with the 'immediate' material city but a set of images. He refers to a 'charming' exhibition of amateur photographs of Berlin that ran concurrently to the Bauwochen in 1962 (Fig. 4). This photographic exhibition illustrates two connected technologies of the museal urban gaze. First, there was the gaze of the photographer, whose 'beam of attention'[15] is motivated by a 'will to remember'[16] place in resisting the threat of destruction by the production of a 'spatial image' of a particular detail of the vernacular urban landscape. Second, there was the display of the photographs in the exhibition, which resituated that initial moment of resistance into the form of civic seeing organized by the city authorities who were ultimately responsible for the competition and the exhibition of its results (with the associated evaluative ranking).

Posener described these photographers as 'lovers of the city, in the true sense of the word, [who] have represented Berlin scenes with a romantic magic which the eye that is used to the everyday in Berlin scarcely expects.'[17] Many motifs in the exhibition, such as the Charlottenburg Palace

4. Opening of the exhibition of the amateur photograph competition, 'History in the Cityscape'. 30 August 1962. Left, first-prize winner Heinz Gronau; right, Senator Rolf Schwedler. Photograph: Johann Willa. Courtesy of Berlin Landesarchiv.

for example, are also present in photobooks of the period, such as *Junges altes Berlin*. Posener in fact remarked on the omnipresent phenomenon of the Berlin photobook, observing that 'on average there appear about two a week.' *Junges, altes Berlin* and other photobooks of this ilk, work much more ambivalently than Artus's book, mentioned earlier, in their sympathetic presentation of the former cityscapes. Whereas the exhibition showed many vernacular elements, the photobooks, Posener argued, focused on the 'monumental.' In the exhibition, 'one sees old street lamps and iron cast sewer hole covers, the like of which are still to be found in side streets'; one also sees houses, house fronts and parts of house fronts from the previous century.' This focus on detail is striking and typical of what would become a more general museal urban gaze. Posener concluded that 'we have to keep hold of the Charlottenburg Palace, of the old house fronts in the Christstrasse, of the green squares in Kreuzberg. We have to preserve them, just as we have to preserve the street lamps and the old water pumps. [...] We have to preserve them, because we are poor.'[18] Posener is here giving voice to what Halbwachs calls the 'resistance of local tradition', albeit one that is mediated through the official channels of exhibition.

Remembering the 'murdered' city

This resistance, and its concern with vernacular remains, had also been taking on a more concrete form in the public sphere in the voice of the publicist
Wolf Jobst Siedler's essays, which had been appearing in the *Tagesspiegel* from
the late 1950s onwards. Siedler's essays were collected in a book, *The Murdered
City* (*Die Gemordete Stadt*), first published in 1961, along with photographs
by the recently graduated Elisabeth Niggemeyer. While Siedler's book had a
claim to general validity for the Federal Republic, it is Berlin that remained the
focus, both in his text and in Niggemeyer's photographs. The essays originally
appeared in the newspaper without illustration, but now the essays and the
images combined to dissect the synchronic urban gaze, and formulate place
memory with 'an ironic affection for yesterday'.[19] Siedler's textual critique of
the synchronic urban gaze and verbal exposition of a museal urban gaze was
accompanied by photographs that reiterated and professionally evolved the
practice of the Bauwochen exhibition. The tenor of Siedler's essays echoed the
cultural critique of the contributors to the Bauwochen discussion. His central
critique of the synchronic urban gaze was derived from Ernst Jünger and
1920s conservative critiques of modernity and mass society. This is evident
in the introduction to the first edition, where he makes it clear that, in his
opinion, the city square did not fall victim to modern urban planning, but
to 'new forms of order in society'. At the conclusion to the essay entitled
'Farewell to Nineveh', his position finds perhaps its clearest expression:

> At midnight it makes no difference if one is standing amongst the sky-
> scrapers of Houston or the ruins of Berlin. In these two ways the spirit of
> the age of the masses has achieved its aim: emptiness.[20]

In their 'self-deprecating romanticization' of the encounter with urban
phenomena such as the back courtyard, the essays invoke an 'emotional
experience of the urban environment', that is particularly visual. Siedler
may want to facilitate a memory of 'the urban', but urban memory is not
always explicitly invoked. It is implicit in certain formulations regarding
the 'atmosphere' or 'living quality' of a quarter; and always has less to do
with individual buildings than with ways of looking at a city's milieu, a
focus on the vernacular rather than the monumental.

   The introduction to the opening essay, 'Romanticization of the Back
Courtyard' (*Verklärung des Hinterhofs*) highlights the importance of the
gaze, as it remarks not so much on the loss produced by new urban planning,
as upon the fact that this loss has now become *visible*, as a spatial image. Up

to this point, there had been a blindness to this loss, but 'even someone who had no desire to defend rickets-inducing back courtyards' must now see it. [21] What disappears is the visual evidence of the past. In the essay, 'Requiem for Putti' he talks of the 'spirit of the nineteenth century' having been legible from the house walls and street vistas that bore witness to the increasing representative presence of the Wilhelmine empire, and draws attention to the gaze that generates this memory value in a manner that echoes Halbwachs's formulation of understanding how the built environment of the past functioned. For this memory value only exists now 'if our eyes even only slowly become aware of the quality of building in the second half of the previous century, and even if we still have to learn to comprehend that generation in their particular intentions.'[22] Siedler invokes key aspects of Halbwachs's model of place memory: this visibility is predicated on a particular form of gaze that echoes Halbwachs's observations on how place memory was to be remembered, but also adds a rejection of homogeniza-tion, which is at the heart of Siedler's argument: the local and particular versus the homogenized. The perception of 'place' is based on local spatial practices, but the prerequisite of the visibility of 'local' place memory is, in fact, the recognition of loss. Siedler's essays are profoundly attuned to the conditions that produce a museal urban gaze, in that he recognizes that it is linked to vanishing features of the urban environment.

> It is the tragedy of the reconstruction that we are able to recognize the bare facade structures of the Schinkel-inheritors of the [eighteen] sixties and seventies and the vegetative stucco of the *Gruenderzeit* houses of 1880 to 1895 only at that moment when the plaster-addicted wave of modernization in association with household-style calculations liberates the facades of the German cities from all ornamental decoration, in order to cover them with plain unified plaster.[23]

The moment of recognition coincides with the moment of disappearance, but always through the visual perception of atmosphere, as he suggests in 'World without Shadows':

> Atmospheric transformations of this kind are almost always tangible through the visual. In the case [of the shift to purpose-driven perception – SW], the bird's eye perspective would already signal that changes in a society's 'structure of feeling' have taken place: alongside the gaslit green of the old quarters of town comes the bright glare of the new treeless environments.[24]

It is not just the sensual impact of the visual that is invoked, but the contrast with a synchronic urban gaze that dismantles the visual experience of the city. Siedler describes the aura of an obsolete modernity that becomes visible at a moment of technological transformation.

For Siedler, the 'office, shopping and housing centres' are seldom seen as a menace to the 'culture that is being threatened at its roots' by the synchronic urban gaze (which he terms a 'rationalistic drawing-board mentality'). As Siedler describes it, the signature of that culture was the clear togetherness of its citizens in a milieu that had up to now been 'historical', i.e. rooted in historical experience. By implication, the new space will be 'without history', just as it is without (rooted) trees. Siedler's analysis of the synchronic urban gaze also observes that gaze's concern with circulation:

> [For the city renewers,] the city should be made to function again. The concept of the functioning of streets, squares and city areas relates to frictionlessness ... like all words that come from the water-economy. Water as a stream flowing ceaselessly and irreversibly in the same direction is the ideal of urban planning. This is an ideal that is opposed to the spirit of the urban, which lives from the blockage, friction and congestion, from the back and forth, to and fro; the push and shove of the streets draws our attention to cities that are full of life, and *only* those boulevards that are full of people and invite us to stroll (*flanieren*).[25]

Elisabeth Niggemeyer's photographs inserted between the essays are the visual manifestation of a 'stroll' through the city, and the idea of the flâneur is here central, as it is a form of movement without direction and purpose. Niggemeyer's photographs are organized into categories of minor urban objects that one might easily overlook; streets, lamps, façades, windows, trees, squares, doors, doorhandles, halls, greenhouses, courtyards, shops, public houses, villas, towers and gardens. These are particulary highlighted in part of the final section of the book, which is devoted to Chamissoplatz (in Kreuzberg) and, in contrast, the new housing development in Britz-Süd. This final section encapsulates one particular strategy in the visual part of the book: the juxtaposition of 'old' and 'new', but any definition of 'old' and 'new' is shaped by the gaze which has selected the fragment of the city to photograph; in other words, in each case, the framing is directed towards the generation of an auratic effect of 'age value.' The framing seeks to generate the place memory embodied in the form of city square.

The photographs' emphasis is on the face of the square; the façades, but also the more literal inscriptions on the walls. There is a celebration of

5. *Die gemordete Stadt*, pp. 182/183. Photograph: Elisabeth Niggemeyer. Courtesy of Elisabeth Niggemeyer-Pfefferkorn.

the non-linear, both in the formal framing of the scenes and in the layout on the page (Fig. 5). On the first double-page of photographs, there is a large-format picture of one corner of the square, alongside which are placed six smaller images, all of the same size, presenting aspects of the square; on the third page are twelve images, arranged in rows of three images of equal heights, but of irregular width. The subject of the photographs is interestingly balanced between people and architecture. In the set of six, there are four whose main subject is the façade or streetscape, one focused on young girls with a doll, and one where the presence of the people is evident but marginal to the dominant effect of the façade.

In the set of twelve, there are three devoted solely to the façade (two verandas, one shop window); of the other nine, two seem exclusively concentrated on the human subject, but even they explicitly set the human subject within the urban environment, so there is the implication of an interactive relationship. In other words, this set of photographs highlights the connection between spatial practice and the production of space. They reveal spatial practice as a set of human traces left specifically by the inscriptions on the façades, but also on the street, such as the cart standing outside the 'wood and coal' shop. This is a photograph apparently without human presence, but actually gesturing towards the continuity of human presence.

This sequence produces a spatial image of urban memory, but, as in Siedler's essays, it is also placed in contrast to a framing of the synchronic urban gaze in the set of photographs that document Britz-Süd, a social housing development built in the south-east of West Berlin in 1956-57. These are printed over two pages: the first, as on the facing page from Chamissoplatz, has twelve images, but these are of a uniform size. The focus is uniformly on the architecture; there are no human subjects and only one photograph contains a single car. The images appear as a panoramic series taken from a single standpoint, and this serves to draw attention to the varied standpoints from which the Chamissoplatz photographs were taken. The camera thus mimics the static viewpoint of the synchronic urban gaze, but also *demonstrates* through *imitation* the sterility of that gaze. The camera deliberately chooses subjects that do not function as coherent photographic subjects, implying this absence of coherence is a result of the design. The notion of serial repetition, which is generated by the uniformity, is underscored by placing the images in a grid, and by the fact that the first and last images are almost identical (in fact they are not, the last one is tighter to the balcony, and thus cuts off the two furthest windows in the first photograph).

This final photographic section of the book functions as the culmination of a strategy that has been visible throughout the photographic sections in the book, one that includes the juxtaposition of 'new' and 'old', illustrating how the synchronic gaze envisions the urban environment by reproducing that gaze. The photographs in this section make sense as part of a series: children appear captured *in motion* on the next two pages, running over cardboard boxes on the pavement of the Nehringstrasse, whereas the following large-format photograph spread over two pages, offers a bird's eye perspective of a spartan playpark in the Goethestrasse in Charlottenburg, with two children sitting statically on a geometrically situated bench. The synchronic urban gaze is visually associated with stasis and emptiness. The supplementary captions in this section include a list of the 'vocabulary of the urban planners, building authorities and architects', accompanying another grid arrangement of images of 'prohibition'.[26] The linguistic regulation of spatial practice is complemented by the (monotonous) regulation of seeing imitated by the camera. [27]

By contrast, elsewhere in the book, where the camera projects a museal gaze, the focus is on specific objects, such as the full-page photograph of a cast-iron water pump from the Karl-August-Platz in Charlottenburg. The accompanying caption's topographical detail here and elsewhere reminds us not to draw too clear a distinction between text and image in the book;

this is underlined by the fact that the essays are interspersed between the photographic series. The new Hansa quarter is a key reference point for the camera that is dissecting the synchronic urban gaze, and a full page is devoted to the image (which also appears on the book's cover) of a builder apparently carelessly tossing a piece of decorative stucco from the roof of a building; the caption simply describes the location as 'Old Hansa Quarter, demolished'. This is the camera as documenter of the city; the collection of photographs then as the production of an archive of cultural memory.[28]

The image of Riehmer's Hofgarten (from 1964, one of five areas protected by the city façade regulations) is accompanied by a textual narrative about its builder, Wilhelm Riehmer. This is an archetypal example of cultural memory underpinned by communicative strategies, in that the image becomes the evidence for the story that is told, but the encounter with the images of the 'age value' of the place plays a key role as a guarantee for the validity of the narrative.[29]

(Psycho-) analysing the inhospitable city

The Murdered City developed the technology of recovering place memory through a certain mode of encounter. The book illustrates the importance of the visual as a means of communicating the critique of a synchronic gaze and the formulation of a museal urban gaze. Whereas Siedler's verbal formulation of the memorial urban gaze was complemented and expanded in the photographs and captions of Elisabeth Niggemeyer, Alexander Mitscherlich's invocation of 'collective place memory' in *The Inhospitability of Our Cities* was exclusively textual. Central to Mitscherlich's gaze is the assumption that post-war reconstruction represents a form of wilful collective amnesia. The maintenance of the built environment could, then, ideally, construct a different kind of collective – identity. He analyses post-war West German society as a 'society which carries out its atonement – which equates to a healing of the soul – by pretending there had been no catastrophe and moreover, as if the process of ongoing industrialization and bureaucratization would have no pressing consequences for the whole calibre of their life [...]'. Mitscherlich implies that the built environment is the expression of a collective psychological state of amnesia. Dieter Bartetzko also suggests that the towns became the architectural expression of Mitscherlich's central socio-psychological concept, the Germans' 'inability to mourn'.[30] This is predicated on the model of place memory in which the built environment is a faithful mirror of a collective:

> We have wasted the chance granted us after the war to build more cleverly
> thought-out, genuinely new cities. Or, to put it another way, if cities are
> collective self-representations, then that which we encounter here in
> terms of self-representation, is alarming.[31]

Siedler and Mitscherlich have in common a critique of technocratic modern
rationalization, as it was symptomatically manifested in the synchronic
urban gaze that disregards the value of tradition. Mitscherlich views post-
war reconstruction as a thoughtless, technocratic destruction of tradition,
but identifies the historical roots of that gaze in National Socialism, arguing
that 'the reconstruction, which we have experienced and permitted, is still
an awkward after-phase of the collective psychosis that was "National Socialism", which led to the destruction of our most noble urban substance.'[32]
This is an important argument, as it suggests that the interrogation of the
experiences under National Socialism, absent other than subliminally in
references to 'the war' in Siedler's book, is central to an 'overcoming' of
the authoritarian, anti-democratic worldview of which the synchronic
urban gaze is a symptom. This approach is important to understanding the
forms of the museal gaze and the associated 'place memory work' that will
emerge in the 1970s. Initially, as with Mitscherlich, this work is not based
on identifying and working through traces of the past, but on identifying the psychological roots of the synchronic urban gaze. Mitscherlich
claims that 'inadequate urban planning participates in the destruction
of public consciousness whenever it takes only commercial interests and
traffic infrastructure into account.'[33] He thus introduces a conception of a
cohesive, democratic public sphere that is absent in Siedler's considerations,
and thereby implies that the maintenance of the built environment could
construct a different kind of collective identity through a different kind of
consciousness, in other words, a different kind of relationship with the built
environment. What this might mean in practical terms is not explained
by Mitscherlich, but, at the end of *The Murdered City*, Siedler offers a way
forward that addresses contemporary developments and seeks to move
beyond 'islands of tradition' to 'milieux of memory' (where the rhythm is
determinate), which will become increasingly important in coming years:

> We are not dealing here with a 'save the stucco' movement, which has only
> been the fig leaf for reckless interventions in the historical substance of
> the city, and cityscape preservation [*Stadtbildpflege*] can, in its conserva-
> tion of islands of tradition, only be of secondary importance for an overall
> building policy which deals with the revitalization of old quarters – from

the medieval Spandau, exclusively ruined by planning, down to the Wedding of the nineteenth century. This, and not another new quarter, would be a bold and future-directing task for an IBA in Berlin.[34]

The start of this excerpt refers to a Senate policy of the time, 'Save the Stucco' (*Rettet den Stuck*), one of the ways in which the authorities in West Berlin sought to soften the resistance of local tradition to its urban renewal plans. In institutional terms, the Senate subordinated the 'memory value' of urban space to the exchange value of space, primarily by situating the section for 'monumental preservation and museal art objects' as one of five sections within the department of 'State and Urban Planning', within the Senate Administration for Building and Housing. The Head of Conservation for the (West) Berlin region had been administratively situated outside this framework (being part of the Senate Administration for Science and Art). The 'Office for Monument Preservation' was however described in the commentary to the 'Building Regulations' of 1959, as a subordinate office of the Senator for Building and Housing, which took on the tasks of the former Head of Conservation. The position of Head of Conservation had remained unfilled after the departure of Prof. Hinnerk Scheper in that watershed year of 1957. At that point, Wolfgang Konwiarz had taken on the supervision of 'monument preservation' in his role within the State and Urban Planning department. The complex relationship between *Stadtbildpflege* (preservation of the city image) and *Denkmalpflege* (monument preservation) finds expression in the administrative structures that evolve at this point: *Stadtbildpflege* is separated off from *Denkmalpflege* and becomes the responsibility of Konwiarz and his department. It is therefore ever more clearly bound within planning structures and its dictates.

   Stadtbildpflege as a form of museal urban gaze is a technology that aims to preserve the visual mode of encounter with the cityscape. As urban memory, it involves not the explicit narrativization of a collective past that it preserves – as would be the model in cultural memory – but rather an inexplicit encounter with the façade as an 'unintended monument' which possesses age value. The principle is directed towards the 'surface value' rather than 'historical value' of the building; though it is often equated with the slogan 'Save the Stucco', *Stadtbildpflege* works not just with the 'old', but also with the harmonious in the cityscape. In 1964 five areas in Berlin were selected to be protected from alterations which would affect their 'uniqueness': these were the aforementioned Riehmers Hofgarten, Chamissoplatz and Planufer in Kreuzberg, the Schloß-/ Christstraße in

Charlottenburg und a part of Alt-Spandau. Here the plaster and stucco decorations from the pre-1914 era, along with the gas lanterns, water pumps and other aspects of street furniture were to be maintained.

The museal urban gaze in East Berlin

International modernist architecture had been frowned upon in the early, Stalinist-dominated years of the GDR. While, as a result, it is possible to read the GDR cityscape in terms of the intentional ideological codings embedded within them, this can lead us to neglect the role played by remnants and their ambiguous codes, but also the way in which the GDR's vision of the cityscape, like that in the West of the city, corresponded, post-Stalin, with other international tendencies in urban planning. Yet the conception of the cityscape as a 'technical problem' in East Berlin becomes evident if we return to the infamous decision to demolish the Stadtschloss in the heart of the city centre in 1950. Bernd Maether, in his study of the 'destruction' of the Berlin Palace follows the conventional line of argument that it was the leadership of the SED, and in particular Walter Ulbricht, who was responsible for the decision to demolish the Stadtschloss, because the destruction of the historical heritage of the Prussian monarchy was a fundamental component of their ideology: 'the idea was to rewrite history by ignoring, indeed destroying the old.'[35] Elsewhere Maether asserts that the Communist Party (KPD) was in favour of demolition from the very start.[36] This is the archetypal 'ideological' reading of the cityscape, but this explanation is only rarely evident in the documents relating to the Palace. These documents can be productively read in terms of how they regard or disregard the site, highlighting the important distinction which Maether elides in his use of 'ignored and 'destroyed'.

On June 26 1950, at a session of the ZK of the SED, point 5 of the agenda considered the order for the removal of ruins and the reconstruction of those cities in the GDR destroyed by the war. The financial cost of reconstruction was central to these proposals: the reconfiguration of useable ruins was to be allowed as long as the cost of reconstruction was below that of demolition and new build; in other words, this was an economic calculation.[37]

A report prepared by the Institute for Urban Planning in the Ministry of Construction addressed not the fate of the Palace, but rather the construction of a large-scale space for political demonstrations in the centre of Berlin and in its calculations it considers the demolition of both the Dom and the Schloss.[38] Although the space was to serve an ideological purpose, the conclusion drawn is formulated in terms of a calculation framed within historical coordinates: the Lustgarten was the 'historical location for demonstrations', and has space for 140,000 demonstrators taking part in a non-mobile demonstration; with the demolition of both the Palace and the Cathedral, that number would increase to 300,000.[39] The report then suggested that if a decision were made in favour of a space for mobile demonstrations, the 'historical' square could be retained. The wall of the Schloss would form the background to the demonstrations. This certainly does not imply, as Maether infers, that the demolition of the Palace was a foregone conclusion, but rather that the value of the space was primarily being calculated according to the principles of urban circulation.[40]

Maether asserts that Walter Ulbricht expressed himself very strongly against the maintenance of the Palace in his speech at the 3rd Party Conference of the SED on 22 July 1950. Yet, again, the focus in Ulbricht's speech in the section 'Large-Scale Buildings in the Five Year Plan' betrays a fundamental disregard for the Stadtschloss, which appears almost marginally in the section:

> The centre of the city is to be determined by monumental buildings and an architectonic composition which does justice to the importance of the German capital [...] The centre of our capital, the Lustgarten and the area taken up now by the ruin of the Schloss must become a space for demonstrations in which the willingness of people to struggle and build must find its expression.[41]

While it is clear that the future cityscape is to serve ideological ends, the reference to the *area* occupied by the Schloss ruin indicates, from Ulbricht's perspective, both the neutral emptiness of the space and the soon-to-be-removed obsolescence of the Palace. The debate documented in Maether's collection in fact highlights the question of the Schloss's supposed obsolescence, revolving around, on the one hand, the cultural-historical and antiquarian-historical value of the architecture as asserted from the Western perspective, and on the other, the question of the extent of the Palace's ruination (estimated at 80%) and the cost of renovation, as opposed to demolition and new construction.[42] Gerhard Strauss, who was leading the preservationist activities at the demolition site, posted his 'Theses' about the Schloss both in the Palace and in the Humboldt University. This was the one point at which the ideological obsolescence of the building was cited as an obstacle to the construction of a new socialist city.[43]

The urban planning questions addressed so far contain an implicit visualization of urban space, but on 10 October 1950, Strauss wrote to Kurt Liebknecht, director of the Institute for Urban Planning in the Ministry of Construction, reminding him that he had previously suggested making a *Kulturfilm* about the work being carried out at the Palace, with the intention of demonstrating two things: the necessity of demolition as well as the painstaking work being undertaken by the government in salvaging valuable material. He appended to this letter an outline for the proposed film.[44]

The film was to begin by juxtaposing images of the undestroyed and the destroyed Palace, illustrating the culturally hostile barbarism of the Fascist war and the Allied terror attacks. It would also demonstrate that the government's decision to demolish the Palace was the right one, through the great extent of the destruction, i.e. the building's physical obsolescence, while simultaneously pointing to the maintenance of all extant valuable elements. In order to provide a context for the Schloss's situation and the need to deal with the obsolescence brought about by the war, this would be followed by images of destroyed parts of Berlin and other cities in Germany. Again emphasizing the technical problem of the city, it would be made clear that the demolition of the Palace ruin would be shown to open up the centre of the German capital for a comprehensive restructuring, which would allow for the large-scale solution of most of the long-term urban infrastructure problems. The film was then to conclude with images of models for the new city centre.[45]

While there was doubtless an ideological dimension to the demolition of the Stadtschloss, the building was not demolished because of what it represented. Rather, what it represented meant that it was not accorded any value as an element of the past. Instead there was an interplay of technocratic and ideological concerns in which the calculable and visually demonstrable obsolescence of the building grounded an argument that was aligned with the perception of its ideological obsolescence. The 'empty space' created by the demolition of the Palace was to be filled by ideological content, but the principle which underpinned the clearing of the site was a calculation about space that pays no attention to the historical time present in the Palace buildings. Laurenz Demps comes to this conclusion on the basis that, for the GDR regime, 'the total urban environment was material at its disposal, whose historical contours they believed they had every right to ignore.[46] As the sixteen principles of urban planning, published during considerations of the Palace on 27 July 1950, made clear, the organization of urban space was ultimately subordinate to the needs of circulation.[47]

The initial phase of (re)construction, under the guidelines of the Sixteen Principles, was underpinned by a search for a 'national German architectural style', as in the first phase of the Stalinallee, and by plans that proposed the 'careful renewal' of old districts such as the Fischerkiez.[48] Urban planning in East Berlin and beyond was however increasingly dominated by what Simone Hain terms the 'establishment of the most modern building structures within conventional international parameters.'[49] This meant a continuing disregard for existing urban structures and habitual spatial practices, as seen in Henselmann's 1956 vision for the Friedrichshain district, and the plans submitted for the 'socialist restructuring of the city centre' in 1958. Allied to this was an emphasis on a more efficient industrialization of building production.[50] At the heart of this was a synchronic urban gaze that had no conception of former time and space, and envisioned the future as a site of circulatory automobile activity, just as the fomer site of the Schloss had been viewed as a site of synchronic marching. This vision was disseminated to the GDR public in a series of photobooks produced throughout the 1950s, such as *Berlin: Yesterday, Today, Tomorrow* (*Berlin: Gestern, Heute, Morgen*) or *Ten Years of National Construction Work in the Capital Berlin* (*10 Jahre Nationales Aufbauwerk Hauptstadt Berlin*),[51] which juxtaposed images of the 'obsolescent' city of 1945 with images of the emerging 'new' city, or *Berlin Heute und Morgen* or *Unser Berlin: Die Hauptstadt Berlin*, which celebrated the new architectural and industrial achievements of the nascent socialist state.[52] These volumes demonstrate how, in a manner similar to that intended by Strauss, the conceptual vision was translated into the media of visual culture.

From the post-Stalin era onwards, the production of the East Berlin cityscape was primarily visualized as a technical problem, as the 'creation of an intelligible city without a memory of everyday life.'[53] Nevertheless we can begin to chart how the remembrance of everyday life begins to emerge almost in spite of itself against the dominance of an economic evaluation of the built environment.

This new perspective manifests itself in two renovation projects in previously disregarded areas of East Berlin in the Prenzlauer Berg in the late 1960s/early 1970s: Arkonaplatz and Arnimplatz. In a 1968 edition of the official state architectural journal, *Deutsche Architektur*, Klaus Pöschk outlined the principles concerning the renovation of Arkonaplatz.[54] Pöschk had concluded in a prior article in 1967 that earlier renovations nearby had not been effective enough from economic or socio-political perspectives. Although the exchange value of the site remained predominant, Pöschk proposed the renovation of the Arkonaplatz as a model by which the 'obsolescent and out-dated structure of the residential district' could be overcome.[55] Within this model, a different visualisation of the value of the cityscape, its 'memory value', began to make itself evident in Pöschk's thinking:

> The individual streets form a particular focus of the architectural design of the reconstructed 'Altbausubstanz'. The requirement here is that the characteristics of the typical Berlin streetscape are retained, and a meaningful colour scheme, which in a newly developed colourfulness takes into account an adaptation of the original colours, in order to reflect the new social content. It is important to note that the residential district does not belong to those 'reserved zones', such as the Marienstrasse [close to the Friedrichstrasse railway station – SW], which fall under the special conditions of Berlin's monument preservation regulations.[56]

Pöschk's final point is a crucial one: what is being preserved is not an object of 'historical value', but a memory of the network of relationships to the built environment, a 'spatial image' of the past. Attention was to be paid to the relationship of the new colours to the original, as well as the maintenance of certain sections of wall (*Mauerwerksteile*). While the renovation paid attention to the way the buildings looked in the past, Pöschk stressed that any expense incurred was justifiable, and that the underlying criterion, remained the 'physical and moral obsolescence' of the building. This was underlined by the use of illustrative photographs, in particular an image of the 'urban structure and form of the residential area', a dilapidated back courtyard that, according to the caption, was the inheritance of 'the capitalist past' and bore the 'characteristics of the rental barracks of the *Gründerzeit*'. While the caption identified the structure's 'moral obsolescence', this was elided with the photograph's visible evidence of physical obsolescence and juxtaposed a page later with a photograph of a renovated façade.

Two years later, again in *Deutsche Architektur*, Manfred Zache was also keen to justify such remedial maintenance through the evidence of calculations. Despite his emphasis on the calculability of renovation, one of the guiding principles was, as with the Arkonaplatz, an emphasis on the effect of the visual impact of the buildings through the integration of material elements (façades) that are 'culturally historically valuable' or indeed merely 'partially still in existence'.[57] Zache introduced into the equation a factor ('cultural history') that was subjected neither to the calculability of economics nor to a clear ideologically approved historical narrative. Yet this did not involve a fundamental change of revaluation of the way in which former structures were viewed.[58] The objective quantifiability of the cityscape was still the dominant paradigm for visualizing the city.

Rejecting the synchronic city in West Berlin

This quantifiability paradigm was largely still the case in the west of the city, where, however, the generational unrest of the late 1960s also spilled over into concerns about the built environment. Mitscherlich had argued in *The Inhospitability of Our Cities* that 'such [an amnesiac] society awakens in different parts of its body at different times from their dreams and their denials – but it does awaken.'[59] This process of awakening manifests itself very strikingly in the place memory work of the 1970s, which the next chapter discusses, but it also begins to become visible in the 1967 protests against the proposed demolition of plot 210 on the Kurfürstendamm. The protests questioned whether Berlin should become 'like Frankfurt' (i.e. a city dominated by financial transactions). These protests are evident in 'Aktion 507', named after the room in the Technical University appropriated by a set of young architects to make use of the money (18,000 marks) the Senate had provided them with to present their work and ideas. The young architects had taken the money and, after some hesitation from Bausenator Schwedler, had been allowed to use it for their 'critical engagement with contemporary building practice.' Following the pattern developed by the emergent extra-parliamentary opposition in the city, the event formed a self-styled 'anti-Bauwochen', and was organized in the style of a revolutionary council: 120 architects met in the room, discussing photographs of various building plans. The main target for their opprobrium was the, at that time half-completed, Märkisches Viertel development in the north of the city. By 1972 this new quarter was intended to be housing more than 60,000 people who had been moved out of the 'obsolete' workers' districts of Wedding and Kreuzberg that were in the process of being demolished. The critique was predominately directed against what the young architects saw as the mere transposition of the 'slums' from one district to a new one. In line with the argument of Mitscherlich, which had emphasized the continuity of economic structures as one key dimension of Germany's failure to think itself anew after the war, they also criticized the particular structure of the Berlin building economy that made financial gain the prime driver of housing production. Memory value was not (yet) an element in the discussion. The critique manifests itself primarily within the terms of exchange value. It was, ironically, the former Nazi architect, Werner March, who produced a *Gutachten* outlining that the renovation and modernization of one particular house (Wassertorstrasse 5 in Kreuzberg) would cost 91,500 marks, whereas the demolition would cost 250,000 marks. Similar calculations were made by the West Berlin sociologist, Ilsa Balg, which suggested that renovation of the Kreuzberg districts would cost 6.4 million marks as opposed to 18.1 million for new building.[60]

This is not a critique of the synchronic urban gaze in terms of how it frames a relationship to time and the city, but accepts the principle of the exchange value of space. The critique accepts, at least on the surface, that a better system of exchange value would produce a more efficient solution; in other words, as with East Berlin's urban renovation policy, the argument accepted the economic and technocratic principles of spatial organization.

The idea that the cityscape might contain value different to a quantifiable exchange value had however begun to manifest itself by the end of the 1960s. The institutional regulation of this shift is visible in the announcement by the *Stadtbildpflege* department in January 1970 that it would be making an inventory of 'historically valuable' house façades in the inner districts of West Berlin, effectively transferring them from the urban repository into a relatively more ordered archive. This act of curating the city was described as a task of 'discovery' and initial results suggested that 229 houses in Kreuzberg were under consideration.[61] None of the official forms of the museal gaze seek to reframe the rhythm of the encounter with the cityscape as a movement through urban space and as such it will ultimately be susceptible to the synchronic rhythms of consumption. It is film where this examination of urban rhythms first emerged.

Summer in the city: Moving through urban space

Wim Wenders's first film, *Summer in the City* (1970) is an investigation of movement through urban spaces. The film's title seems ironic, as the action takes place in winter, and there is little 'urbanity' in the film's depictions of the cityscapes of Munich and Berlin.

Wenders's film explicitly addresses transformations in the built environment when the central character, Hans, addresses his partner across the breakfast table. He remarks (in a non-sychronized voice-over) that jack-hammer noise had awoken him at 7am, and that he was thinking of going to Berlin, where, he reports, a house had been demolished on the corner of Kurfürstendamm and Bleibtreustrasse. In the terse, almost non-communicative verbal style of the film, he continues:

> A grey, five-storey house. There were a bunch of people there and two big bulldozers. It was in the late afternoon. It was almost dark and the sky was blue even though it was November. Over the hole in the ground the sky was divided vertically. On the left side it was blue and on the right side there was a wall of dust and smoke that reached into the horizon. It is said that the sky was almost too blue and too dark.

The city described verbally here is topographically generic, an effect which the rest of the film does little to dispel. Yet it is a film that examines city-scapes and their encounter very closely. This is done most explicitly in those sequences which examine the mode of travelling through urban space. There are eight travelling sequences in the film; the first three in Munich, the fourth a plane journey to Berlin, and the final four in Berlin, but there is little that is specific to either city in any of these journeys. The meandering journeys presented in the film take up approximately a third of the film's running time (ca. 40 minutes of 2 hours), but it is central to these journeys that they have no apparent direction; the absence of narrative thrust, of cause and effect, of action and reaction, allows them to be read as abstract investigations of rhythm and movement in cinema and the city.

The second journey through Berlin begins with a static shot of a news-paper kiosk at a road intersection; the camera moves, and we slowly realize this was a non-character-aligned view from a car that had been waiting at a traffic light; the car turns a corner and comes alongside Hans, who is walking through the snow. The car/camera matches his pace as it follows him for about a minute; at which point the film cuts to a streetscape of an old 'rental barrack' thoroughfare replete with ornate façades, viewed statically from a position in the centre of the road. There is a sudden, low-pitched noise that scatters pigeons across the frame; a distant car moves off, leading us automatically to associate the noise with the car, although the juxtaposition is awkward enough to make this seem a little unlikely (it is more the 'boom' of a demolition). This auditory association of the car with the disruption of the peaceful/old cityscape is one that makes sense within a film in which moving through the city is gradually adapted to walking pace, rejecting automobile movement in favour of contemplation of the built environment, as seen in the concluding view of the 'old' façades in this sequence, as the camera remains static, allowing us to contemplate the static streetscape for another thirty seconds.

This trajectory from automobile transport to walking is taken to its conclusion in the final travelling sequence of the film, which follows Hans as he walks along a snowy path by a canal in Berlin. The camera is not signalled as being transported via car, nor do we have any human figure with whom to identify the gaze beyond that of the camera. In any case, the camera moves at Hans's pace to the accompaniment of the powerful rhythms of The Lovin' Spoonful's 'Summer in the City'. This walk continues uninterrupted for over two minutes until the camera halts while Hans walks on, leaving the spectator to contemplate the 'rhythmic' architectural structure before the music stops.[62] At this point the built environment, the camera and the soundtrack combine; we are no longer looking at the image of movement (walking). We thought the object of our attention was the (now unlit) walking protagonist, but in fact we realize that it was the brightly lit building behind him for the duration of the shot. The camera allows the protagonist to disappear from the frame as it comes to a halt and we are invited to contemplate the modernist building. Wenders interrupts the habitual regime of cinematic seeing, which focuses on the movement of the body of the protagonist, and engages us in a form of museal gaze, a contemplation of the city through which he (and we) conventionally move without looking – crucially, the protagonist here is *also* not looking at the building, thus causing the encounter with the building to be framed as indirect.

The film's presentation of the encounter with a generic modern city determined by a synchronic urban gaze, is not wholly negative; it is important to note the hypnotic pleasure of the view from the car in the film, one that is underpinned by the use of the rhythmic soundtrack. Nevertheless, the trajectory is towards a contemplative gaze directed at the built environment, away from the 'view from a car' that is the ground-level form of the synchronic gaze. The film analyses how the synchronic urban gaze shapes the automated subject at 'ground level' and the analysis moves towards a positive formulation of an museal urban gaze within the film form, a phenomenological encounter with the 'new' is contrasted with a different gaze that foregrounds different rhythms of space and time as central to the substantive, durational experience of the urban environment.

Film and obsolescent places in East Berlin

The Berlin of *Summer in the City* is also resolutely a Western one. Its diagnosis of the modern city disregards the political divisions that undoubtedly shaped Berlin and the spatial experience of the city. In East Berlin, film, for more pragmatic reasons, was silent on the capital division, but was also being used as a way of interrogating the urban environment and its relationship to time. In the GDR, a critique of interchangeability now began to manifest itself in the reassertion of an individualism that insists on the stubborn detail in contrast to the grand narrative. This individualism is also a rejection of the *modern* individual with his individualized living cell (apartment) and travelling cell (car), part of the more general critique of modernized existence that emerges in the GDR from the early 1970s onwards. [63] This critique is focalized through the figure of Paul at the beginning of *The Legend of Paul and Paula* (*Die Legende von Paul und Paula*, 1973). In *The Legend of Paul and Paula*, the distinction between 'obsolete' and 'modern' is conveyed in the juxtaposition of two forms of dwelling (the ostensibly obsolete rental barracks and the new apartment block) within the same streetscape. The critique of automobility as a modern urban rhythm is implied within the narrative by the fact that Paula's son is knocked down by a car, and the fact that Paula is initially offered a way out of her situation by Harry Saft, who owns a tyre workshop, and frequently acts as Paula's chauffeur. Paula's refusal to accept this solution is both a gendered response and, in a more subtle way, a refusal to submit the body to the rhythms demanded by the city. Similarly, while Paul and Paula's refuge is an interstitial marginalized location amongst the building sites, it is also the place where Paul keeps his stylishly obsolete car as a kind of hidden relic. As my analysis here suggests, the obsolescent works here, as a silent, but visible emblem of dissent towards the synchronic regime of the GDR city (and state). The formulation of a specifically museal urban gaze remains cinematically unworked-through in GDR film at this point, but will be developed in *Solo Sunny*, released in the GDR in 1979 and discussed in the next chapter.

Public discourse and the urban past

By the mid-1970s in both halves of divided Berlin, the memory value of the urban past was emerging as a key motif. While it remains largely 'sub-textual' within public discourse in the East, the growing interest in the urban past in West Berlin was manifesting itself in public discourse before 1975. For example, *Der Tagesspiegel* had a long-running series on structures that were 'amongst Berlin's listed buildings', which ran from the end of March 1971, just after the publication of the official 'List of Building

Monuments' in February, through to 1974. That official list contained 'only' 192 buildings for the 12 districts. The series mutated in June 1971 to run in a parallel with a series of buildings that were 'not listed' and thus can be thought of as unintended vernacular monuments to the urban past.

The first article in this parallel series, authored by Günter Kühne, presented Kurfürstendamm 37, a spatial image of a building under threat (with an explicit reference to the demolition of Kurfürstendamm 210). It was not so much the building which is at stake, but the 'typical atmosphere' of the milieu, to which the individual façade contributes. Kühne's gaze produces a spatial image of the former city but the form of memory value is simultaneously superficial and intangible, and certainly imprecise in terms of its conception of 'the past', other than in contrast to a system that does not value a building other than for its exchange value. As Kühne writes of Block 37, 'a new owner can do the calculation, and work out that a complete new structure would be more profitable in terms of rent income.'[64]

Kühne followed these parallel series with another, more prominent and regular series for the Sunday edition of the *Tagesspiegel*, from April 1974 onwards, entitled 'Is Berlin losing its Face?'[65] The programmatic focus on the street's display of the vernacular past is striking, although Kühne's initial article, subtitled *Stadtbild in Gefahr* (The Cityscape in Danger), was effectively a history of post-war planning in Berlin. In this article, he bemoaned the dominance of unspecified 'economic interests' in planning decisions and included a discussion of the concept of the cityscape, in which, reiterating Mitscherlich's critique, the post-1945 era was invoked as a missed opportunity in which 'a convincing planning conception never became visible.' This was expanded in the second article, which described the Hansaviertel in precisely these terms. Kühne's critique of post-war urban planning extended over six articles in total, and despite the overarching title, he rarely referred to the presence or disappearance of past structures (although in the fourth article, he does discuss the disappearance of the *Grundriss* of the medieval settlements of Berlin and Cölln at the centre of the now-divided city). While the visual motif repeated at the top of each article was of a *Gründerzeit* façade gradually crumbling from view, Kühne's article took up a different historical lineage, suggesting that what was missed in the post-war era was a connection to the modernist traditions of the Weimar era, but he took this no further, and indeed it is a lineage that has rarely managed to find much traction even in post-wall Berlin, other than in a most superficial fashion.[66] The valuing of the 'urban past' at this point was intended at 'making good' the mistakes of the post-war era. Kühne's articles were aimed at an amelioration of the synchronic urban gaze, primarily through a critique of a misrecognition of spatial practice and the dominance of 'traffic planning', which leads to 'an atomization of the urban structure'. Kühne lamented the absence of public involvement in urban planning at any level. He noted, however, the popularity of the activity of the *Stadtbildpflege* department, though saw this activity as still symptomatic of a piecemeal approach that had determined post-war planning, underpinned by what he saw as the dubious and desperate preservationist theory of 'islands of tradition'. Consequently, he called for a revision of urban policy in the sense in which Siedler described it earlier. Kühne also observed the return to 'inner-city living' that was growing in popularity at this time. This inner-city living is structured by a set of spatial practices that are no longer so closely tied to the automobility on which suburban developments such as the Gropiusstadt and the Märkisches Viertel were predicated.

An attempt to address questions of 'inner-city living' was at the core of the Senate's response to this public resistance to the demolition of neighbourhoods. The formation of urban memory, as a memory of the urban environment, but also of memory *in* the urban environment, is at stake in the following decade: the planning, from 1978 onwards, of an International Building Exhibition (IBA), originally slated to take place in 1984, although ultimately it took place in 1987. This process, and how it helps to refine and develop the museal urban gaze through its 'place memory work', is the focus of the next chapter.

2.   'Place Memory Work' in Berlin 1975-1989

This chapter traces how 'place memory work' developed across forms of visual culture in the 1970s and 1980s, a period that sees a generational shift in urban consciousness and the emergence of curators, for whom the need to respond to the traces of the city's past (both from before and after 1945) led them to theorize how to 'work with place' in the production of spatial images through architecture, site-specific intervention, as well as photography and film. As this chapter shows, the dynamics of place memory can be generated through a direct encounter with the material remnant, but also through the indexical recording forms of the photograph and film, whose strategies for displaying the cityscape dovetail with the display strategies of material interventions.

Beyond the piecemeal work of *Stadtbildpflege* and sporadic journalistic spatial images of resistance to demolition, Berlin's Second International Building Exhibition, which had its beginnings in the late 1970s and officially concluded in 1987, established the institutional curation of the built environment within the city, under the guiding principle that 'the fundamental historical structure of the city must become the basis of future urban development.'[1] This involved the institutional incorporation of figures from a younger generation who had previously been on the margins of urban planning. The major actors of this generation include the architect, JP Kleihues (born in 1933) whose 1971 design – 'Block 270' – for a residential building in Berlin-Wedding had been a seminal work in making Berlin's 'block plan' publically visible again after the wholesale disregard for this form of urban organization in the post-war era. They also include Dieter Hoffmann-Axthelm (born in 1940), who was heavily influenced by the alternative politics of Berlin-Kreuzberg in the 1970s, and through his involvement in the critical architectural journal, *Arch+*, and the influential alternative publishing house *Ästhetik und Kommunikation* had begun to address questions of urban planning and architectural history through a varied intellectual career. At the core of the International Building Exhibition (IBA) is the assumption that the built environment has a connection to the past, its fabric has an anamnestic dimension, a 'memory value' in Huyssen's terms. What constitutes that past and how it is to be both curated and displayed are the central concerns of the museal gaze in this period, which sees both the theoretical discussion and practical operation of a museal urban gaze and the production of spatial images. This will be discussed through the lens of the IBA, and its projects, as well as in other forms of visual culture, in particular site-specific installations, photographic practice, and film, all of which enacted forms of the museal urban gaze in this period.

The second IBA

Planning for the IBA took its impetus from developments within the city of Berlin and from the rediscovery of the tradition of the 'European city' by the Italian architect Aldo Rossi (1931-1997). Rossi's influential book, *The Architecture of the City* (*L'architettura della città*) had been published in 1966, and played a major role in convincing the European Council to establish the European Year of Architecture, and its adoption of the European Charter of the Architectural Heritage in 1975. Rossi's understanding of 'monumental urban architecture' that was neither a specific monument to a past event, nor sought to dominate its citizens, deeply chimed with Halbwachs's theories of collective memory, particularly the persistent street network as the 'genetic code' of the city.[2]

The slogan for the European Year of Architecture, 'A Future for Our Past', invoked a collective temporality within the city. Berlin's IBA was intended to take account of an emerging new urbanism, in terms of an engagement with a philosophy of urban history. As we shall see, in practice, it cultivated an image of the past, through the post-modern, playful appropriation of previous architectural forms by the architects invited to become involved, who included Peter Eisenman, Zaha Hadid, Aldo Rossi, and Rem Koolhaas, and whose brief expected them to respond to the requirements of modern life, and the social, economic and technical requirements of the city. While the Interbau of 1957 had been focused on a particular district (the Hansaviertel) quite distinct from the rest of the city (though the principle had been gradually and less sophisticatedly extended to other areas, such as Kreuzberg), the IBA's emphasis on 'urban repair' meant gap-filling in the urban landscape. While this was not restricted to any particular part of the city, many of the projects were located in the 'southern Friedrichstadt', in the western part of Kreuzberg. It is here that the differences in the museal urban gaze emerge between the two distinct parts of the exhibition, the IBA-Neu and IBA-Alt, the former concerned with 'reconstruction' of urban living, the latter with the maintenance of the old built structures. It is these differences that will be delineated in the following discussion of their underpinning principles, for the IBA-Alt and IBA-Neu developed two very different conceptions of urban memory.

The museal gaze of the IBA-Neu

The first central formulation of the philosophy of IBA-Neu was to be found in the newspaper series, 'Models for a City' (*Modelle für eine Stadt*), published in the *Berliner Morgenpost* in early 1977. The repair of the cityscape that is promoted in the articles by Josef Kleihues and the architectural theorist Heinrich Klotz is founded on a vision of the contemporary cityscape as 'fragmented' and 'empty'. Direct reference to an urban past is not made explicit in these articles, but evident in all of them is the implicit remembrance of a former building tradition and its incorporation in a narrative of cultural memory.

The specific aims of the IBA were discussed at length by Kleihues after the fact and indeed after German unification in 1993.[3] This particular essay has much to do with debates about the meaning of the key concept of the IBA, 'critical reconstruction', in terms of the reconstruction of Berlin after 1989, but it is also significant in outlining the principles of the IBA as Kleihues understood them, and as they were practised by the loose collective of architects involved from the late 1970s onwards. The essay is entitled *Städtebau ist Erinnerung* (Urban Construction is Rembrance), and yet 'collective memory' is less significant than the architect's relationship with tradition.

The first iteration of memory in the essay is connected to the Senate prescriptions for the IBA, which stated that 'the fundamental historical structure of the city must become the basis of future urban development.[4] The fundamental historical structure of the city is itself not historicized, but conceived as something that is profoundly set in stone. While after 1990 Kleihues retrospectively criticized Aldo Rossi's fetishization of classical urban unity and the neo-classical architectural structures of Leon Krier for their rejection of experiment, he remained still committed to a recuperation of a generic 'city', since 'the layout [of Berlin] bears witness to the spiritual and cultural idea of the founding of a city.'[5] These 'authenticated traces' signify, even after their decay, a former mode of urban experience that predates the over-rationalization of city structures and their subservience to mere functionalist dictates: the 'wrong path' which the IBA sets out to correct.

The second iteration of memory is related to the work of Peter Eisenman, for whom, programmatically, 'where history ends, memory begins'.[6] This post-modern position that rejects the historical mission of the architect, gets to the heart of the complexity of Kleihues' relationship to the past in this essay. The architect's remembering of past forms and styles is founded on a rejection of a modernism that had now itself become classical. When Kleihues claimed that urban planning after 1945 took 'no notice' of the historical evolution of the city, these post-war developments were framed as failing to pay 'attention' to the past, and so the recovery of urban experience through the IBA was also the recovery of attention to the city structure by the architects designing spatial images (through) the museal urban gaze.

Kleihues' reflections are memory traces of a tradition that itself emerged as a particular form of socio-economic organization. The post-war deindustrialized status of West Berlin is a defining factor in being able to recuperate a former conception of the city. Nostalgia is avoided through the historical narrative of urban modernism as a wrong path. The IBA's (re)production of the spatial image of a cityscape is, however, founded on a quite specific historical perspective – the original *points de vue* which Karl Friedrich Schinkel constructed in the southern Friedrichstadt in the nineteenth century, which enable, according to Kleihues, forms of social interaction which connect to a possibility of spatial experience.[7]

In a second, shorter essay on the southern Friedrichstadt,[8] Kleihues admits that it was not so much urban reconstruction that was at the heart of this second IBA as the curation of 'memory traces' (*Gedächtnisspuren*). Within the autonomous development of the individual projects of the IBA, an ordered history is experienced, in line with the way the order of the cityscape can be experienced as a whole. Kleihues names three strategies for organizing the museal urban gaze: first, the literal reconstruction of a former situation; second, where the past is extended in a defamiliarizing, collage-like fashion, which 'activates the silent reserves of the place' through a respectfully playful engagement with historical traces; and third, the 'self-conscious contradiction', an intensification of the second strategy through the 'calculated break, the political, intellectual or artistic provocation through the intervention of the new and different.'[9] The distinction between strategies two and three would seem only to be grounded in the architect's intention, and indeed this is implicit in Kleihues' analysis of Peter Eisenman's constructions which, he claims, embody a 'refreshing conceptual idea' that still has to be recognized by a *lesenden Betrachter* ['reading observer'].

Reframing the parking lot

The specific example discussed by Kleihues and Klotz in the 1977 article is James Stirling's proposal for a 'repair' of the corner of Meinekestrasse/

Kurfürstendamm, which had been demolished after the war and replaced by a high-rise parking lot. The understanding of 'emptiness' and 'fragmentation' in the cityscape is telling: for Klotz, 'the meaninglessly loitering fragments' of the city (of which the parking lot is a typical example) need to be brought together to form an intact 'environment'.[10] Kleihues similarly refers to the site as an 'unused or badly used' plot of land, complete with 'left-over' spaces that need to be reactivated and 'grey zones' that need to be removed.[11] This empty space is to be replaced by buildings such as that proposed by Stirling, which is designed to reinstate the 'original' urban structure of the 'block edge' (*Blockrand*). Although this block structure is the element of the urban past that is to be recuperated within contemporary cultural memory, its collective experience is to be tactile, in the mode of a recovered place memory. Such buildings were intended to create an interactive urban experience (the German term used here is *Erlebnis*), in contrast to the façade of the parking lot, which 'merely happens' (according to Klotz). Central to this assertion is the construction of 'streetscapes' that can be reclaimed for 'urban life', where the encounter is a kind of event. In Klotz's terms, the parking lot disregards the citizen, much as the citizen, in synchronic sensory-motor mode, does not encounter it in a meaningful way.

Klotz identifies an ironic relationship to the past in the transformation of the 'banal' petrol station on the street corner into an 'urban(e) situation full of experience' (*erlebnisreich*). The corner of Stirling's planned building has the addition of a lift shaft that rises above the traditional Berlin eaves height. For Klotz, this mundane element has the quality of an 'unmonumental monument', creating an *erfahrbaren* [visually experential] context that can be *erlebt* [encountered] as a recognizable 'place'. Such a 'place' would be beautiful, in Klotz's view, since 'the building regains a face' in which the reality of its function is not hidden, but remains visible. Indeed the parking lot at times 'nakedly announces itself' in the structure, or 'peeks out unexpectedly'. Klotz describes this effect as a 'dramatization' of the problem posed by the post-war situation: urban experience is again conceived as a dramatic event. Although this engagement with the past is not only visual, it is unclear how such a partial reconstruction has any effect on the body of the inhabitant. The citizen in Klotz's vision is still a spectator in a car, waiting to go into a parking lot that is still present, if almost invisible from the street.

The museal gaze of the IBA-Alt

The identity of this spectator-citizen is not addressed by the IBA-Neu architects, who remain the 'reading observers' of their own constructions. The

identity of the observer is, however, central to a seminal article published
in 1978 in the architecture journal *Arch+* by the architectural critic Dieter
Hoffmann-Axthelm. The article, entitled *On the Treatment of Destroyed
Urban History*, was clearly a response to the ideas of the IBA-Neu.[12] As such,
the essay is a critique of the policy of 'urban repair' (*Stadtreparatur*) as an
aesthetic response to the two waves of destruction that had been visited
upon the city. Nevertheless the essay shared with the IBA-Neu a critique
of the synchronic urban gaze that had dominated urban planning since
the end of the Second World War in West Berlin. Hoffmann-Axthelm's
position is a refinement of the 'second destruction' argument (made by
Siedler in particular, as discussed in the previous chapter), in that he
identifies the clearances of the centre of Berlin as a 'primarily technical'
exercise; the centre of Berlin became empty through 'a tirelessly technical
clearing-away'.[13] He distinguishes between the fate of those districts at the
centre which 'developed as an urban desert under a sky barely impinged
upon by buildings, with their own vegetation and a subterranean aesthetic
eccentric charm', and the neighbouring intact proletarian districts (such
as Wedding and Kreuzberg) that were then being demolished under the
principle of 'large-scale rehabilitation' (*Flächensanierung*). Such renewal
had also been seen as only a technical process. Importantly, these proletarian neighbourhoods had not been left in ruins by the war; rather these were
intact communities and, according to Hoffmann-Axthelm, a 'historical
cityscape' that had not yet become a 'commodity mask'.

Hoffmann-Axthelm recognized that the IBA-Neu contained a critique
of the post-war reconstruction process, but condemned it as an 'aesthetic
programme', for it was the *image* of the city, streets, squares, courtyards and
parks that was being repaired.[14] The city was ultimately still being viewed
as a machine, and a broken machine can be made to function again. One
part of the city was being repaired, but without reference to the whole, since
the 'broken social relationships' were not being repaired:

> The new buildings contain no dialectic; the historical substance leaves
> behind no traces, it is simply taken away by digger, and the new buildings
> stand there, as if the destroyed city had never existed.[15]

For Hoffmann-Axthelm, the removal of all traces meant not simply the disappearance of particular buildings, but also the extinction of an authentic
past; the destruction caused by the Second World War is also part of urban
history, as a rupture it generates its own historical urban environment: 'we
only have "historical" buildings as a result of the destruction', he claims,

adding that one may not, and indeed cannot, build up a destroyed city as if nothing had happened, more precisely, one cannot rebuild this city Berlin, as if it were any other city, as if it had (merely) been subject to an earthquake.

At this point, Hoffmann-Axthelm introduces the *morality* of a relationship to the past into the curation of both the built environment and of its memory value. What has been 'excluded', according to Hoffmann-Axthelm, is what happened and originated in Berlin as the seat of a 'terror organization' that tortured, gassed and murdered many millions of people: Jews, resistance fighters, Socialists, the mentally disabled and homosexuals. For that reason, according to Hoffmann-Axthelm, attempts to build over these spaces in Berlin could only lead to further denial of that past. With IBA-Neu, he argued, what was emerging is an urban history without victims, 'interchangeable and without age'. The return of (neo-) classical forms (in the architecture of Rob Krier, for example) is for Hoffmann-Axthelm simply the 'return of the repressed'.[16] The framings of the past, and the monuments that have been constructed, are 'incomplete, biased, [they] render harmless, or simply melancholic (as expressed in the cliché, "in difficult times").'

Hoffmann-Axthelm rejected the (re)construction of the urban environment as the source of a comforting narrative of cultural memory. He proposed instead a history that 'should' be told, founded on emerging models of collection and curation of the past, driven by a growing interest in a history 'from below'. As he noted, within the workers' districts there was remembrance of the class struggles of the past, but this had not taken on the public form of commemoration, i.e. it had not been accepted as cultural memory. Similarly, there was the oral testimony that was being recorded by historians and video documentarists. For Hoffmann-Axthelm, however, the demolition of whole housing blocks destroys a system of orientation. The population changes and quite different forms of urban experience come into play, in particular, the individualization of urban experience.[17] For the new inhabitants, the history of the quarter is not their history, is unknown and ungraspable for them. For Hoffmann-Axthelm, such an individualization of history means that the criticism directed against post-war urban planning had no collective focus and merely became a way of expressing an unproductive and harmful social discontent: protests against the urban motorway served ultimately as a conduit for xenophobia. The reconstruction of the 'southern Friedrichstadt' had produced an area that is now inhabited by people who have no historical relationship to the quarter and are getting used to the interstitial spaces ('this confusion of ruin fields, snack bars, remainders of houses from the former business district'). For these inhabitants, the historical process has become fundamentally abstract.

Their relationship to history is a symptom of a wider abstract relationship to civic society in general.

This describes a model of how place memory is eradicated, along the lines described by Connerton, whereby the synchronic urban gaze produces a related form of attention at ground level. Importantly, Hoffmann-Axthelm claimed that the area did, in fact, contain a legible prehistory of the foundational urban structures within it. He formulated a museal urban gaze that is structurally similar to the principles of the IBA, except that this 'prehistory' is not founded on recovering and recuperating an 'original' city. Hoffmann-Axthelm attempted to describe an appropriate way of dealing with 'destroyed urban history', or of writing the 'history of urban destruction.'[18] He did this with reference to an area in the southern Friedrichstadt that had been the site of the SS headquarters during the 'Third Reich' and had been demolished after the war. As Hoffmann-Axthelm notes (at this point becoming collector and curator of the city as a repository of the past), an engagement with this empty site means producing the visibility of the historical process as duration, which was to form the basis of a critical relationship to the 'memory value' of the remnants. He asks:

> which are the signs contained within the destroyed area that can orientate the expansion and collation of the existing patches, without the erratic historic-aesthetic pattern that has been woven by urban repair in the area. It is history that reaches from the past into the planning of current living conditions, the prehistory of the current situation, not as an image to be observed, but a process that is connected with current conditions and gives them the perspectival depth.[19]

The material remnant ensures the cityscape possesses 'perspectival depth': one of the earliest definitions of the 'critical dimension' of the anamnestic dimension evoked by the museal urban gaze and its spatial images. The abandoned object, like De Certeau's ruins, is both far away and close, because the remnant 'reaches' into the present. The past is apprehended as a living process within that present. 'The ruin fields of the southern Friedrichstadt are closer to being a legible history of the city than the formal corpse we are promised [by the IBA]. [...] History is there. It does not need to be invented, merely liberated from its repression.'[20] For this to happen, the southern Friedrichstadt should not become an official monument. There should be no sense of an absence of age but rather the presence of the historical process. Hoffmann-Axthelm imagines this as a different form of cultural memory from that offered by the IBA-Neu, albeit one that is similarly grounded in an immediate experience of the built environment. The urban experience that returns here is an experience of historical time through the spatial image.

This is a museal urban gaze that is developed in rejection of the synchronic gaze, which is associated here clearly with the removal of the past (and a particular form of the past). The question of 'legibility' however still haunts Hoffmann-Axthelm's work of curation. He makes no suggestions as to how these 'ruin fields' should be 'curated' other than as a critique of other framings and their (ahistorical) philosophy of history. For Hoffmann-Axthelm, city repair treats urban destruction as a natural catastrophe not worthy of representation. While he recognizes that the arrogance of the post-war urban planning paradigm had passed, no new way of seeing the city had emerged other than as a return to the former state of affairs.

Two different theories of the museal gaze, of memory value and the anamnestic dimension of the material cityscape are thus elaborated within IBA-Neu and IBA-Alt. In both cases, the memory value must be first generated within urban experience. Although they share key dynamics of place memory, in their resistance to homogenization and their emphasis on a non-instrumentalized and unmediated encounter with an inexplicit spatial image, they nevertheless differ fundamentally in the way they shape a perception of the past. The built environment may contain the anamnestic dimension Andreas Huyssen associates with the memory value of the material object, but that memory value can, however, be extrapolated in two directions, either as a memory of former urban experience, or as a way into understanding the present's relationship to the past.[21]

The 'memory value' of the material object *from* the past derives its auratic quality from the implied testimony to historical time. Kleihues' model of memory value in the cityscape is founded on the testimony it bears and the transmission it enables, of the city's architectural origins, whereas the authenticity of the cityscape for Hoffmann-Axthelm is founded on both substantive duration and historical testimony. While this explains their differing claims to authenticity, their differing instrumentalizations of place memory can be described through Nietzsche's analysis of history in *On the Uses and Abuses of History for Life* in terms of 'monumental memory value' and 'critical memory value'.[22] In the former, the 'monumental memory value' of a place is founded on the *construction* of an unmediated experience of the past that emphasizes its poetic qualities: the encounter with 'the silent reserves of place' generates a poetic and fundamentally affirmative, coherent and resolved understanding of the past, whereas in the latter the encounter with 'place' generates a critical, unresolved understanding of the past. 'Critical memory value' tries to organize those poetic qualities in order to induce critical insight without becoming so legible as to override the glancing encounter on which it relies for its authenticity.

The sited practice of the museal urban gaze

How does this form of the museal urban gaze emerge in practice, and how does it address the question of an evocative 'legibility' of the past. The museal gaze, as a form of remembering well, formulates itself in contradistinction to what it views as the hegemonic urban gaze. We shall now look at a series of examples, beginning with the framing of the former SS-headquarters discussed by Hoffmann-Axthelm in his essay and then contextualizing what was practised here through other examples of site-specific framing of remnants in Berlin, such as the Anhalter Bahnhof and the former Embassy quarter, which will open out the question of the various media (photography and film in particular) through which the museal urban gaze operates in this period.

1.   The Topography of the Terror: 'No place for roads'

As discussed above, the former SS-headquarters in the Prinz-Albrecht Strasse had been demolished after the war. Hoffmann-Axthelm suggested that urban planning after 1945 had no language to deal with the remains of war and 'simply demolished, and allowed grass or asphalt to grow over everything [...]'.[23] The language that it did have at its disposal was the grammar of abstract space.[24] The directive that came from Bonn in 1962 merely described the clearing away of administrative buildings (*Abräumung von Verwaltungsgebäuden*), as part of the preparations for a new urban motorway.

The location was not recognized as a ruin site with memory value at this stage. Indeed it was also disregarded for a long time by the synchronic gaze of the planners, as it was rendered low in exchange value due to its proximity to the Wall, only coming into view as a relatively late part of Berlin's urban motorway project. One part of the site was a dumping ground for rubble from demolished buildings in nearby parts of Kreuz-berg. Another, as Hoffmann-Axthelm discusses, was asphalted over and formed an unregulated track for driving without a licence. The ruins were not even tentatively identified as an 'unintended monument' until 1978.[25] James Young follows both Mitscherlich's socio-psychological reading of the built environment and De Certeau's imputation of agency to ruins, when he suggests that the remains lay dormant until this point, but, 'as is the wont of repressed memories, however, the site returned to public consciousness with an obsessive, ferocious vengeance.'[26] In fact, 1978 is the year of Hoffmann-Axthelm's essay and the urban archivist curated the unintended monument through a key form of the urban museal gaze's collective address: the guided tour. In January 1978 Hoffmann-Axthelm led tours of the site during a convention of environmentalists and anarchists (the 'TUNIX', or 'Do Nothing Congress', a notable rejection of the 'active city'), effectively conducting a training in the museal urban gaze as an act of discovering counter-histories. In contrast to Kleihues, the curator of the silent reserves of 'place', Hoffmann-Axthelm is the activator of the silent reserves of place as a counter-historical 'movement' through the city.

In 1979, the IBA-Alt attempted to intervene in the plans to run the motorway over the terrain. In a move analogous to Hoffmann-Axthelm's invocation of the history of victims of National Socialism, Michael Kraus, a member of IBA-Alt, recalls the moment in February 1980 when he introduced the question of the site's former usage into the context of a planning meeting about the site:

> It was not unproblematic to depart suddenly from the level at which the conversation had taken place up to that point and to allude to the political and moral background, for that could be understood – and was indeed understood by the supporters of the road-building programme – as a purely tactical manoeuvre, as an non-objective, emotional and unfair move into an area which could not be rationally grasped with the criteria which had been used up to now.[27]

Kraus's invocation of the memory value of the site, in terms of understanding the site's material presence as a 'place of memory', radically breaks the frame of discussions about the rational ordering of space in terms of the synchronic gaze. This terrain is, in the title of his essay', 'no place for roads'. This is the first step in the establishing of the memory value of the place: its relationship to authenticity is established in terms of historical testimony. The next problem that arises: how is the authenticity of encounter to be framed in a spatial image?

One of the tensions between 'critical memory value' and 'monumental memory value' lies in the fact that critical memory value introduces a potentially intellectual, abstract engagement with a site that would deprive it of the qualities of place memory that rendered it auratic in the first place. This tension can be followed through the protracted discussions and competitions that ensued in the past twenty-five years, as people have attempted to maintain this interstitial location as a site of the historical imagination. A critical understanding of memory value has to grapple with the paradox that once the unintended monument becomes the location of a verbalized, conceptualized critical history, it can no longer function as its own point of historical reference. The debates surrounding the Topography of the Terror demonstrate uncertainty about whether this site of memory *can* be its own referent, although little doubt that it *should* be.

Descriptions and visualizations of the site from the early 1980s emphasize spatial images of absence. The site is described as empty, an emptiness in contrast to the traces of the site's usage over the past decades: the rubble from the building work and the rubber tyres of the racing track. Hoffmann-Axthelm suggested that the 'fundamental emptiness' is the 'message itself'; the site was an unintended monument to post-war indifference to the crimes of the Nazi state and that lack of intention is central to its initial significance, as is clear from the journalistic tours of the site which foreground the act of discovery.

The discovery of an 'unintended monument' led to reflection on how the 'message itself' was to be made legible. The tension between aesthetic effect and ethical meaning in the work of curation was picked out by Hoffmann-Axthelm in considering how one might turn this 'unintended monument' into something more durable. He pointed to the dangers of 'aesthetic legibility', arguing that 'one cannot simply relate to the location in a visual manner', and that the last thing that should be enabled is 'a cultivated shiver down the spine' of the bussed-in tourists. The tension between the sensory impact of the encounter with the location and its potential didactic function was drawn out by Ulrich Eckhardt, who made a distinction between an emotional reaction resolving into 'self-satisfaction' and its status as a 'place of reflection' (*Denkort* – a reworking of *Denkmal*), a 'strange, questioning site.'[28]

The 'critical memory value' of the site was, however, not the only value placed upon this space. This became evident in the first competition to find an adequate way of marking the site, where it was also stipulated that the designs had to include an area of recreation for the inhabitants of Kreuzberg. This compromise illustrates that area of tension between 'habitable space' and 'historical consciousness' that marks the conflict within the IBA as a whole. The museal gaze for that first competition was framed by the then Mayor of Berlin, Richard von Weizsäcker:

> Reshaping the terrain where the Prinz-Albrecht-Palais formerly stood is
> one of the most important responsibilities our city faces both for reasons
> of history and urban development. For better or worse, Berlin is the cus-
> todian of German history, which here has left worse scars than anywhere
> else. [...] The terrain adjacent to the Martin Gropius Bau [...] contains
> invisible traces of a heavy historic legacy: invisible are the buildings from
> which the SS state operated its levers of terror. Visible is the Wall, cutting
> like a knife across the former Prinz-Albrecht-Strasse. [...] As we go about
> reconstructing this area, it will be our task to proceed with contemporary
> history in mind while also providing a place for contemplation. Yet at
> the same time we must not miss the opportunity to give the Kreuzberg
> district a terrain where life can unfold and leisure is possible.[29]

Three aspects of the speech can be highlighted. First, there is the emphasis
on visibility/invisibility at the site. Second, and connected to this, the idea
that spatial practice should be directed towards contemplation, one of the
key tropes of the museal urban gaze. Third, the fact that, nevertheless,
a contemplative site did not count as a functioning/useful space within
the city: it has to be functionalized as a leisure space. In this light, Ulrich
Conrads's commentary on the 1983 winning design by Jürgen Wenzel and
Nikolaus Leng is revealing:

> What one enters there can be called neither grove nor park nor wood.
> One will enter into something dead but alive, in an absolutely artificial
> landscape, which, however, is not entirely devoid of nature. [...] The docu-
> ments, laid out on the ground, will say why this is the case. [30]

The Wenzel/Leng solution combined the aesthetics of the ruin, between
life and death, artifice and nature, image and materiality, with the didactic
abstraction of the verbal. The value of the documents, reproductions of
Gestapo and SS policy records, is a combination of 'age value' (in their
testimonial authenticity), 'exhibition value' (in that they are displayed)
and 'critical memory value' (in that they serve a didactic purpose for
the present and work with a disruptive juxtaposition between past and
present). The winning design was by no means universally acclaimed. It
was attacked by neighbourhood groups who realized that it had not really
provided them with a recreational space. It was also criticized by those
who thought that the design, which sealed the ground with cast-iron plates,
'closed off' the site, rather than leaving it as an open wound. Dissatisfaction
with the solutions offered established once more the peculiarity of this

space: Hoffmann-Axthelm observed that it would have been interpreted as a cursed space by premodern societies, while Ulrich Conrads talked of the site being 'poisoned.'[31] There was consensus for Hämer's observation that the site can have no functional role to play in the city.[32] Indeed the dangers of abstract space are invoked in Conrads's concern that compromises could lead to the influence of 'a calculating administration', and Hoffmann-Axthelm's warning that the 'administration of space' should not be allowed to dictate the treatment of a site that was richly layered in history.

A number of the 194 entries for the 1983 competition had made use of architectural metaphors of excavation but the memory value of the site was heightened when actual archaeological finds from the Gestapo era were made during the 1986 excavations, which followed on from the polemical intervention by local historical activists a year before. These remnants dealt the Wenzel-Leng plan a final blow and greatly enhanced the auratic power of the site. Thomas Friedrich called the uncovered Gestapo cells the 'most expressive part' of the area.[33] The expressive fallacy is perhaps best illustrated by the fact that in 1981 Hoffmann-Axthelm had argued that the site was to speak, 'and indeed without display signs',[34] although he did later suggest that the power of the site to speak had in fact been proven by the signs that had been erected.[35] The site uncovers the tension between the intended and unintended monument, or the monument of mourning and that of melancholia.[36] The testimonial aura of the site had been secured by excavations displaying themselves in the centre of the city, ensuring the direct, visual 'memory value' of the encounter with the site; the signs ensured the exhibition value of the remnants. How to ensure the establishment of 'critical memory', or a critical awareness of the historical process?

The Topography of the Terror site illustrates formal questions surrounding the technological construction of the spatial image of urban memory. The museal urban gaze is related to the interactive construction of aura, but how is time ('past time') framed for experience in the urban environment? The recovery of place memory is also the recovery of a way of relating to history. The case of the Topography of the Terror is clearly a significant moment in the history of national memory discourse in post-war Germany – for Young, it became 'the controlling focal point for all German memory.'[37] In terms of the emergence of urban memory, its significance lies principally in the shift away from the dominance of the synchronic urban gaze and the grounding of a different form of memory value, namely the 'critical memory value' of the built environment, in the way that it produced the presence of a (repressed) past through the dynamics of the encounter, aiming for a moment of discovery that is also a moment of preservation. While the

Topography of the Terror has been subject to much public and academic discussion, it has not previously been contextualized with other projects of the late 1970s and early 1980s that were grappling with the appropriate form of a museal urban gaze in relation to other, less immediately charged, ruin sites in the western half of the city. The first concerns a site just a short walk from the Prinz-Albrecht Strasse, a location that was equally disregarded by the post-war authorities, though perhaps without the claim to social amnesia through which the Topography of the Terror has been framed. That site is the Anhalter Bahnhof.

2.   Anhalter Bahnhof: Ruin or temple?

The cover of the photograph book produced to accompany the Federal Republic's contribution to the 1975 focus on the European city, juxtaposes the remnant of the façade of the Anhalter Bahnhof with the Europahaus behind it. The railway station's status as an official monument related only to this portico remnant. As with any unintended monument, the historical meaning of the remnant was ambiguous: the ruination of the Anhalter Bahnhof had only been partially shaped by the war, but had been completed thanks to its demolition by the city authorities in 1959.[38] The image of the ruined station façade was refunctionalized in a variety of contexts. The image also reappeared on the cover of the booklet 'Antifascist City Plan for Kreuzberg' (Antifaschistischer Stadtplan Kreuzberg), set against the backdrop of a schematic map of the district, a spatial image again signifying the auratic encounter with the past, vouching for the authenticity of the historical labour contained within the booklet. The portico appears in Figure 1 of this book, as an image staged in front of the actual ruin. Its form also appeared in December 1977, with the staging of an updated version of Hölderlin's 'Hyperion' in the Olympic Stadium in the west of the city.[39] A football goal had been replaced by the ruin silhouette of the portico, around which was gathered a group of those marginalized from society, in that RAF-overshadowed autumn of 1977. It was however not just a ruin gaze that was in play here, but the spatial practice of the post-war interstitial space and its marginalized characters. Within the ruin gaze, the definition of the monument remains unresolved; is this ruin the product of the war, or of the product of the 'second destruction' of urban reconstruction? Contextualized within the setting of Hitler's Olympic Stadium, it would seem to be the former, but it can also be seen as a revisiting of the immediate post-war period, with the façade standing in for an abandoned ruin that can be recuperated for an experience of the past.

While the façade has an iconic value as it circulates as the image of a post-war ruin, the remainder of the space previously occupied by the station was a kind of no-man's land that was used as a free car park.[40] The iconic 'face value' of the portico was interrogated by the curatorial approach taken by Raffael Rheinsberg, for which the site-specificity of the authentic object was central. In 1979 he constructed an 'installation-exhibition' about the station in the Galerie Gianozzo in the Suarezstrasse in Grünewald in south-west Berlin. The installation began already on the pavement outside the gallery where 54 railway sleepers were laid out. Inside, two display rows of photographs vouched for the substantive duration and testimonial value of the site by showing the history of the Anhalter Bahnhof from its busy days to its post-war usage to its demolition. Among those photographs, Rheinsberg exhibited his own Polaroids of the current state of the site, details and documentation of his own traversing of the site. Displayed alongside those photographs were commentaries on the site made by nearby residents, without any clear connection of specific commentary to image. It was not just images that were on display, though; on a podium in the gallery a series of objects were exhibited: a bent fork, five-pfennig pieces, a lock, a brush, photographic mementoes, an old sole of a shoe and a football. In the cellar space, which was laid out with railway gravel, Rheinsberg had spread old coins, shrapnel, the fragments of a KPM-mug, broken MITROPA cutlery, and iron tools. The objects of a relatively recent everyday spatial practice were presented as if in an archaeological museum, placing in question conventional boundaries between past and present.

Rheinsberg enacted a museal gaze and also constructed a spatial image for the viewers of his exhibition, reconfiguring their relationship to the original object in its urban location, by moving beyond the visual appropriation of the iconic façade while generating a multidimensional spatial image. The exhibition engaged with levels of mediation (of time and the built environment); the historical photographs, themselves taken from a photographic archive and exhibited, the contemporary photographs, and then the objects themselves, framed within the gallery space.

While Rheinsberg was not bound to the didactic intentions in play at the Topography of the Terror, his installation speaks to similar concerns with social history that informed the work of the IBA-Alt and processes of urban memory in its formulation of a mode of encounter with the object, as well as interrogating the process of the transmission of historical knowledge through captions, something that was highlighted in the book publication.

This book publication, *Anhalter Bahnhof: Ruine oder Tempel?*, inevitably diminished the spatial dimension of the installation. The structure of the

6. Raffael Rheinsberg, *Anhalter Bahnhof: Ruine oder Tempel?* (1979). Courtesy of the artist.

book organizes a linear framework, in that (following the introductory essay, discussed below), historical photographs of the Anhalter Bahnhof are placed before an essay by Janos Frecot. Then follow Rheinsberg's photographs of the site, but presented as follows: each photograph is preceded by a not quite translucent piece of 'tracing' paper on which is printed a hand-written commentary, so that the photographic image is slightly obscured and certainly rendered opaque. This heightens awareness of the act of seeing and deciphering (though the handwriting is mechanically reproduced and is all from the same hand, as if Rheinsberg has appropriated authorship of the comments).

This first text/image combination also highlights the act of seeing, taken from an elevated vantage point looking down on the portal remains and to the former bunker in the back right of the image (Fig. 6). The quality of the reproduced Polaroid is sufficiently poor that the buildings at the back of the image/site become unidentifiable, lending the photograph an impressionistic quality. The textual supplement on the tracing paper – 'looks like an old temple' – is paradigmatically ambiguous as a supplement. Rather than resolving the enigmatic image, it actually only throws us back to the attempt to determine the object. The image is itself ambiguously composed: the elevated vantage point means that the portico is to the front right of the image, the bunker to back right – as if the subject of the photograph were the empty space and the temple could be the bunker. The disjunction between inscription (and much play is made of graffiti on the walls of the buildings) and visual evocation is highlighted with a photograph of the bunker overlaid with a commentary that reads 'This is supposed to be a railway station.' Rheinsberg highlights here the ambiguity of a defunct site (defunct also in terms of spatial practices). Similarly a photograph of a concrete slab set against a backdrop of winter trees is captioned 'When a person is dead, then he has died', rendering the banal slab the image of a gravestone; the next image, a more closely cropped image of a gravestone is captioned 'I see no train.' The question of value is highlighted by a statement (directed we might presume to Rheinsberg, but also to us as readers), 'what you have there is valuable', that frames an almost unidentifiable image. Similarly, the phrase 'that is worth it' (which could also be a question) captions a photograph of objects on the gallery dais.

'Do you want to clear up here?' (*aufräumen*) can be read as an ironic refer- ence to the official language of clearing up the rubble spaces, accompanying an image of spades found at the site and displayed in the gallery. This is the final image, addressing Rheinsberg's purpose in 'ordering' the material; he clears it up, renders it museal (ready for the museum) – one of the captions reads 'that is all in the museum.' Yet Rheinsberg does not produce a museum, but an open site where the everyday and the banal has memory value, rooted in the materiality of its objects, a value that remains open as the result of an encounter that generates both presence and distance.

Rheinsberg achieves what Hoffmann-Axthelm saw as the necessary function of an engagement with the history of the urban environment: he makes the historical process perceptible. Nevertheless, the aesthetic framing of the perception of the fragments of the urban environment leaves their 'memory value' only ambivalently incorporated into a historical nar- rative that is not provided textually – although it is provided in the book by a visual history of the Anhalter Bahnhof up to 1959. Rheinsberg's urban museal gaze engages with the people who live close to the site, but not in the sense of constructing a coherent collective; their voices are present, but anonymous and incoherent.

The aesthetic framing of perception enables the visibility of the process to remain open-ended. Removed from the processes of circulation, the site can be framed with the qualities of the encounter with place memory that Rheinsberg seeks to enact through his sacralization of the encounter with everyday objects. Their meaning is embedded in the nature of the encounter with them. This does, however, have to be set against Andreas Huyssen's

observation that a traditional aesthetic of monumental ruins points towards the durability of origins. Indeed the place memory work at both the
Topography of the Terror and the Anhalter Bahnhof, which both pursues and
interrogates a melancholy ruin aesthetic, is also aimed at uncovering (and
conserving) the origins of the current German state.[41] Most importantly,
Rheinsberg shows that critical visual culture can analyse the technologies at
use in the narrativization of the remnant in urban space through mobilizing
an encounter with place that is at odds with the synchronic gaze.

3.   Embassy quarter: 'Messages' from the past?

This engagement with technologies of narrativization is evident in another
Rheinsberg installation, this time from 1983, when the competition to
frame the Gestapo site was ongoing. This project was entitled 'Embassies'
(*Botschaften* – the German term can also mean 'messages', and the ambiguity
was not unintentional). The exhibition was held in the Berlin-Museum from
27 March to 9 May 1982. The exhibition followed the archaeological principle
that had determined the Anhalter Bahnhof exhibition: in the museum space
Rheinsberg exhibited the 'found objects' that had attracted his attention
(e.g. a rusted bomb, the remains of carpeting, Nazi propaganda, invitation
cards to a diplomatic ball, old embassy signs) as a barely ordered 'storage
facility' of the everyday that did not explicitly distinguish between the
sacred and the banal. Memory value was not instrumentalized according to
a historical narrative. While Rheinsberg's exhibition sought to establish the
memory value of the location, its exchange value was also being established:
the Danish embassy had been sold off to Berlin's (at that time) largest real
estate owner, *Neue Heimat* ('New Home(land') in 1980, and the nearby Zoo
Station had an eye on the site as part of a possible expansion.[42]

    In addition to the exhibition, Rheinsberg's curatorial activities included
guided tours, like Hoffmann-Axthelm at the Prinz-Albrecht-Strasse, through
the embassy district, offering the 'view on foot.' The terrain had apparently
been the location for a film about the end of the Second World War and had
been subject to the destructive spatial practices of squatters and homeless
people in the meantime. As with the Prinz-Albrecht terrain, the remnants
of past time were not simply those of the war, but traces of the time that
had passed since the war.

    The exhibition catalogue established the distinction between the syn-
chronic urban gaze and Rheinsberg's own gaze through its opening image,
the reproduction of the 1938/39 GBI (General Building Inspection) plan for
the diplomatic residences, which takes a bird's eye of the surface of the site.

The black-and-white photographs that follow, by contrast, are taken from ground level.[43]

One of the major differences to the Anhalter Bahnhof catalogue is that there are photographic series that document the encounter with the terrain, imitating the guided tour and also the excavation, in the production of 'spatial images', where the bodily presence of the photographer is implicated in the image. Whereas the Anhalter Bahnhof exhibition framed the ambiguity of the undetermined remnant through the interplay of image and text, the Embassies exhibition alludes in its title to the ostensible presence of a message, but then seems to express visually a refusal of communication. This is evident in the choice of photographs from the first series (of the Spanish embassy). Gates are closed (18); windows and doors are bricked over (19, 23, 24); even bricked-over windows have iron grills over them (24-27). The concluding image, of a bricked-over doorway was the one chosen for the catalogue cover (Fig. 7).

In this opening series, Rheinsberg thematizes the problem of access to the past while also engaging with the visual effect of 'age value' through focusing attention on the way in which, for example, weathering has affected the eagle insignia on the embassy façade. The 'tour' section (*Begehung*) is simply four photographs; the first of which shows an empty streetscape with a (barely legible) street sign as the only marker; the three that follow show mosaics laid into the pavement of the street. These mosaics also display evidence of the passage of time and even attempted repairs, and iconographically recall the mosaics uncovered at Pompeii.

The section entitled 'Tour on Foot' is also short. Rheinsberg's photographic series of the various embassies remains directed towards their exteriors, cataloguing the crumbling façades, but also gesturing towards the theme of the 'message', the crude graffitied inscriptions (also political ones, as on p. 81). The centrepiece of the volume, though, is the Danish embassy. As if geographically specifying the location, while gradually training our gaze to the perception of the transmission of 'messages' in the encounter with the cityscape, the first photograph is of the street sign ('Thomas-Dehler-Strasse, 51-48'), but a large part of the sign has been rendered illegible by some process of erosion/defacing/violation. The next photograph is of the house number '48', the third a photograph of the stone inscription that commemorates the architect of the building (Johann Emil Schaudt), with the date of the building's completion (1939). There follows a wide panorama of the building's frontage and then, focusing on a detail perhaps not immediately evident in that photograph, an image of a provisional entrance door, which has been inscribed with graffiti ('Your palace

7. Front cover of Raffael Rheinsberg, *Botschaften* (1983). Courtesy of the artist.

is your prison', 'here wants to live') and also the name 'Raffael Rheinsberg' (alongside inscriptions on individual bricks). The act of photographic appropriation is marked as an act of inscription. From here the photographs enter the building and there follow 72 images from the interior, images of the detritus of forty years' neglect that construct a tour through the building. The concluding section of photographs shows objects collected from the Danish embassy.

As with the Anhalter Bahnhof project, these images are accompanied in the catalogue by a series of historical photographs. On this occasion, Rheinsberg highlighted the process of translation from archive to exhibition through the reproduction not only of the photograph, but also the archival record card from the 'Ullstein Bilderdienst' (which includes references to newspaper articles from which the images derived). The record card is thus itself a palimpsest of traces (from the period 1938 to 1960), and breaks the topographical frame of the project in that there are images of the American Embassy on Pariser Platz during the Second World War, as well as one of the former Spanish embassy in the Hitzigallee in south-west Berlin immediately prior to its demolition in 1958).

Whereas the archaeological project around the Anhalter Bahnhof translated objects directly from repository to exhibition, Rheinsberg here highlighted the process of transition from photographic archive to exhibition, while also recording that process of cataloguing through the inclusion of the record cards. It would be an oversimplification to suggest that Rheinsberg's projects are only reactivations of objects through the encounter with the urban repository, for there is also the reactivation of the historical photograph of the cityscape. Indeed this use of historical photographs in both of Rheinsberg's projects is an interesting phenomenon of the period, as it forms a different technology of the museal urban gaze, a looking back at the gaze upon the former city, which we shall turn to shortly.

The catalogue is accompanied by a number of essays. The first, which precedes the photographs, by Ulrich Bischoff, contains a clear delineation of Rheinsberg's gaze which is described as 'comparable with the initial investigations which a child undertakes in an alien terrain' and differs from the 'selective mode of seeing (*betrachten*) of the tourist or the businessman.'[44] The synchronic urban gaze, 'the abstract reference point of utilization, of profit [...] fires the imagination of the housing speculator, who already can see a wide variety of chic apartments growing out of the still standing and intact representative buildings.' Rheinsberg, says Bischoff, is drawn to the ruin 'where the language of things begins quite audibly and looks for someone who will lend them an ear, will take them on, preserve them and communicate them further.'[45] This illustrates how Rheinsberg's museal gaze, not that of a nostalgic inhabitant of the original place, produces place memory after the fact. Recalling the idea of the non-assimilated body within the city, which we discussed in the introduction, Rheinsberg's gaze upon the Deleuzian 'any-space-whatever' sees beneath the 'asphalt carpet of forgetting' that was laid over the urban environment and is out of joint with the synchronic rhythms of the tourist or the businessman. For Bischoff,

Rheinsberg's work resolves the paradox of aesthetic and critical perception through the work of art, with the artist as curator of the museal urban gaze for a collective. Rheinsberg's method is 'exemplary', producing in the spectator a moment of recognition 'about ourselves and our history that encompasses both intellect and emotion.' What Bischoff does not recognize is that Rheinsberg is unlocking both the asynchronic and allegorical potential of the remnant, but is foregrounding the process of transmission.

The synchronic urban gaze, which only pays attention to surface, is contrasted by Bischoff with the child's gaze. This idea is evoked by 'Postscript 1981', an essay later in the volume by Janos Frecot which follows his piece on 'Tiergarten Quarter 1965', in which he recalled the former embassy space in that era in a poetically associative prose. Frecot's 'Postscript 1981' is in fact a reminiscence of the space in 1947, when he experienced it as a young boy on his route to school. Frecot's essay concludes with a plea for the preservation of the space in its current form(lessness):

The terrain has not yet been comprehended neither in urban planning terms nor as a space between park and canal or as an historical environment. Therefore, one should fence it off, preserve it, and charge admission until something proper has been thought of. 'Archaeology of a War' should help us think of it as a historical site. The Tiergarten quarter should not be merely a free space at/for disposal.[46]

'Place memory work' and the photographic archive

Frecot presents Rheinsberg here as the facilitator of a collective museal gaze, but he himself is also operating as a curator of the urban past, creating an encounter with past material.

This period sees the archiving and display not only of the Berlin cityscape, but also of photographs of the former Berlin cityscape, both of which are increasingly understood as a palimpsest of history. This was a process in which Frecot himself played a major role as curator and archivist. Frecot was intimately involved in the emerging intellectual-cultural scene in Berlin (he was acquainted, for example, with photographers who would go on to have very successful careers in that field, for instance Michael Schmidt and Bernd and Hilda Becher, with whom he shares an affinity for seriality). Under the direction of Eberhard Roters and Jörn Merkert, Frecot had begun in the winter of 1978 to construct a photographic collection for the Berlinische Galerie, within a newly established institutional context (the Galerie was founded in 1975). This was shaped by more egalitarian understandings of aesthetic value, which meant he was not obliged to try and legitimize the value of photography as a form of visual culture.[47] Here Frecot's role as curator of the archive comes to the fore. The initial collection included architectural photographs from the latter half of the nineteenth century that were presented in the first exhibition of the archive in 1982. Frecot wrote an essay introducing the catalogue to this exhibition, *Berlinfotografisch,* which documented a history of photography in the city between 1860 and 1982, illustrating, as the title suggested, how the history of the city and the history of photography are inextricably linked. Frecot claims that Berlin developed in this period into a 'centre of photography in creative, journalistic, in industrial and scientific terms'.[48] The catalogue effectively functioned as a stocktaking of the collection at this point in its development and thus reflected on the process of archivization. The presentation eschewed chronological order, but instead ordered the images alphabetically according to photographer, as one might find it in an index of an archive rather than as an already ordered history.

Frecot saw the 'Zero Hour' as 'urgently contemporary'[49] in 1982 and his perception of this urgency clearly informed his curation of the collection. From the very beginning, the archive's major focus was the 'rubble photography' of the immediate post-war years, whose significance had not yet been recognized. When Janos Frecot was interviewed (in 1989) about the collections of the Berlinische Galerie, he distinguished between artistic photography (as 'creative', in the sense of *darstellend*) and a representational photography (*abbildend*) that was more the matter of the institutional archives (the *Landesbildstellen*).[50] Frecot, however, immediately undid this neat distinction by observing that the Galerie's collection did include the likes of Fritz Eschen and Henry Ries, described as prominent examples of journalist photographers.[51] For Frecot in 1982 it was clear that 'where art can be understood as a force for spiritual as well as a political resistance, it is clear that merely aesthetic criteria of value no longer suffice.'[52] This lends a particular resonance to the quotation from Werner Schmalenbach with which Frecot concluded his remarks in the *Berliner Kunstblatt* volume from 1989: 'It is less the task of the museum to concern itself with living art than with the art that has survived.'[53] This suggests that, just as material remnants abandoned in the post-war urban environment were being translated from the city's repository into a functional cultural memory, so a corresponding translation was happening with a variety of photographic images from the post-war period. The photography of the 'Zero Hour' was being recuperated within cultural memory, but beyond the assertion of its

artistic merit, what was the memory value of such photographs? Another
exhibition that Frecot was working on from 1979 onwards, *Berlin im Abriss*,
the catalogue of which was published by the Berlinische Galerie in 1981,
offers an answer to this question.

Berlin im Abriss translates literally as 'Berlin in Outline', but it is also
a play on words: 'Abriss' also denotes 'demolition', so 'Berlin within the
Demolition/under Demolition', or 'Berlin: A Survey' are possible translations
that capture some of what is at stake in Frecot's work ('Survey' refers neatly
to the dominance of the visual economy of urban planning to which the
exhibition responds). Indeed Frecot's introduction to the exhibition catalogue outlines a 'history of demolition' (*Abrissgeschichte*) that is different
from a standard architectural history in that it does not study constructed
but demolished buildings. It is founded on the premise that building has
demolition as its precondition and that urban history has to be recognized
as a series of destructions. That history is set, according to Frecot, within
two opposing conceptions of time. These two conceptions propose, on the
one hand, time as intimately connected with 'life' as a process whose course
is not calculable and whose end is not foreseeable; and on the other hand,
a conception of time as linear, which means that life can be planned and
administered: it is calculable and can be made subject to statistical analysis.[54] Frecot also argues against the dominance of such analytical procedures
as an epistemological mode for engaging with the spatial dimension of
the city, arguing that the central method for such an engagement should
understand urban experience, beyond 'mere' gazing, as a sense of being
engulfed, since all senses are being involved in the act of perception. Frecot's
central method of capturing urban experience is suggestively reminiscent
of psychogeographical approaches. He describes it as a form of creatively
losing one's way: 'Dead ends open up the opportunity for the disorientated
to become aware of the finite nature of space and time.'[55]

As a result, *Berlin im Abriss* works with the photographic archive in
order to formulate a particular experience of time and space in the city.
One example – a sequence that treats the Potsdamer Platz and its main
tributary, the Potsdamer Strasse – serves to illustrate this. The series on
the Potsdamer Platz (123-37) begins with a photograph of the abandoned
Potsdamer Strasse from 1981 that shows trees lining grassed-over tarmac.
This image, far from being self-evident, is only made to speak through
Frecot's image-archaeological procedure that follows. As such, it suggests
Frecot's own form of 'media archaeology', a recent approach to questions
of archivization developed by theorists such as Wolfgang Ernst. Read in
this way, Frecot's approach could be seen as producing a form of cultural

memory that has become technical memory. Whereas media archaeology emphasizes the medium over the message, Frecot's approach, due to its interest in the representation of the cityscape, remains indebted to the 'indexical' quality of the image, which 'points' to the cityscape that the photograph has recorded.[56]

The next images are of the Vox-Haus, built, as the caption notes, in 1923 and demolished in 1969 (though the photograph is not dated) and of the house at Potsdamer Strasse 9 (dated to 1910). There follow two photographs of the *Bayern-Brunnen*, the first showing it in its current location in 1981, and the second in its original location in the ruin of the *Haus Bayern*, which, as the caption notes, was at Potsdamer Strasse 24. This photograph is dated as prior to the house's demolition in 1972. The fascinating aspect here is that Frecot is given as the author of the 1981 photograph, whereas the 1972 photograph was sourced from the *Landesbildstelle* (the regional photographic archive). Frecot's media archaeology moves back and forth between the cityscape and the production of the photographic archive to illustrate how engaging with the latter can in fact inform contemporary photographic production. Here Frecot has highlighted the way that the synchronic urban infrastructure of the road system has impeded the encounter with the cityscape.

The next photograph, from 1910, shows the house in its former function as a Wertheim department store. This is accompanied by an extensive caption outlining the history of the building that makes clear its various uses over time. This photograph then has only a limited connection to the history that is narrated in the caption – here Frecot has foregrounded the variety of media at his disposal in the exhibition process: the caption comes at the end of the series, as a supplement to the initial encounter with the images. The next sequence begins with an image of traffic at the Potsdamer Bridge in 1979, and follows this with a photograph of the construction work at the bridge in 1966, when it was realigned to take account of the Kulturforum buildings that had been and were being erected there. This image is accompanied by a caption that outlines much of the history of the bridge, revealing that it had already been structurally realigned in the 1930s by Albert Speer. The next image shows the 1945 ruins of Speer's 'House of Tourism' which was built in the 1930s close to the bridge in 1945, and the one that follows shows the bridge in 1913. The final image reproduces an engraving of the location, with a much more rudimentary bridge, around 1780, prior to its urbanization.

This is, of course, not a complete photographic history of the Potsdamer Strasse. In his introduction, Frecot explicitly rejects a totalizing impulse:

'We know of countless further examples and reject the attempt to aim for completeness where the matter at hand is a consciousness of an almost totally destroyed history.'[57] Frecot manipulates this photographic archive through an archaeology of urban image-making that reveals the forms of image-making as well as the layers of urban spatial practice that are to be discovered through non-chronological ordering, that is, not according to the dictates of linear time, which one might anticipate as a formal method of ordering within an archive. Frecot plays with the 'explicatory' role of textual supplementation and focuses on the past, bypassing almost entirely any linear narrative of political history in favour of a history of the architectural layers of the cityscape. It presents here a model for making the passage of time visible in an archiving procedure through a series of historical photographs selected from the repository. Photographs that were not necessarily the product of a conservationist focus on the vanishing site are now seen through one, although the intention is not to conserve these photographs in themselves, but to generate a new form of juxtaposition that undermines the self-evidence of the contemporary cityscape.

This approach is founded not on a simple juxtaposition between old and new, as with the use of archival photographs in earlier decades, but on forcing the viewer to consider history as non-teleological, and on fragments of the past being recombined in a different way. As a result, the Potsdamer Platz can now be seen as a space that is infused with history. Frecot's engagement with the photographic archive seeks to frame, both in the exhibition and in the printed catalogue, a 'sensual' experience of passing through layers of time rather than thinking of urban space as a merely quantifiable entity at the viewer's disposal. It is in this evocation of a 'tactile' encounter with the archive that Frecot comes close to the kind of media archaeology that would, as Jussi Parikka has formulated, 'focus on archives and archaeology [as a] mode of analysing [...] media in the way they channel and synchronize patterns of "cultural" life.'[58]

This principle underpins the re-emergence of 'rubble photographers' such as Fritz Eschen and Henry Ries within the exhibitions of the Berlinische Galerie (Eschen in 1985 as part of a series on the 'Aufbaujahre', and then in 1990 in a single retrospective of his work; Ries in 1988). These curations of the photographic archive speak to the same idea of exploring the prehistory and fissures in an allegedly intact contemporary cityscape. This photography of the immediate post-war years looked upon a formerly intact city reduced to fragments and it is the productivity of the intervention of such archival photographs into the present that is emphasized by Frecot in the volume on Eschen. Here Frecot frames Eschen's photography as a point of

contrast to the mythical narratives of the city that were being composed
by governmental institutions on either side of the Wall for the city's 750th
anniversary in 1987.[59] The photographic remnant as evidence of a survival
that bears witness *to the history of its forgetting* is a key premise of the
curatorial activity of this period that seeks to use photography to recover
a misplaced past opportunity for anamnesis. This is the significance of the
photographic archive of the 'Zero Hour' when viewed from this point in the
early 1980s; it becomes a site where a more recent past can be undone and
through its activation of the repository, it allows for a reimagination of the
contemporary city.

The Berlinische Galerie was by no means the only curator of post-war
photography. A striking example is the rediscovery of work by Friedrich
Seidenstücker, a photographer of the immediate post-war era. Seidenstücker,
like Eschen, was not self-consciously an 'art' photographer, but rather a
practising journalistic professional, and was mostly known for his work
for popular magazines, both during the war and in the post-war era. For
this reason, a retrospective of his work in 1962 in the Rathaus Wilmersdorf
clearly focused on the populist aspect of his work, in particular his images
from the Berlin Zoo. While attention was given to these popular images,
which were often reproduced in newspapers, the unpublished body of
work that Seidenstücker had produced in the immediate post-war era, in
which he minutely recorded the ruined city centre, went almost unnoticed.
Seidenstücker's post-war work was salvaged only by the chance intervention
of a zoologist who was interested in his animal photography. Unable to
afford Seidenstücker's collection, the zoologist asked for the support of
the Bildarchiv Preussischer Besitz, which then acquired the images in 1971,
although they showed little interest initially in exhibiting them. It was only
from the mid-1970s that his photographs appeared on display, initially with a
focus on his images from the Weimar period in Kassel and Hamburg, before
his post-war work began to emerge, first in a gallery exhibition in Berlin
in 1980, the curators of which produced the first publication collecting his
work from the 1920s through to the late 1950s.[60]

The photography of Eschen and Seidenstücker had not previously been
regarded in terms of its aesthetic value, although, as noted above, the
documentary value of the former's images had certainly been asserted
and instrumentalized in the 1950s. Within the local context of Berlin, it
is important to stress that the growing awareness for this photography of
the immediate postwar era in the 1970s and 1980s was not only concerned
with 'coming to terms' with the period of the National Socialist regime,
but also, and crucially, meant revisiting the disavowals of the post-war

era. Frecot's assertion that the 'Zero Hour in its openness seems more urgently contemporary than ever' stands as a motto for the emergence of the photographic archive of the immediate post-war period into a critical form of cultural memory work in the late 1970s and early 1980s. This archiving of the 'Zero Hour' more than thirty years after the fact was an attempt to see the 'open city' once more following the impact of the post-war reconstruction. Through Frecot's media-archaeological approach to the photographic archive, 'excavation sites' become speculative 'reconstruction sites' for an imagining of the history and future of the city as an antidote to a melancholic memory culture that views the historical as little more than one of traumatic loss.[61]

Contemporary urban photography and the museal gaze

In this same interview in the *Kunstblatt*, Frecot also referred to 'Stadt-photographie' in the list of photographic categories that spanned the art/documentary photograph distinction. While he meant this primarily historically (listing earlier photographers such as Schwartz, Rückwardt, Mende and Lange), it could also refer to another name he mentions later in the interview: the contemporary photographer, Michael Schmidt. His volume *Berlin-Kreuzberg*, from 1973, is a subtle examination of the interplay of old and new, which also picks up on and replays some of the tropes of Siedler/Niggemeyer's *Murdered City*, particularly in its depiction of children at play, but also through the framing of the water pump and the pissoir, and through the layout of the photographs that plays with the grid structure of representation and which contrast empty streetscapes with scenes of spatial practice.[62] The perspective is so repetitively that of a ground-level pedestrian that any very infrequent deviations are immediately striking. It also juxtaposes old and new in key ways; either through the use of facing pages, such as an old façade versus a renewed façade, or within the same image, as most strikingly in the book's final image, captioned 'Contrasts at Askanischer Platz' (the captions are listed at the back of the book, leaving the images primarily to 'speak for themselves').[63]

The important development in *Berlin-Kreuzberg* is Schmidt's presentation of 'obsolescence' as a critique of a new that proclaims the obsolescence of the old. The ruins have been 'overcome', but the 'memory value' of the vernacular cityscape is becoming evident in the kind of spatial images that Schmidt is producing, as a way of seeing West Berlin.

8. Michael Schmidt, o.T (Untitled), from *Berlin nach 45* (1980), Silver bromide gelatine print, framed 23,4 x 29,2 cm. ©Stiftung für Fotografie und Medienkunst mit Archiv Michael Schmidt. Courtesy Galerie Nordenhake Berlin/Stockholm.

As with Niggemeyer's photography, the spatial image of 'obsolescence', when juxtaposed with cityscapes formed by the synchronic urban gaze, becomes a critique of the synchronic urban gaze. In photography, as in text, the formulation of the museal urban gaze is rhetorically dependent on the formulation of the synchronic urban gaze (i.e. of the modern). The experience of the asynchronous city is dependent on the construction of a synchronic city that it seeks to resist.

We see this, too, in the work of one of the most significant photographers within the East Berlin context in this period, Ulrich Wüst. His collection, *Fotografien*, was published in 1986, and the introduction to this slim catalogue, published by the Berlin-Friedrichshain Photography Gallery, was written by the GDR architect and critic, Wolfgang Kil, who cited an 1980 article written by Hein Köster in the critically oriented journal *form + zweck*, in an issue which also included some of Wüst's images. Köster's commentary on Wüst's photographs formulates an important dimension of the museal urban gaze.

Images only speak to the person who first of all trusts his own eyes. Anyone, on the other hand, is already finished with things when he can

say their name or finds his prejudice about them confirmed, overlooks
the freedom on offer here to fill the scene with actions and to let himself
be told history ['Geschichte'].[64]

Köster here formulates two forms of gaze: the instrumentalizing gaze that
reduces the object to what it signifies and another gaze that opens out
the image as a process and involves the paradigmatic loss of control. Kil's
1986 introduction expands on Köster's observation, proposing that Wüst's
'architect eyes' closely observed the built environment and 'encountered
time',[65] in a manner which fulfils Halbwachs's injunction about remembering place well that was discussed in the introduction:

> Lived life that engraved its traces into formerly pristine surfaces: the
> remains of countless, anonymous existences, in the course of which
> houses were not admired like works of art, but used, used up.[66]

Key here is a Rieglian definition of 'age value' that, as with the official
GDR line expressed in *Deutsche Architektur* in the early 1970s, clearly
distinguishes between the official monument and vernacular remnants
that attest to the passage of social time. Through this close observation,
Kil argues that Wüst discovered that:

> everyday life [is] more interesting than academic architectural history
> in the mundanity of the many generations who make the life-history of a
> street, of a house, of a square metre of plaster. At first Ulrich Wüst refused
> aesthetic strategies, began with an enlightened gaze to engage in analysis:
> urban space as living space, newly built areas, small city streets, and always
> with a particular eye for those difficult to grasp zones in which the obsolete
> and the recently added collide with one another (a collision of the eras
> materialized through building structures: the city appears thus not simply
> as a collage of different architectural styles, but of different cultures).[67]

Kil contrasts the abstract calculations of the synchronic urban gaze with
the effect which Wüst's photography achieves:

> What was created was photography, inspired by general knowledge about
> the phenomenon of the city, but driven by the very concrete experiences
> of one's own – urban – existence [...] as if the mountain of stone and
> concrete, of numbers and facts and geometries had gradually been cleared
> away and enabled the gaze to grasp a wider terrain.

He then explains the quality of Wüst's museal gaze upon the city: it is no longer simply observation (*Betrachten*) but seeing (*Schauen*), which implies something more 'profound', a perception of the process of time, for in Wüst's photography reality is no longer being 'documented in concrete detail' but as a 'fleeting fragment' – 'the moment becomes important, with everything that it evokes – atmosphere, mood, subjectivity.[68]

The fragment here is both spatial and temporal: a material fragment *momentarily* perceived. Wüst's museal gaze is contrasted with the pseudo-objectivity of the synchronic urban gaze that renders the object (and thus the subject) intact and impermeable, also to time. Such a perception of 'obsolescence' in the GDR contrasts with the state's vision of the intact, coherent built environment.

Turning to the photographs in Wüst's book, we find that the opening image (Fig. 9) appears at first glance to be a typical evocation of 'age value;' the remains of an eroded sign gives a clue to a topographical location (the second-half of a street name), but the window is bricked over, implying inaccessibility. Obsolescence is only superficially self-evident and not as transparent nor as calculable as the synchronic urban gaze would have it. This opening image appears as part of a juxtaposition between the 'empti-ness' of a new housing block, but this façade too exhibits signs, but signs that are signs of urban regulation (no parking/direction).[69] Having established a contract with the viewer through these distinctive forms of gaze, the rest of the photographs do not dwell on obsolescence, but rather offer ways of bringing 'process' into the ostensibly sterile cityscapes of the new buildings and their environs, principally through unconventional angles on spatial practice or the way in which spatial practice negotiates with the regulations of urban space that have been imposed.

The pictures are not captioned in any way, heightening their potential for ambiguity, simultaneously invoking and complexifying the self-evidence of the images; neither are the catalogue pages numbered (which creates a further difficulty of referentiality). The text within the images on occasion suggests legibility: an image of what might be an old factory has the old *Fraktur* inscription above the entrance, but letters are missing. By contrast, a photograph two pages later of a fragment of a new apartment includes the signs (with arrows) directing pedestrians to a series of streets and house numbers. This again sets the ostensible transparency of the synchronic urban gaze (the streets/houses are themselves NOT visible) against the ambiguity of the museal urban gaze (the factory might be identifiable, in a Halbwachsian sense, to those inhabitants familiar with the site through their long-term, historical spatial practices). This illustrates that Wüst's

9. Ulrich Wüst, Untitled, *Fotografien* (1986). Courtesy of the artist.

architectural photography is directed not towards our acknowledgement of what is being represented, but we are required to pay attention to the ways in which we recognize and are asked to recognize the urban environment around us.

Michael Schmidt, already discussed above, published a further volume of photographs in 1978, entitled *Berlin: Cityscape and People* (*Berlin: Stadtlandschaft und Menschen*).[70] The introduction by Heinz Ohff highlighted a connection with Wüst's focus on the fragmentary detail, suggesting that Schmidt 'documents an excerpt, a part of the cityscape.' Ohff's introduction points to the longer-term historical trend of the tourist appropriation of the cityscape, but it is marked by an ambiguity:

> There have been and are many photograph volumes about Berlin. Anyone who wanted to keep a city, possibly his city, in his memory and place it as a second visual memory (*Gedächtnis*) on his bookshelf or hang it on his wall, would have bought in the past the veduta of the travelling artist.[71]

In addressing the popularity of the photobook, this is a very striking analogy, for it implies a process of translation of the 'memory' from the storage repository to a display situation, while also affording the curator of the museal gaze a crucial outsider status as neither visitor nor citizen. Perhaps the clearest example of this interrogation of the threshold between tourist and non-tourist gaze is provided in the opening photograph of Schmidt's book, which is a view – not from a car, but from the S-Bahn – of the approach to Zoo Station.

The correlations between the urban photography of Schmidt and Wüst speak to a broader sense of convergence in the museal gaze between East and West. This convergence finds its expression in 1980 in two films released in East and West respectively: *Solo Sunny* and *Chamissoplatz*, in which the critique of the destruction of 'place' is conjoined with the promise of a place memory.

Film and the museal gaze around 1980

In Chapter One, we discussed *The Legend of Paul and Paula* (1973) as part of an emergent critique of the synchronic designs of the GDR state. *Solo Sunny* (1980) is very aware of the codes which shape the structure of its forebear.[72] Nevertheless, unlike the earlier film, *Solo Sunny* refuses to sentimentalize the community networks of the old apartment block, which is shown to be a place of petty jealousies and suspicions amongst its long-term residents, as well as a not always positively portrayed upwardly mobile bohemian clique. The film is also more ambiguous in its presentation of the relationship between the obsolete and the modern. Although the camera frequently lingers on decaying façades in front of which Sunny walks, it seldom directly juxtaposes this with a vision of the new. This ambiguity is derived from its more subtle exploration of the cinematic gaze as a way of framing the built environment.

The film's opening titles seem to offer us a static image of an 'obsolescent', decaying façade, but as we watch, Sunny comes into view, introducing movement into an apparently still image. A later shot is of demolition, but it is followed by a shot of Sunny's shopping on the kitchen table, as if to imply that such demolition is now simply part of the everyday, rather than the visceral interruption that it is in *Paul und Paula*.

Solo Sunny reflects on the gaze upon and from the built environment in the sequences set in the new apartment block where Sunny's friend has moved. In the first scene set there, we see Sunny putting up wallpaper that is a life-size scale version of a sunlit and fertile classical arcade. The trompe l'oeil effect is perfect as we see the back of Sunny framed by this illusion of harmonious urban living. During the next scene set in the apartment block, we see a black silhouette of Sunny from behind as she gazes out of

10. The view of the cityscape in *Solo Sunny* (1980). ©DEFA-Stiftung/Dieter Lück.

the window; the next shot (Fig. 10) shows us what she sees: a grey, desolate, empty streetscape with a single car. This is less the critical gaze at the product of the synchronic urban gaze, as with *Paul and Paula*, but rather a demonstration of how the subjective gaze (of Sunny) has been shaped by the synchronic urban gaze.

As with Paula in the earlier film, Sunny is also offered a way out of her situation by a man with a car. In this case it is Harry, a taxi driver. Her alternative (in more than one sense) is Ralph, who describes himself at one point, in a rejection of the culture of the synchronic city, as 'not living in a new apartment block, *not having a registered car* nor a television' [my italics – SW], and whom the mise-en-scène associates with the decaying back courtyards of the former 'rental barracks', as these tenements of the late nineteenth century were typically described. One scene locates Sunny and Ralph in a graveyard framed in ivy. Ralph is, perhaps unsurprisingly writing about 'death and society', addressing the question of decay which the GDR state with its synchronic gaze was refusing to address.

Such contemplative views of obsolescence and decay are examples of a museal gaze that attends to the (passage of) time within the built environment, offering by extension a critique of the ostensible quantifiability of the cityscape and its ideological rejection of obsolescence.

This framing of the visual power of obsolescence is not however situated within a clear narrative of history or cultural memory, due to the absence of historical commentary, but is closer to the indeterminate 'age value' of obsolescence. *Solo Sunny*'s rejection of automobility is central to establishing a perception of the city that offers an alternative to the rhythms dictated by urban planning and takes us back to the 'alternative' photographic framing of the Berlin cityscape in the east and west of the city from the 1970s onwards. This was demonstrated in the work of Ulrich Wüst and Michael Schmidt, but can also be seen in the East in the photography of Evelyn Richter, Helga Paris, Christian Borchert, Manfred Paul and Uwe Steinberg. In the West, a striking comparison can be made with Helke Sander's 1978 film, *Redupers*, a remarkably subtle portrayal of the everyday life of a female photographer, Edda Chiemnyjewski, struggling to make a career in West Berlin. While the film is generally considered in terms of its investigation of gender, it is also susceptible to the approach undertaken in this book. The film begins with, and often reiterates, a long, unedited sequence of the view of the West Berlin cityscape from the side window of a car. This synchronic gaze imitates the endless, monotonous rhythm of urban life that produces the 'all-round reduced personality', the film's English title that captures, in its parody of the GDR's claim to produce the 'all-round Socialist personality', precisely that convergence of the pernicious effects of urban living on both sides of the Wall.

Edda is working on many photographic projects simultaneously, always in the hope of generating, with site-specific interventions and critical photographic practice, an insight into the gaps in the Wall, but also, by extension, in the apparently seamless urban fabric.[73] Edda is interested in images of demolition, and many of the car sequences captures elements of obsolescence, but there are only two particular sequences when the car halts. First, when it encounters on a billboard one of the Wall images (which strikingly contains a car parked front on to the Wall) and secondly, in conclusion, when Edda is observed walking down a street away from the camera, ultimately vanishing from view.

As a further point of comparison with *Solo Sunny*, Rudolf Thome's 1980 West Berlin film, *Chamissoplatz*, is on the surface an issue-based film taking a realistic look at the debates surrounding modernization and renovation in the Kreuzberg district around the time of the IBA (not mentioned directly in the film). These debates are filtered predominantly through two perspectives. On the one hand, that of a young female Sociology student, Anna Bach, who is making a documentary film as part of her involvement with a group of activists seeking to fight the demolition of, in their eyes, still viable housing stock. On the other, a rather disillusioned architect,

11. Credit sequence in *Chamissoplatz* (1980). Courtesy of Rudolf Thome.

Martin, entangled in the processes of city planning (one shot shows him in supervisory mode standing atop a new housing development, framed by tower blocks).

The film operates with a series of juxtapositions, starting with a crane-shot gaze upon the city: the opening sequence (Fig. 11) is a long, slow pan across the rooftops of the city before descending to street level, where a local street event is underway.

A loudspeaker intones the following piece of exposition, which also aligns the spectator with Anna, the student with a camera, and implicates a specific collective audience:

> 'Ladies and Gentleman! You being the affected residents of Chamis-soplatz, I wish to call for your attention for a moment. The area around Chamissoplatz is the last remaining in Berlin where the original buildings of the nineteenth century have been completely preserved. This lends a particular historical value to the quarter.'

This 'historical value' is not explicated directly in the rest of the film, but remains implicit in the shots of the façades that form the film's mise-en-scene. In the discussion between the student and the architect that follows this exposition, Martin accuses Anna of personalizing questions that are actually system-related. This point is a crucial juxtaposition in the film, which obviously creates a more nuanced investigation of its ostensible topic through the initially tentative, but growing, emotional connection between the two figures.

The film investigates the impact of the cityscape on its protagonists, both of whom are products of an urban system that they cannot ultimately escape. For example, the film sets up an explicit contrast between automobile Martin and pedestrian Anna, who refuses lifts in order to take the subway and who, to begin with, is seen walking around the streets of her neighbourhood and shopping at her local market. If, as in *Summer in the City, Solo Sunny* and *Paul and Paula*, automobility is figured as one particular form of encounter with the cityscape, then *Chamissoplatz* follows this pattern. At the film's opening, Martin's wife, from whom he is separated, has had a car accident. The space he goes to in order to pick her up in his car is a functional space for a functional transaction founded on an empty contractual arrangement (a marriage that only exists in name).

The relationship between Anna and Martin is set, by contrast, in 'natural spaces' outside the domain of the urban infrastructure. For example, linking back to Frecot's focus on the Potsdamer Strasse as a palimpsestic space of the post-war city, they walk and talk in an untended patch of grass just north of the Neue Nationalgalerie near the unshown Wall at Potsdamer Platz. They also go to Wannsee: we see their car arrive at a barrier, over which they leap as they head out towards the lake. In both cases, their relationship is figured as an escape from urban infrastructure. This is most explicit in the remarkable sequence towards the end of the film, where the couple drive, overnight, from Berlin to a sun-kissed Italy. Of course, this is the reiteration of a familiar German trope, reaching back to Goethe, and indeed, the car stops in front of a ruined castle, as Goethe does in Malcesine on his Italian journey. Yet, as with the earlier 'nature' sequences, this escape from the urban infrastructure is only a brief one, undone by an argument that ensues when Anna reveals she is pregnant, although she neither wants to keep the baby, nor indeed accept Martin's offer of marriage.

The most striking sequences in the film are the 'night drives', analogous to the car journeys in Wenders's *Summer in the* City, that serve no functional plot purpose. Rather than offering us a view of the city by night, they frame the isolated driver in an environment devoid of detail, merely composed of dark and blinking neon lights set to an aryhythmic non-diegetic jazz soundtrack that accompanies the relationship between Anna and Martin throughout. This, along with the drive to Italy, proposes a gaze from within the synchronic system that is blind and lost, something mirrored in their earlier visit to the dark of the cinema.

The plot follows the growing dysfunctionality of Martin, the city functionary. The penultimate driving sequence illustrates this clearly, where his night drive leads him to Chamissoplatz. The camera frames him asleep in the car, being closely observed by a traffic warden. Martin is clearly now 'homeless', the logical consequence of his automobile dependence. This is reinforced on the return from Italy, where it becomes clear at a party that Anna's friends have published the clandestinely recorded, very revealing remarks by Martin about the inner workings of renovation processes in the city. He storms out of the party and drives off. Anna, catching sight of him, follows in a borrowed VW beetle (the same model crashed by Martin's wife). They disappear into the automobile labyrinth of the city. At this point the film ends, implying there is ultimately no escape from the automobile urban infrastructure.

Other than the opening sequence discussed above, the film rarely offers the obsolescent cityscape as a specific object of contemplation (this is the most explicit contrast with *Solo Sunny*). The one exception is a sequence involving Martin's investigation of Anna's tenement's foundations. Here we watch Anna filming Martin and also the dilapidated exterior of the building; this is an interrogation of the surface assumption that that which looks old is necessarily obsolescent. While it similarly critiques the mode of encounter with the city that is generated by urban gaze, unlike *Solo Sunny*, the film does not celebrate 'age value' over the new. This has much to do with the systems in which the films are made: the valuing of obsolescence has a subtle but, to the initiated, clear political subtext in East Berlin as a form of clandestine, unspoken resistance to dominant state discourse. The urgent demands of a socially acceptable housing policy dominate the valuing of the obsolescent in the housing debate in the West, though there is obviously a crossover within the memory discourse of the period. The state discourse is less clear-cut in the West, not least because the Senate, through its policies of *Stadtbildpflege* and support for the IBA-Neu, had paid lip service to preservation. This sequence, which looks behind (and below) the façade in *Chamissoplatz*, serves that same purpose of the museal urban gaze of looking behind the surface of the city, towards a different kind of display of the built environment, rendering visible (through the camera) what is usually invisible, or not put on display, other than as a strategy of devaluation, as in the city-sponsored films of the 1960s, which showed conditions in the 'rental barracks' of the proletarian district of Wedding.

We have seen how the museal urban gaze is shaped by slightly different focuses in East and West on the neighbourhood as 'abandoned remnant' in these two films. Beyond this, neither engages in an elaboration of the 'memory value' of the cityscape in terms of a historical narrative. It is the asynchronic dimension of the material remnant that comes to the fore, primarily shaped through a critique of the automobile gaze and its impact on the subjectivity of its synchronized protagonists.

3. The Remembered City On Display, 1984-1993

The 'place memory work' discussed in the previous chapter becomes codified in forms of display which establish the paradigm of the city as a museal space in itself between 1984 and the early 1990s, spanning the caesura of the fall of the Wall. This is evident in the outcomes of the IBA-Neu and -Alt projects, and then a series of projects related to the 750th anniversary of the city's founding in 1987, which establishes a new technique of place memory production: the installation as 'collective' event. The 1986 Mythos Berlin exhibition on the site of the Anhalter Bahnhof illustrates site-specific urban memory production ('the city as museum') as a specific technology in the evocation of past time and experience, but also as a development of an embryonic event culture. An extended analysis of Wim Wenders's *Wings of Desire* (1986) focuses on how the film shapes the viewer's encounter with the 'empty spaces' of the southern Friedrichstadt, the Anhalter Bahnhof and the Hotel Esplanade. Wenders curates the city in such a way as to (re) formulate the viewer's experience of the cityscape through the undoing of the sensory-motor habits of the urban environment. The Nikolaiviertel reconstruction in East Berlin allows for a broader consideration of the display of the urban and its role in monument preservation and reconstruction in the period, especially in comparison with the aims of the West Berlin IBA-Neu. It is read alongside the late GDR film, *The Architects* (1991) which revisits the themes of critical visual culture, the built environment and the urban gaze that were also visible in Chapter Two. *The Architects* points to a continuity in the museal urban gaze that is to be found in a number of works from the immediate post-wall era. Jürgen Böttcher's documentary film about the fall of the Wall and its aftermath, *Die Mauer* (1991), works with the visual language of obsolescence we are familiar with from the GDR – not however now as a tacit form of state dissidence, but as a form of resistance to the synchronic time regime and the new post-unification order with its associated historical narratives. A similar continuity is evident in Christian Boltanski's *Missing House*, and Shimon Attie's *Writing on the Wall*, both of which are explicit interventions in the urban fabric that foreground the palimpsestic city as simultaneously repository, archive and museum.

The IBA on display

In the previous chapter, we discussed the IBA primarily in terms of the theories of the museal urban gaze that its leading curators formulated. How did the application of those theories relate to the exhibition and display of the city that followed at the end of its process? In 1984, the year of the interim report of the Berlin IBA, the urban renewal section on the ground floor of the 'Martin Gropius Bauhaus', as the project manager and designer Bernhard Strecker named the venerable building in an invocation of architectural tradition, displayed a project which sought to do justice to the concerns of careful urban repair. Jürg Steiner was commissioned to develop a typical Kreuzberg scene, using streetscapes aligned with old buildings and the 'new Kreuzberg centre.' The street corners of Kreuzberg were shown as large-format photographs and the incremental reduction in scale created an impression of perspective for the exhibition visitor. This was an attempt to construct an encounter with place, or perhaps more correctly, the memory of place memory in an exhibition setting.

The display side of the IBA-Neu is, however, best read through the new constructions themselves, which were, however, limited in 1984 to largely unobtrusive signs that described the either fulfilled or yet to be fulfilled intentions of the IBA (for example, James Stirling's intervention at Meinekestrasse, discussed earlier, has no indication of the architect's input). The philosophical coherence of this 'urban repair' was conceptualized in the 1984 exhibition, 'Architecture and Philosophy since the Industrial Revolution', curated by Vittorio Magnagno Lampugnani at the New National Gallery. This exhibition continued the theoretical line of discussion and sought to present architectural history as intellectual history, largely through sketches and designs, rather than representations of actual buildings. The critical architectural journals, *ARCH+*, took a sceptical view of the exhibition's limited social contextualization of architectural theory, contrasting it unfavourably with the exhibition, 'Berlin around 1900', in the Akademie der Künste (curated by, amongst others, Janos Frecot) which it considered a much more historically informed and informative reflection on questions of urban planning and architecture.[1]

For the specific display of spatial images, however, one must turn to the work done by IBA-Alt in Kreuzberg, which created a series of 'site-specific' (*vor Ort*) exhibitions. It is here that the practice of the museal urban gaze becomes highly visible, with the use of existing structures (such as the hall of the Schlesisches Tor underground station) and a pedestrian 'guided tour' of the work being done by IBA-Alt in a series of blocks, starting from

Admiralstrasse 17, via Admiralstrasse 23, Liegnitzer Strasse 18, Cuvrystrasse 20, Oppelner Strasse 41, Wrangelstrasse 69, Silbersteinstrasse 97, Ohlauer Strasse 37, to the Paul-Lincke-Ufer 20-22. Significantly, the encounter with these acts of urban curation culminated in an exhibition in the former multi-storey car park at the Kottbusser Tor. The exhibition, Baller und Kennedy's 'Brave New World – Ecological Projections from a dilapidated garage', allowed, according to Peterek in *ARCH+*, 'the desired radical break with the past to be experienced with all one's senses.'[2] The same reviewer also considered that there remained, in the whole IBA exhibition process, a problem of address: 'the site-specific exhibitions are not always addressed to those who live in the area.' The IBA-Neu offered the visual and philosophical encounter with the cityscape in an exhibition space, the IBA-Alt demanded an encounter on foot that recreated forms of place memory. The display aspect demonstrates the fundamental distinctions in the conceptions and address of the museal urban gaze of the two sides of the IBA.

The IBA's museal urban gaze culminated not in 1984's exhibitions, but in its incorporation into the 750th anniversary of the founding of the city of Berlin in 1987. This anniversary, celebrated on both sides of the Wall, brought together the developing paradigms of urban memory, such as the encounter with the anamnestic dimensions of the material site and its implication in the generation of cultural memory narratives and asynchronicity. Rather than looking at the 'official' commemorations organized by the regimes on either side of the divide, I want to look at how the museal urban gaze was formulated in three projects of this period. First, the 'Mythos Berlin' exhibition, which described itself as a 'history of the perception of an industrial metropolis', enacted through a 'scenic representation' of a variety of installations at the Anhalter Bahnhof. Second, the major East Berlin 'urban renewal' project for the 750th anniversary, the reconstruction of the Nikolai Quarter, which had been all but razed to the ground at the end of the Second World War. And third, Wim Wenders's 1986 film, *Wings of Desire* (*Der Himmel über Berlin*), which is a profound meditation on the encounter with the presence of the past in (the western half of) the city.

Mythos Berlin

'Mythos Berlin' was an institutionally supported project, but as befits the generational change of the period, the institutions themselves were now populated by those for whom the radical shifts in urban politics and aesthetics in the late 1960s were part of their own education. It is, unsurprisingly,

12. Exhibition Opening at the Anhalter Bahnhof, 'Mythos Berlin', 13 June 1987. Photograph: Ingeborg Lommatsch. Courtesy of Berlin Landesarchiv.

a project that also saw the incorporation of critical visual culture into the institutional making of urban memory.

Eberhard Knödler-Bunte, the director of the project, indicated that a major impulse for the 'Mythos Berlin' project had been the discussions around the fate of the southern Friedrichstadt (see previous chapter). 'Mythos Berlin' recapitulates the narrative of the 'second destruction' of the post-war era and restates the importance of the 'search for a method for dealing with urban spaces that do not lend themselves to being displayed as representative' (i.e. that are not overlaid with narrativizations).[3] The rhetoric of place memory is evident throughout the conception of the project, in its production of a spatial image. As Knödler-Bunte stated:

> Perception and myth always relate to a place of social interaction. [...]
> Place here [in Berlin] is not only what is on one side of the Wall, but
> on the other side as well, present as a remnant of remembrance even
> there where its visibility has faded. [...] The Anhalter Railway Station
> with its remaining portico and the few remnants of its function, is a
> necessary prerequisite, a reference-point which shapes (*entlanghangelt*)
> our perception; the materiality of the remains are an irreplaceable clue
> (*Anhaltspunkt*) to make history visible.[4]

The key difference, perhaps, to the Topography of the Terror discussed earlier, is the distinction between the demand there for 'legibility' and the rhetoric here of 'visibility.' The original German is strikingly tortured, in its almost tautological 'prerequisite' and 'reference point' in attempting to describe the object and its function in shaping perception.

The exhibition as a whole experiments with the technologies of the museal gaze's work of transmission, in that it 'formulates clues' that are triggers rather than solutions for its addressees. Different modes of encounter are embedded in the exhibition beyond the initial prerequisite of the material remnants. There is a collective dimension to the experience of the exhibition space, but the varying objects and stagings imply a differentiated response, which, for Knödler-Bunte, is a sign of the metropolitan.[5] The framings involve montage, gestural signs and spatial sequences which seek to create a fluid encounter with space. The experience of place and scale is reinforced not in order to revivify old narratives of the location, but to understand the present moment in contact with history.

As Knödler-Bunte described the Anhalter Bahnhof at this point, it is interstitial, poised not only between ruin and renewal, but also between the pulsing commercialism of the Kudamm and the stability of the local neighbourhood. For Knödler-Bunte, this interstitial quality describes 'the cultural', which is related to specific forms of perception that are at odds with the perceptions shaped by commerce. He also draws a contrast with theatre: the Anhalter Bahnhof is not an artificial stage, but a space of experience (*Erlebnisraum*). The fundamental structure is hidden behind the 'aura' of the exhibited objects and for Knödler-Bunte, this enchanting form of presentation is crucial for the production of aura, since, if the objects were removed from this form of museal context, they would disappear into the continuum of everyday perception. Only the particular framing here, removed from their original context, and combined in an 'elevated' space, allows their particular and unique meanings to be evoked (*hervortreten*).

While this seems to privilege sensation, and a certain kind of sensationalism, a consideration of one of the art projects on display in the terrain of the former station helps to get a more tangible sense of the kind of spatial image that was produced under these conditions. Wolf Vostell, a central conceptual artist of the previous two decades through his involvement in the FLUXUS movement, designed an installation, 'La Tortuga' (The Tortoise) which, in Vostell's words, sought to manifest the 'ongoing death throes of the socio-aesthetic environment in the recent history of Berlin.'[6]

The installation, which consisted of an upturned steam locomotive, situated in the terrain without explanatory signs, certainly addressed the

polemical combination of social and aesthetic work that was underpinned
by Vostell's concern with perception in the urban environment and the
specific exhibition space. Enhanced by its partial casing in concrete,
the building material of the synchronic post-war city, the implication
that an obsolescent 'modernity' has come to a standstill was, for Vostell,
counteracted by the dynamism inherent in the still potentially mobile
wheels (which were driven by an installed electric motor). The presence
of 'the past' was suggested not just by the obsolescent locomotive, but
also through the dynamics of communicative memory, voices which
evoke 'the victims of German history, which precisely in this part of
Berlin still float around reproachfully in the atmosphere.' The mode of
encounter was central to the work: the public was able to come right up
to the sculpture and, 'by PLACING THEIR EARS [capitals in original] on
the engine' hear the sounds of screams, conversations, heartbeats and
fragments of music.[7]

Here Vostell created a spatial image for the encounter with obsolescence
that evokes the attentional dynamics of place memory. Another work by
Vostell created for the 1987 anniversary that reinforced and enhanced these
concerns in the context of another collective large-scale art project, the
'sculpture boulevard', which ran along the Kurfürstendamm in 1987.[8] The
seven artists involved were a mixture of international and local artists,
brought together for a project that, like the Mythos Berlin event, would only
be present in the cityscape for a short time. The tension between 'art work'
and 'temporary urban environment' proved creative and disruptive, as in
the work of Olaf Metzel, whose 'sculpture', '13.04.81', consisted of a tower of
shopping trolleys constructed over night at the Joachimsthaler Platz right
in front of the Kranzler Café. As Duchamp had called into question the
nature of the gallery museum with his everyday readymades in the 1920s, so
Metzel called into question the sensory-motor perceptions of the Kudamm
as 'shopping boulevard.' The undoing of mobility, and the 'stumbling' of
the Berlin citizens on the morning after its erection, was echoed in the
response to Vostell's 'Beton-Cadillacs' (Concrete-Cadillacs) (Fig. 13), which
was positioned in the centre of the roundabout at Rathenau-Platz, at the far
western end of the Kudamm, where it meets up with the 'Stadtautobahn'
at Halensee.

The site-specificity of both works is on the one hand, a self-conscious
dissection of the sensory-motor regime which had been dominant in West
Berlin in the past decades and on the other hand, a commentary on forms
of urban memory, founded in an enigmatic refusal to explain. The response
to Metzel's 'parody' of the nearby Kaiser William Memorial Church recalls

13. Wolf Vostell, 'Concrete Cadillacs' at Rathenauplatz (2014) Photograph: Simon Ward.

the response of the Berlin public to Egon Eiermann's design for a 'new' memorial church in the 1950s. Yet site-specificity has more to do with the modes of encounter embedded in a site, rather than any history of the location. Vostell's sculpture, two golden cadillacs, up-ended and encased in cement, spoke to De Certeau's contemporaneously crumbling 'concept-city', while at the same time, like Metzel, creating an unintended monument, in the sense that the artist's intentionality is not explained or denoted. Its effect on the perception of the automobile drivers circulating around the roundabout at Rathenauplatz cannot of course be measured, though the public response to these two pieces was very clear, compared to the setting of the Anhalter Bahnhof, where the framing of the locomotive-monument within an exhibition setting created an expectation of non-conventional perception. Vostell's immobile donation to the socio-aesthetic experience of West Berlin's built environment was certainly incendiary, but not nostalgic. It made a small, but lasting contribution to the 'history of destroyed urban history' and disrupted the synchronic perception of space. It does not operate with an already existing museal space in the manner of Mythos Berlin, nor does it offer the compensations of a memory of urban place as was promised by the IBA-Neu, or indeed by the East Berlin reconstruction of the Nikolaiviertel, which will be discussed later in this chapter.

Curating Berlin in *Wings of Desire*

It is not insignificant that it is Berlin in which this museal gaze and its concomitant memory culture emerges, a culture that is more sophisticated than what might be decried as a conservationist, heritage nostalgia. If, following the implications of De Certeau's argument, non-museified ruins themselves create an implicit form of seeing, then the urban museal gaze that emerges in Berlin in the 1970s and 1980s is perhaps also shaped by the city itself. Wim Wenders spoke to this in an interview around the time of the release of *Wings of Desire*. This is a quotation that we have already cited, but it bears repetition, as it is a rich and suggestive assertion:

> Berlin has a lot of empty spaces... I like the city for its wounds. They show its history better than any history book or document. [...] [The] empty spaces allow the visitor and the people of Berlin to see through the cityscape [...], through these gaps in a sense they can see through time.[9]

Wenders's claim for Berlin has many resonances with De Certeau's version of the museal object within the synchronic post-war urban environment. The wounds of the city possess an anamnestic dimension, give immediate access to the past and counteract the synchronic cityscape that has been imposed on the urban space. Wenders presents the city(scape) as a repository of the past that is activated into a space of museal encounter through an interactive gaze. In line with Huyssen's formulation of the museal gaze, there is a symbiotic relationship between spectator and material object in the production of an anamnestic gaze that can perceive a sense of the past and of non-synchronicity. As with Riegl, the immediate experience of temporality is privileged over the transmission of historical knowledge and understanding – history is shown, not told – but there is also a sense of the recovery of a different relationship to time, which is also implicit in formulations of place memory. Wenders's quotation implies an immediate experience of the cityscape by the visitor or citizen. Given our earlier discussion about the construction of place memory, this elision is significant; the visitor does not have the immediate relationship that binds the citizen to place, as Halbwachs argues in his essays on 'Space and the Collective Memory', but is in the city, thus subject to the practices of 'civic seeing.' Wenders proposes an observer that can be extended to the situation of the cinematic spectator (one which the quotation's context – *Wings of Desire*'s interest in Berlin's cityscape – heavily implies). As suggested in the introduction to this book, film can position the spectator in the 'museal encounter' with the opaque, material object, a spectator who has surrendered synchronic visual mastery.

Before discussing *Wings of Desire* in detail, a point of correlation between Wenders and Andreas Huyssen needs to be elucidated in their conception of the technologies of the synchronic and museal gazes. The oppositions that underlie Huyssen's argument, in particular of the museal object versus television, are very much of their time, though they do not necessarily diminish the relevance of his insistence on the compensatory power of the material object. They are crucial to an understanding of the historical moment out of which the museal gaze emerges and whence it has evolved. Like Huyssen, Wenders is sceptical about television, which brings 'the new idea of being able to view distant events 'live', as they happen [...]': television is a facilitator of synchronicity beyond the city walls. For Wenders, television is 'colder, less emotional' than the movies, and it takes us further away from the idea that an image has a direct link with 'reality' (i.e. a 'register of reality', in Huyssen's terms). Televisual hyperreality could 'only be opposed by our European images, our common art and language, our European cinema.'[10] Cinema emerges as a medium for Wenders that can counteract the 'televisual gaze', through its direct link with reality, an idea which has its roots in Bazin's essay on the 'ontology of the photographic image', which founded the value of the photographic image (and by extension the cinematic image) on its automatic, indexical link with reality.

Wenders's faith in the photographic image as an indexical record of reality is borne out by his observations on the buildings in Berlin that were being sacrificed to urban planning throughout the 1970s and 1980s. When asked in an interview whether he saw film-making as an archival activity, Wenders replied that the fact that a building is about to disappear is always a good reason to include it in a scene, thereby reinforcing the idea that urban memory emerges at a moment of threat. *Wings of Desire* does not, however, only include ruins and threatened buildings as acts of celluloid preservation. As spatial images, those acts of preservation are simultaneously active encounters with the material, opaque remnants that litter the Berlin cityscape.

Wings of Desire presents the cityscape as a repository of the past that is activated into a space of museal encounter through the live gaze of the camera/viewer. This is foregrounded in an early sequence in the film. The angel Damiel, atop the ruin of the war-damaged Kaiser William Memorial Church, looks down on citizens moving across a pedestrian crossing. While almost all the citizens are walking according to the traffic regulations, a child stops in the middle of the pedestrian crossing to look up at Damiel.

The film here contrasts the instrumentalized mode of seeing (in) the city – a 'civic seeing' which is blind to everything except the regulation of circulation – with that of the curious child's mode of perception. The child stops moving and can perceive the angel, but the child also sees the wound, the Kaiser William Memorial Church, which is much more dominant in the long shot of the angel.

Aligned with the child, the cinematic viewer sees the 'wound', and is invited to see, via the 'age value' of the ruin, through the synchronic time of the city. It is of course debatable that the Kaiser William Memorial Church 'shows the history of the city better than any history book or document', as Wenders claimed, but the historical understanding of the object is secondary to the encounter with the anamnestic dimension of the object's 'age value.' Importantly, right from the start, the film establishes a precondition of its museal gaze, one that can be aligned with de Certeau's reflections: to see *through* the cityscape is to see beyond the reduction of the cityscape to a phenomenon of a utilitarian present, the means by which ever-present circulation can be regulated.

The film sets up a contrast between two ways of encountering the cityscape: on the one hand, a form of civic seeing which may itself not be one of 'visual mastery', but that is shaped by the logic of the synchronic organization of time and, on the other, a gaze that performs a different form of perception and a different form of encounter with the material of the city. The dominant regime of seeing the city sees *only* the cityscape; the alternative regime of seeing the city, which *Wings of Desire* proposes to its viewer, is one that sees *through* the cityscape, by not framing the cityscape as a static image. Indeed, this strategy is manifest right from the start of the film, when the mobile camera (imitating the film's angelic perspective) swoops down from above and passes through the walls of a tenement block to reveal the alienated lives of the citizens otherwise inaudible and invisible behind the façades of the cityscape.

Throughout, the film shows how the gaze of the vast majority of citizens is locked into the logic of the concept-city, most explicitly exemplified in the sequences showing them in their cars on the urban motorway (whose construction we have discussed earlier). This 'synchronic urban gaze' from the car is complicated in sections which reflect on film's archiving function and also its potential for constructing a museal encounter. Through the use of archival footage that is montaged into a drive down the Potsdamer Strasse, a taxi journey becomes also a drive through the streets of Berlin towards the end of the Second World War. Wenders aligns the spectator's gaze with that of one of the film's figures, the angel Cassiel, who has a more complex relationship to time than the taxi driver whose thoughts, which we hear, simply follow the logic of the synchronic city (he is, after all, a taxi driver). The gaze of the cinematic spectator thus encounters the material object of film as an indexical record of a past that is conventionally invisible in a cityscape that has expunged past time. This form of museal gaze is illustrated again in a sequence where Homer wanders across the empty space of Potsdamer Platz. As he wanders in a state of disorientation, the film montages colour images of the Platz presumably from the end of the Second World War. Homer's ability to see through time is used as a way of showing film's capacity to store past images of the city and represent them at a later point.

The aforementioned drive down Potsdamer Strasse brings Cassiel to the former air-raid bunker which is being used as a location for *Wings of Desire's* film-within-a-film, which is a melodramatic appropriation of 'Third Reich' history for a mass market. Wenders's film follows the American actor, Peter Falk, who has come to play a role in this American production. Falk, as the visitor to Berlin's walks through the city, 'seeing through time.' In one sequence the camera tracks Falk as he wanders across the vast empty space behind the ruin of the façade of the former Anhalter Bahnhof. The soundtrack allows us to hear Falk's inner monologue, 'spazieren, walking, looking and seeing', at which point he, and the camera, stop to look upon the ruin of the station 'where the station stopped.' The cinematic museal gaze is produced by a live gaze upon an opaque material object in which the spectator's gaze is aligned with that of a character. The special quality of Falk's 'flanerie' ('walking, looking and seeing') is established through a contrast with the Berliners who walk past him in the opposite direction. As Falk disappears from shot, the Berliners wonder whether this figure is Columbo, illustrating their trained fascination with images from American television, as well as their obliviousness to the ruin. Yet the camera has stopped its tracking of Falk, the final shot is of the men aligned with the new building behind the ruin, which is still visible in the margins on the left-hand side of the frame (Fig. 14).

Wenders here makes use of depth of field to maintain the presence of the ruin even when the ostensible curator of the museal gaze, Falk, has disappeared from shot. This focus on the object recalls the Shell House sequence from Wenders's first feature-length film, *Summer in the City* (1970), discussed in the previous chapter. While there are formal parallels to this Falk/Anhalter sequence, perhaps the most striking aspect is that Wenders actually reshot the 1970 sequence during the making of *Wings of Desire*. As Wenders remarks in his audio commentary to the DVD extras, the building in the back of the shot is Emil Fahrenkamp's Shell House that, at the time of filming (in both 1970 and 1986), was threatened with demolition. On the surface, the purpose of reshooting the sequence was to 'preserve' the building one more time on celluloid. Yet Wenders also reshoots the mode of encountering the building, the cinematic museal gaze which makes use of depth of field and tracking shot to induce in the spectator the same temporal duration of the encounter with the material object. Employing a Bazinian long-take, Wenders uses film to construct a museal gaze which both records an indexical reality and reveals that reality to the cinematic viewer.

Wenders's use of the tracking shot in the construction of the spatial image in these sequences shows how cinema can evade the ossification of the material object through a haptic encounter with that object. The film shows that the present cityscape is inhabited by the past, even if that past is not always visible, and also demonstrates that through the encounter with those objects that bear a 'register of reality', an alternative way of seeing the city, a museal gaze, can be redeemed.

Wenders's film is also a display museum for former ways of visualizing the city that construct a counter-narrative of cultural memory in some of the film's more allusive and elusive moments of intertextuality. In one sequence, the camera tracks Damiel as, subject to the synchronic regimes of the city, he is conveyed up an elevator, walks through a shopping arcade and then stops in front of a display window for electrical goods (television, cameras and video recorders). Damiel, munching an apple, is captivated by a television screen, which at that moment is displaying the image of the actor Peter Falk. The image freezes and is then replaced by a clock. Damiel checks his own watch, reminding us of the regulation of 'human' time, before he moves on.

This sequence revisits the famous scene from Fritz Lang's *M* (1931), where M, played by Peter Lorre, munching an apple, stops in front of a metalware shop, attracted by the sheer number of knives displayed in the window (though Wenders, otherwise so keen to point out references to the past in the film, omits to mention this in his commentary to his museum film). Once more, though, it is not simply the display of an object, but also an awareness that the object in its urban environment is subject to a certain regime of seeing. In Lang's film, as M stands before the window, devouring both the apple and the knives in a literal and visual sense, we are reminded, as Janet Ward writes, 'how fundamentally the command of advertising on our psyches is based on the promise of gratification' and the deadly way in which the display window fosters scopophilia and voyeurism in the denizen of the city.[11] Lang's film, then, is a critical commentary on the 'commercial forms of popular visual entertainment, which are said to lure the eye into civically unproductive forms of visual pleasure.'[12]

In *Wings of Desire*, however, it is the moving image that has itself become commodified in the display window, and it is moving image technology, and American images and American TV (Columbo) that are on sale. Wenders's observation that 'images once had as a primary purpose to show something, that primary purpose is becoming more and more the tendency to sell something' implies that he displays past images (in his revisiting of Lang's *M*) not just to preserve a threatened object (in this case Lang's legacy), but to preserve and display a different regime of seeing: the images of Lang's films show us how images are being used to sell a mode of seeing.'[13] *Wings of Desire* invites us to see through time back to a different regime of seeing. The cinematic display of the past is thus, for Wenders, an act of show-ing, rather than telling or selling, the past to the spectator. The contrast, implicitly, is with the film being made in the bunker in which the image of the National-Socialist past is being framed to not reveal anything, but to be displayed for profit.

Such intertextuality can be read as a way of preserving a tradition – European traditions – of ways of seeing versus a televisual way of seeing, but precisely not 'pacifying' the fragment's potential. The intertextuality is not signposted or framed in any way. Its very surreptitiousness means that it does not rely on the recognition that this is an opaque object from the past.

The final melodramatic dialogue, framed in close-up, between the angel, Damiel, and the trapeze artist, Marion, is set in the ruins of another threatened object of the Cold War era, the Hotel Esplanade. The Hotel Esplanade is a paradigmatic location for *Wings of Desire*, an interstitial space and time on the ultimate margin of West Berlin, the ruins of Potsdamer Platz where the concept-city has not yet imposed the post-war regime of synchronic time. The scene in the Hotel Esplanade is the culmination of the film's construction of a museal gaze, a way of encountering the city as the repository of past time. The material structure of the Esplanade is crucial in this regard.

Wenders's camera makes use of a tracking shot as the camera follows Marion from the ballroom where Nick Cave and the Bad Seeds are about to perform 'From Her to Eternity' and moves through the bar that is located to one side of it. As it does so, Wenders makes use of depth of field in order to record the material traces of the historic bar, but also mise-en-scène to track past a figure who reproduces, rather indirectly, Otto Dix's 1926 portrait of Sylvia von Harden. This is obliquely suggested in the position of the woman's arm and the cigarette and in the use of colours (red and

14. Peter Falk walks across the space of the former Anhalter Bahnhof in *Wings of Desire* (1987).
Photo ©and courtesy of Road House.

white reversed from the painting; it is, of course, Marion who is wearing
von Harden's red).

Although he does not notice the Dix reference, Friedemann Kreuder,
in his study of the Hotel Esplanade as a cultural-historical object, argues
that the scene provides the 'experience of one's own historicity' in the
Esplanade's atmosphere. In a formulation of the hapticality of the museal
gaze, Kreuder argues that Wenders provides 'an aesthetic experience of
historical material, not in the sense of a critical-pessimistic judgment, but
as a value-free perception, sensation, appreciation of shapes and colors.'[14]
This mise-en-scene invites a museal gaze, the Esplanade is a spatial image
combining past and present in which the city's repository can be reactivated
and put on display for the 'live gaze' of the cinematic spectator. In the almost
invisible presence of the past in the indirect citation of Dix, the film engages
with the problem of musealization and the potential of the monument
whose meaning and intention is not foregrounded.

Throughout the film Wenders cinematically frames the conditions
under which the museal gaze can operate in the city. That gaze is, however,
founded not on a singular and fixed spectatorial vantage point, but utilizes
the medium of film to produce a 'museal gaze' which dislocates the eye and
from the 'pace and speed of modernization' and the synchronic organization
of time that dominates in the city.[15] Under Wenders's curation, film produces
a hapticality that troubles the reification of the object and maintains its
enigmatic opacity. It does not deem the obsolescent object, in the manner

of a subject appropriating an object, but proposes an aesthetic mode of engaging the non-musealized object, a moment of discovery which is at the same time a moment of preservation in a moment of encounter.

The Nikolaiviertel and *The Architects*

Despite the omnipresence of the Wall, Wenders's film fundamentally ignores the existence of the GDR beyond that border. Indeed divided Berlin is metaphorical fodder for the site of a generic reflection on modernist alienation in the musings of a taxi driver at one point.[16] It is not just alienation, but historical stagnation that characterizes the urban present in both halves of Berlin as they carried out their celebrations of the 750th anniversary of the city's grounding.

The Nikolaiviertel, just south-west of Alexanderplatz in the east of the city, had lain, disregarded, since the end of the Second World War. The only building still standing after the removal of rubble had been the Nikolai Church and sacred buildings were not of much interest to the GDR state. The decision to restore the church, and indeed the whole quarter, as part of the 1987 celebrations in the East of the city indicated how far the GDR state was prepared to go in the appropriation of cultural memory for its own legitimation, as well as being a statement to the Western half of the city, implying that the roots of the city lay in the East.

A brief comparison between the ways in which East and West commemorated the city's founding at their underground stations is instructive in the forms of urban memory were being constructed. Close to the Nikolaiviertel was the underground station, Märkisches Museum, and as part of the 1987 commemorations, it was renovated with a new set of panels along the wall where, conventionally, posters would be placed. These panels form a fascinating series, for they represent, through coloured stones and without textual adornment, the ground structure of the centre of Berlin (i.e. the area around the Fischerkiez that was the 'original site' of the founding villages of Berlin and Cölln) from the city's foundation through to the present.

The long historical narrative is explained in a panel on the station platform, but the emphasis on an abstract visual encounter with a largely dehistoricized urban structure is particularly striking when set against the renovations, for example, at Fehrbelliner Platz, a station where the U7 and (now) the U3 cross. While the U7 platform retains its rather tired-looking 1970s futuristic stylings (common to a whole series of stations built along the line at that time), the U3 platform received a refurbishment for the 1987 commemorations that reinforced its 'origins' as one of the first stations on that line, having been opened in 1913.

It is not just a case of period restoration here, but the adornment of the platform panels with photographs from the Wilhelmine period. Where the Märkisches Museum engages with the 'deep' structure of the city, the Fehrbelliner Platz constructs the look of a place from the past and as such has much in common, ironically, with the restoration of the Nikolaiviertel in East Berlin.

This reconstruction was not simply a political exercise, but also belonged in the trajectory of the recovery of place memory in the East of the city since the mid-1970s. This had seen the restoration of further quarters in the hitherto-neglected inner city area (around the Kollwitzplatz).[17] The Nikolaiviertel was constructed as a kind of sophisticated pedestrian zone, an island amidst the high-speed, high-frequency traffic routes that surrounded it on three sides (the fourth was the River Spree). It sought to create a form of 'mixed urban living:' around 800 apartments were built (in the style of the original quarter), along with 30 shops and 22 restaurants. It was a memory of urban living that was accompanied by the façade of the past: the house fronts were constructed out of prefabricated concrete, but with levels of decoration that are visible in other parts of the inner city reconstructed at this time, particularly in the Spandauer Vorstadt. The encounter was mediated through the retro-details of the façades, as well as through the signboards dotted throughout the area which told the story of the location, primarily through 'old' photographs, as was the method at Fehrbelliner Platz.

Both the Fehrbelliner Platz and Nikolaiviertel restorations can be read as a summation of the developments of the 'monumental memory value' dimension of the museal urban gaze, a memory value that seeks to communicate by constructing a stable, spatial image that evokes urban continuity and overrides any sense of rupture in space or time. This is the urban memorial gaze as 'Erlebnis', too, however, the organization of the consumer body in a museal urban space.

The Spandauer Vorstadt appears as a location in *Die Architekten,* Peter Kahane's film about the interlocking professional and personal problems of a young (well, 38-year-old) architect in East Berlin. While developments such as the Nikolaiviertel are not mentioned specifically, the film does engage with questions of cultural memory through the figure of Brenner's friend from earlier days, who is engaged in the restoration of an (unnamed) palace. This restoration is clearly part of official cultural memory, as we see the celebration of its completion on television at one point in the film.

The film has its limitations, in that its discussion of architectural questions is frequently more 'tell' than 'show', especially regarding the problems
of urban planning in the GDR. Some of the film's difficulties were due to
its complex production conditions: it took a long time to get production
permitted, and the historical events of late autumn 1989 turned the as
yet unfinished film into an unintentional monument to the production
conditions for both film and architecture in the GDR.

The perspective of the urban landscape is where the film succeeds in
showing rather than telling, in a subtext about memory that resists the
melodrama of its main plot. Here, the film is an unintended monument
to ways of seeing in East Berlin, something which it subtly thematizes in
visual form throughout. The opening, establishing sequence juxtaposes the
conventionally cut office-bound doling-out of shopping-centre contracts
with a long take of an 'empty' wasteland hemmed in between prefabricated
tower blocks. This sequence emphasizes not only duration, but also 'natural
time' as it draws back from the close-up of two plants thriving tenuously in
the wasteland. This focus on the passage of natural time is reinforced by
the following shots, which show a series of fossils in close-up, the camera
aligning our gaze with that of the film's central protagonist, Daniel Brenner.
Brenner's interest in fossils is not returned to in the film. Instead it is one
of the architect collective, Martin, who demonstrates a fascination for the
presence of 'age value' in the cityscape, collecting images of the decaying
façades of East Berlin. One of the film's rather disjointed closing sequences
takes place at 'Weisser Elefant', a gallery in the aforementioned Spandauer
Vorstadt, at which Martin's photographs are being displayed. These are, as
the credits inform us, actually photographs by Ulrich Wüst (see previous
chapter for a discussion of Wüst's work).[18] The establishing shot mimics
one of Martin's photographs in its interplay of old/new, demolition and
construction that was going on at this time in this part of the city.

As with the earlier cityscape films from both East and West, discussed
in the previous chapter, the dilapidated courtyards of the old tenement
blocks provide the locus of community, again combining 'age value' with
community life, in contrast to the static images of deserted spaces and
desultory conversations between Brenner and his wife.

The film, then, on a subtextual level, is interested in the act of seeing.
This is more blatantly evident in the ultimately ambivalent figure of the
accountant Endler, who is presented as having a reputation for economic
rigour, and yet is persuaded by Brenner's economic arguments for aspects
of his project.[19] Given that Endler is an accountant, rather than an architect/
planner, it is important that the question of 'seeing' is most dramatically

presented through the fate of the calculator of the synchronic urban gaze (the problem is not the architect planner, but the economic rationality that circumscribes his planning). We see him for the last time when visited by Brenner in hospital; his eyes have packed in and are bandaged over. Reminding us of Wolfgang Kil's remarks about Ulrich Wüst, Endler declares that he has learnt that perception is more than 'merely' seeing and that the dangerous ones are the 'one-eyed who only see what they want to see.'

Like the earlier cityscape films, *The Architects* makes use of the view from the car as the ground-level embodiment of the synchronic urban gaze, particularly in the final drive through the uniform, industrial city ironically accompanied by the soundtrack of the Pionier song *Unsere Heimat* (Our Homeland) – perhaps now best known for its comic rendition in *Good Bye, Lenin*.[20] This automobility is contrasted then with the image of Daniel and Johanna haphazardly cycling through the city into the 'wasteland' space, replete with children kicking a ball, which is to house the future development.

By the end of the 1980s, place memory work has been established as a paradigmatic activity in Berlin as a form of urban memory, understood as remembrance that is explicitly concerned with and shapes an encounter with the urban environment through the dynamics of place memory. As Wenders suggested, Berlin's specific topography (ruin spaces, spaces of neglect, Wall-defined marginal space) plays a significant role in the creation of this paradigm. Berlin in that sense can be read as a test case for forms of urban memory that emerged over the 1970s and 1980s in response to the impact of the 'automobilization' of the city on the urban environment, and which developed at a slower pace, and with less overt political implications for memory work (though the economic effects of gentrification are certainly political, as we noted above in Hoffmann-Axthelm's critique of the IBA-Neu).

Berlin's specific history helps us identify the tensions in Huyssen's model of the anamnestic dimensions of the material object, in particular, its capacity to generate the experience of asynchronicity. That specific history is, by the late 1980s, expanding to encompass narratives of cultural memory that extend back beyond the Second World War. The figure of the curator, a kind of archaeologist breaking through the ostensibly intact surface of the cityscape, has emerged as central in this period, with the IBA demonstrating the tensions between institutional and non-institutional curation of urban space. Artist-curators in both East and West working in the media of critical visual culture (site-specific installations, photography and film) also operated on the margins of the institutions, and have been central to the investigation of the attentional dynamics and narrative elaborations of urban memory. The figure of the curator, as both citizen of and visitor to the city, brings to the fore tensions in the production of spatial images of place memory, where the connection to the local is no longer a given, and thus the connection between the spatial image and the collective is no longer that of a faithful mirror, but requires the allegorical activity of a 'reading observer.'

Film and the remnants of the wall: *Die Mauer* (1991)

The forms of museal urban gaze do not disappear with the fall of the wall. The forms of visual engagement with the East Berlin cityscape continue to be marked by the typical mode of critical GDR cultural production in the visual field. As Barton Byg observed:

> any critique or opposition had to come from the seemingly 'objective' depiction of life in the GDR as it really was. The results were at times simply stunning: aesthetically sophisticated films that investigate the irreducible gap between personal experience and public history, and the contradictions of the film medium itself in speaking for and to the 'subjects' of history in a socialist state.[21]

We saw how the GDR films generated (without explicit commentary) the distinction between the state's synchronic urban gaze and a museal urban gaze, as well as the gap between the ostensible self-evidence of the image (its 'immediate' communicative potential) and the ongoing requirement for interpretation. This eschewal of direct statement remains the model in Jürgen Böttcher's 1991 film, *The Wall* (*Die Mauer*). On one level, Böttcher's film, which documents the rendering obsolete of the Wall, translates this former part of the city infrastructure into the realm of cultural memory. On the other, in its eschewal of verbal commentary, it seeks to preserve the immediate communicative potential of the built environment.

The film does not open in an urban environment, but with the camera slowly panning across a landscape in which we see random piles of concrete slabs, identifiable through their form and graffiti as fragments of the Wall. This section before the film's title already indicates the eschewal of 'linear time', film's ability both to archive time and reorder it, as the sky above the rubble site, filled with birds, progressively shifts to become the sky over a Berlin in which the Wall is still standing.

This initial sequence at the Wall shows 'amateur' wall-peckers (not only, but also, Asian tourists with shopping bags and Burberry scarves and, later, Turkish youths) trying to break off fragments. The camera watches passers-by watching them, a ground-level engagement with and appropriation of the Wall, both with hammers and cameras. The film reflects on its own work of recording and reprojecting the passing of time, and the work of others to attempt to capture history/historical time (and space) through the multitude of recording apparatuses that Böttcher's camera itself documents. Böttcher uses film to interrogate the 'ghost' (i.e. disused) Potsdamer Platz underground station, showing a shift from ground-level erosion to systematic removal of remains.

Although the film eschews verbal commentary, it explicitly demonstrates the problem with such narration. At one point, during the opening of the Brandenburg Gate, it records a radio journalist constructing a cityscape for his listeners close to the Brandenburg Gate, revealing to the film viewers that he is making it up, for, as he speaks, he is still on the 'Western' side of the pillars. He knows what he is going to see, conjuring up the memory value of the street sign, embedding it within a pre-Second World War narrative that establishes continuity above and beyond the history of the GDR, invoking the familiarity of the landmarks cited (Unter den Linden, Red Rathaus, Palace of the Republic) that are not visible to the film viewers, ironically complementing his assertion that this cityscape was previously one that was not visible from the west.

We then see an American television journalist talking to camera. His speech runs as follows:

> No parades will be coming through these arches for a long time and the Wall over there will remain a blot on West Berlin's landscape. But the gate going nowhere now goes somewhere, and all of East Germany knows where it goes. Richard Blystone, CNN, at the Brandenburg Gate.

Blystone repeats this text four times in all. Although Böttcher's film refrains from explicit commentary, this is blatant. The more Richard Blystone repeats his summation for the global CNN audience of the moment when the Brandenburg Gate is opened, the less convincing it sounds, revealed as a performance whose image must be perfect and uninterrupted, much like the 'West Berlin' cityscape. Unsurprisingly, in Blystone's narrative, the 'landscape' is now in the ownership of West Berlin, and the East German remnant, defined as a 'blot' on that landscape, is condemned to vanish.

This particular section from Böttcher's film is concerned with how the material GDR cityscape is translated into a projection screen for triumphalist narratives at the moment when it is recorded as 'becoming obsolete.' The film also illustrates that this form of memory value is not the only way in which the material cityscape can be used as a projection screen. For example, there are sections when archive film from the history of Germany and Berlin is run through a projector and beamed on to a fragment of the dismantled Berlin Wall. These sequences of the film are not straightforward to interpret, given the many layers of visuality being interrogated. To begin with, we see an audience behind crash barriers watching a projection on to a section of Wall so covered with graffiti as to render it almost indecipherable (Fig. 15). The next sequence presents within a tighter frame sequences of film fragments relating to the building of the Wall. Although the graffiti is now absent, there is a doubling of 'age value' here: as Andrew Webber has noted, the 'pocked and striated surface' of the Wall fragment 'has the effect of appearing before the images projected on to it here, as a veil or partial screen.'[22] There is also a back and forth, as at times the archive footage fills the frame, and at times it is only a small section within an otherwise black screen. These latter sequences comprise mostly footage of escapes, including the repetition of one sequence, implying that aspects of the 'bigger picture' remain 'blacked out' by such an instrumentalized selection.

In addition, this second section replays, in the smaller frame, propaganda from an earlier period (the outbreak of the First World War, soldiers marching through the Brandenburg Gate, then a Nazi parade – but in full screen – the end of the second world war); to the accompanying soundtrack of both the bulldozers and the whirring projector).

The material Wall here is not a straightforward projection surface. There is material interference within the image that draws attention both to the image as image (by rendering it less immediately legible) and to the medium through which the image is transmitted. Böttcher's emphasis on surface is interesting: these are not the traces of graffiti on the fragment of wall that would render the image illegible, but rather material traces of the passage of time that intervene in the ostensibly transparent presentation of history. The implication is that the Wall is a material repository of the city's history, but its translation into cultural memory is complex, neither the wall nor the archive footage give immediate access to the past, despite the illusion.

This film is a history of a dismantling, quite possibly its own. The film itself is 'becoming obsolete' as it illustrates when the projector shows footage from 9 November 1989. Here it not only documents the obsolescence of the GDR cityscape, but this activity is always in the process of 'becoming

15. Still image from *Die Mauer* (1991). ©DEFA-Stiftung/Thomas Plenert.

obsolete.' Nevertheless, through the reactivation of the past within the present, it cancels out the state of 'being out-of-date.' There is a distinction to be made between the stasis of 'being obsolete' and the process of 'becoming obsolete.' Böttcher's film documents the structures by which a state of 'obsolescence' is imposed.

The film's final images are of a pair of eyes on a slab of Wall; the camera moves up this final slab of Wall and halts at the top, with the creation of the visual illusion that a winter tree is growing out of the slab. This can be read as the memory of an image – Caspar David Friedrich's *Abbey in an Oak Forest* (*1809*). Friedrich's image is ambiguous: on one level, it symbolized the decline of the old Church, leaving behind only impressive monuments of the faith that once sustained it. On another level, it stands for nature reclaiming its place, as oak trees now rather impiously grow where cultivated gardens and chapels once stood. Beyond this, it also symbolizes obsolescence. The trees and shrubs of the film are as lifeless now as the chapel and abbey. If we consider these final images in conjunction with the opening 'Wall graveyard', we see that the film also contains an argument; what was 'simply' rubble at the beginning has now been transformed into a site/sight of cultural memory. The old nation-state religion has declined, leaving behind its monuments.

The commentary remains visual, but the focus on the eyes in the conclusion reminds us that the memorial gaze is an act of seeing that involves supplementing the image through interpretation. The film invites that interpretation through a form of haptic encounter that revitalizes the dynamics of place memory.

Site-specific interventions after 1990

One of the most striking features of Böttcher's film is that it translates material remnants into the ambiguous medium of cultural memory *so soon* after the event that rendered the remnants redundant. This is one key feature of memorialization of the remnants of the GDR regime after 1989, and is a function of the return of the synchronic urban gaze in this period of urban transformation. Having been subject to a critique, which led to a paradigmatic shift by the end of the 1980s, the change in the perceived value of certain spaces in the city led to a whole rash of engagements with these unintended monuments. One example would be Sophie Calle's *The Detachment* (1996), an art project that, through reported conversations with Berlin citizens, demonstrated the unreliability of communicative memory, albeit through a non-site specificity in its gallery setting. Other projects demonstrate the continuities of the periods before and after 1989. An example of this is the Finitude of Freedom (*Endlichkeit der Freiheit*) project, originally designed to cross the divided city. This was planned from 1986 onwards, but was radically altered by the intervention of the Wende that took place before its implementation. The project was originated by the playwright, Heiner Müller, and the artists Rebecca Hor and Jannis Kounellis, and was finally accomplished in the autumn of 1990, overlapping with the unification of the two German states in October of that year. There were ultimately 17 projects, dotted around the now unifying city, in a manner akin to the structure of 'Mythos Berlin' and, particularly, the urban interventions of the Sculpture Boulevard. The artworks frequently involved the curation of obsolescent material, something which Kounellis described as 'more a moral happening than an exhibition.' Kounellis's own work engaged with the temporal rhythms of the city: he uncovered an old rail line running between two factory buildings in the industrial ruins of a former transformer station in the Otto-Grotewohl-Strasse and ran a coal carriage at snail's pace between the halls. A similar project was planned by Raffael Rheinsberg, who, in his 'joint venture', wanted to situate large cable rolls in the once-divided Otto-Grotewohl and Wilhelmstrasse. This was ironically deemed not possible, since it would have disrupted the circulation of traffic, and so it was ultimately located beside a remaining piece of wall close to the Martin-Gropius-Bau.[23]

Another of the pieces conceived as part of this overall project was Christian Boltanski's *Missing House* (1990), which 'framed' a gap within the housing stock of the Grosse Hamburger Strasse in Berlin-Mitte, in the former Scheunenviertel.

The initial impetus for Boltanski's work came from a concern with the fate of the Jews of Berlin. His work is formally concerned with the moment of translation of the material fragment from the storehouse repository of the city to the functional realm of cultural memory and *Missing House* enacted (and continues to enact) this in a number of ways.

The absence of conventional communicative memory is reflected both in the absence of both those who lived there and of the house itself, and leads to the production of two memorial sites that are *lieux de mémoire, in lieu of* a (Jewish) '*milieu de mémoire*.' One of these was the missing house on the Grosse Hamburger Strasse, the other was the 'Museum', the exhibition of the historical documentation, gathered by Boltanski and his team of researchers, which was displayed about four kilometres away on a piece of open ground near the Hamburger Bahnhof in what had become the former West Berlin over the course of the piece's development.

Like Rheinsberg in the late 1970s, Boltanski figured here as both collector and curator.[24] He collected a series of marginalized objects (the site of the house, the archival documentation) and curates them principally through the use of signage. The 'walls' of the 'missing house' site are marked by forms of framing that mimic newspaper death notices. Boltanski thus stages an encounter with Victor Burgin's 'mnemic trace' of the past, without providing a straightforward narrative. The concern that this encounter might not be sufficiently mediated is addressed by John Czaplicka in his article on commemoration in post-unification Berlin: 'The aesthetic and empathetic evocation of [such a] situation is best combined with the controlling instance of historical documentation, lest the aesthetic means merely call forth from the beholder a response that plays on the emotions and delves into sentimentality or worse.'[25] In Czaplicka's account, history can 'control' memory. Yet, since in Boltanski's case the historical documentation was located somewhere else in the city, his work explicitly addressed the mechanisms by which the 'memory trace' becomes translated into a memory narrative. Czaplicka gives one explanation of how this mechanism works: 'In the terseness of artistic language, in the significance of insignificant siting, and in a dignified reserve in subjective artistic expression, the viewer will recognize a receptive framework for the contemplative mind.'[26] In reflecting on Boltanski's work,

16. Christian Boltanski, 'Missing House', Grosse Hamburger Strasse, Berlin, 2012. Photograph: Simon Ward.

Czaplicka also identifies a central factor in the dynamics of urban memory: 'Separated and secluded from the systemic workings of its modern urban context, this space has been rightly termed a "contemplative place".'[27]

As we saw in the previous chapter, in an environment that is not dominated by the frameworks of communicative memory, a key constitutive factor for the production of urban memory is a technology which establishes the conditions for a kind of receptive attention that is at odds with the 'systemic workings' of the city. It can thus be seen how Boltanski's work seeks to shape one of the key dynamics of urban memory: an appropriate form of attentiveness.

Boltanski identified the site, but also curated it in such a way as to delay narrative closure within the framework of cultural memory. The notices record the names of former residents, not just the Jews who were deported by the Nazi regime, but also those who were resident in the house at the time of its bombing. This is of course not made explicit by the abbreviated information at the site, so the viewer is not immediately aware what exactly is being contemplated. To what extent is this a productive lacuna, produced by the aesthetics of framing perception? The question is highlighted by the allegorical reading of the installation proposed by Abigail Solomon-Godeau. She argues that 'Boltanski's *Missing House* is an appropriate work for contemporary Berlin because it is fundamentally structured around an absence, a vacancy, a loss.' For Solomon-Godeau, this absence presents '*obvious* [my emphasis - SW] analogies to what is now absent in German national life, namely, the presence of its once flourishing Jewish community.'[28] Solomon-Godeau reduces the ambiguity of Boltanski's framing of the traces to a specific meaning. However, more troubling than the specificity is the ostensibly self-evident over-determination of Solomon-Godeau's interpretation, especially since the accompanying museum and the brief explanatory panel at the *Missing House* have since been removed, meaning that the uninformed visitor at that time would have struggled to contemplate anything other than the anomaly of empty urban space in a milieu dominated by the practices of consumption.

Solomon-Godeau translates *Missing House* from its ambiguous status by functionalizing it as a narrative of cultural memory of the absence of Jewish 'communicative memory'. Nevertheless, *Missing House* has also been translated into the framework of cultural memory: the work passed into the ownership of the district office of Berlin-Mitte and the archival findings are now on display at the district's local museum. The site itself remains in place but, given the exchange value of the surroundings as part of a regenerating city centre, the nature of its visibility has changed. Brian Ladd, returning to the site in the late 1990s, observed that, 'some passers-by see only the new restaurant garden in front of the installation.'[29] Perhaps the growing monumental invisibility of the object illustrates the dynamics of urban memory, as it is gradually translated back into the city's storehouse repository (Fig. 16). For example, it is included in Stefanie Endlich's encyclopedic volume of NS monuments, but it was not mentioned in the official 'City as Exhibition' guide, which is discussed in Chapter Four.[30]

Missing House invokes two anamnestic dimensions of the opaque object in different ways: it evokes asynchronicity by generating a form of attention in the city that is not determined by the systemic workings of the city; and it produces counter-memory through a 'delayed' meaning that undermines the swift consumption of its narrative significance. It is also not located in the 'city centre', and thus, at least when first executed, was marginal to the tourist itineraries as well as being related to a marginalized set of spatial practices. It illustrates the centrifugal nature of both pre- and post-unification Berlin, with its reconfigured centres and margins. When moved to the city centre, the kind of artistic practice in which Boltanski engages becomes transformed into a tourist spectacle, as I shall discuss in Chapter Four.

Boltanski's work can be read profitably alongside Shimon Attie's 1992-3 project, *Writing on the Wall*, also produced in Berlin's former Jewish quarter, the Scheunenviertel, a centre for Eastern European Jewish immigrants from the end of the nineteenth century located close to the Alexanderplatz. Attie's work is a textbook example of the translation of documents from the repository into the functional archive of cultural memory, reactivating historical photographs of the Scheunenviertel that reflected the world of the Jewish working class rather than that of the more affluent, assimilated German Jews who lived mostly in the western part of the city.

Yet this work of cultural memory also relied on the dynamics of place memory, the spatial image of the unintended monument. Attie slide-projected portions of pre-war photographs of Jewish street life in Berlin onto the same or nearby addresses today. By using slide projection on location, fragments of the past were introduced into the visual field of the present, in a method similar to that used at the Brandenburg Gate installation by Hans Hoheisel discussed in the introduction. Parts of long-destroyed Jewish community life were visually simulated and momentarily reactivated, becoming visible to street traffic, neighbourhood residents, and passers-by. This momentary intersection of past and present as an aesthetic strategy does not present an 'old face' alongside the 'new', but rather defaces the contemporary face with the 'old' face, creating a much more complex object that fractures and places in question the contemporary experience of time in the city, producing 'critical memory value' through temporal discontinuity.

Attie also noted that, in the early 1990s, the Scheunenviertel was a neighbourhood undergoing rapid gentrification. His own commentary runs as follows:

> After the fall of the Berlin Wall, it has become the new chic quarter and frontier for many West Berliners. As a result, the neighborhood has seen a huge influx of new residents and capital from the West. Within the course of only a few years, block after block of houses and buildings in the Scheunenviertel had become completely transformed. Most have been

entirely renovated, from the inside out. Others have been transformed into fashionable and trendy bars and restaurants.

As a result, Attie observed in 1996, the Scheunenviertel had become almost unrecognizable even in the few years since the *Writing on the Wall* project was realized. The 'remaking' of the Scheunenviertel affects both Jewish as well as post-war East German collective memory and identity, as the last physical evidence of these pasts disappeared as well.[31]

It is clear from the photographs taken by Attie of his project that it involves the layering of the everyday visual field of the urban environment, turning the city into a spatial image. Like Boltanski's work, Attie's commentary also makes clear that he has perceived that what begins as a comment on post-war German amnesia becomes through time a more general comment on the effacing of time in the urban environment through the workings of capital.

The 'preservation' of obsolescence in these refinements of the museal gaze results from the construction of a 'spatial image' that resists the disappearance of the past in the East. The projects of Boltanski and Attie curate 'empty spaces' abandoned during the GDR and by the disappearance of the GDR state to create an encounter with urban space that is still 'momentary', and concerned with the disruption of temporal rhythms in the city, working with modulations of attention.[32]

These projects also alert us to a shift in the coordinates of urban memory culture. The museal gaze is less addressed to resisting the impact of the synchronic gaze and more with confronting the shifts in the value of 'real estate' and their impact on these spaces of uncertainty.

The reconstruction of the German nation after 1989, both literally and metaphorically, was largely focused on Berlin as the new capital, and indeed the massive and radical transformations in the built environment are a productive example for how the dynamics of urban memory function in a rapidly transforming city on a global scale. At the same time, this model of urban memory is one that builds upon a certain set of practices that had become largely institutionalized by the time of the fall of the Wall. This has implications for the response in the East of the city, which was obviously going to be more affected by the economic shifts (changes in ownership and in the exchange value of space, both public and private) and was thus more likely to resist change through the production of 'spatial images'. The two different halves of the city represented two different forms of collective experience, the analysis of which sheds lights on how urban memory practices responded to the challenge of framing urban memory in post-wall Berlin.

4.   In Search of a City?

Urban Memory in Unified Berlin

At the conclusion of her chapter on 'Re-Centering Berlin', Janet Ward writes:

> By the middle of the twenty-first century, when Berlin may well have
> recovered from its present bankruptcy, the Hauptbahnhof will be there
> smoothly connecting not just the city, but the European continental east,
> west, north, and south.[1]

This is a vision of the synchronic city for the global age, beyond the dreams
of Rolf Schwedler in its celebration of technological time.[2] Where is the
asynchronous city and does it have any value in the global age?[3] Paul Virilio
sardonically declared the end of the 'city' in a 1984 essay that emphasized
the increasing synchronicity of a post-urban regime:

> Where once an entire 'downtown' area indicated a long historical period,
> now only a few monuments will do. Further, the new technological time
> has no relation to any calendar of events nor to any collective memory.
> What is a monument within this regime? Instead of an intricately wrought
> portico or a monumental walk punctuated by sumptuous buildings, we
> now have idleness and monumental waiting for service from a machine.[4]

Virilio's melancholy has much in common with the lamentations of Paul
Connerton about the disappearance of collective memory in a synchronized
environment. The questions which Virilio raises about the technologized,
synchronized body of the citizen and the obsolescent encounter with 'old'
architecture are ones that are germane to Berlin in its post-unification
context.

   This chapter traces the ongoing presence of the asynchronous city and
its role in the construction of urban memory. It looks not so much for the
descendants of the wounds and 'strange emptiness of which postwar Berlin
was full', but to focus on how the museal gaze operated in those large,
obsolescent spaces that were left behind by the collapse of the GDR regime:
the Potsdamer Platz, which had been crisscrossed by the Wall, and the
renamed Schlossplatz, which had housed the Palace of the Republic from
1973 onwards. Here we continue to see urban memory at work, albeit an
urban memory that addresses an even more tenuous collective than had

existed in Berlin before the fall of the Wall. Wim Wenders had seamlessly elided inhabitant and visitor in his description of those who encountered Berlin's wounded cityscape, but perhaps we need to rethink these terms when considering the tenuous collective that the spatial images of urban memory might address in our contemporary moment.

In one of the images used in her 2004 essay on 'Berlin, the Virtual, Global City', Janet Ward presents a photograph she took in 2002 of a poster for the renovation of the corner building of Oderberger Strasse and Kastanienallee in Prenzlauer Berg, the very building over which the poster had been imposed. This is a curiously 'minor' example of a phenomenon that had been virulent in Berlin since the fall of the Wall, most notoriously demonstrated by the Schloss façade draped over the Palace of the Republic (discussed below). What the advertisement and the photograph render invisible is the economic pressure being exerted on the 'crumbling' tenement's current occupants. Yet in terms of an encounter with urban space, the advertisement also blocks the spatial recognition of place that would otherwise be available to those same occupants, their familiar urban environment. The poster has no human figures in its spatial image, merely cars. Ward's position as visitor and photographer (and thus co-constructor of the spatial image) is not one that she reflects upon.

This ongoing process of commercial rehabilitation of 'obsolete' housing structures is not a process unique to Berlin,[5] or even to the post-89 period, as our discussion of the 1970s illustrated, but this particular object, presumably chosen 'at random', in fact illustrates how, in contemporary Berlin, the 'spatial image' operates as a form of resistance. Ward's article was published in 2004, but a year later the proclaimed renovation had yet to begin, and an interstitial use of the building had emerged in the meantime, an occupation (albeit legal) of the site, which has many resonances with the more illustrious example of the Tacheles building on the Oranienburgerstrasse eight stops further down the tramline. While the spatial image of Tacheles was ultimately co-opted into a tourist itinerary of the city[6] – the shock value of obsolescence framed and incorporated for the Lonely Planet generation – this house in the Oderbergerstrasse allows us to think about a site that is not explicitly framed for visitors, but where the complex overlap between developer/artist and visitor/citizen in the transforming city makes itself disruptively visible. An article in the Tagesspiegel from 15 October 2005 began with a phrase that invoked the question of urban attention:

> During the day you hardly take any notice of the house at the Oderberg-erstraße, on the corner of Kastanienallee. The walls are almost black.

Imposing posters announce that you can buy condos here and renovation will be beginning soon. In truth, it should be standing empty. But suddenly a window opens. A white tip exposes itself. Then a rocket comes into view. In other windows light is now visible. A young woman peers out from a balcony door. In a green-painted room a man in red sportswear is doing gymnastics. In the distance you can hear aircraft noise. These strange neighbours are artists and students.[7]

The article was written two weeks before the renovations were due to begin. Here playfulness was part of the game, as Wolfgang Krause, who had taken on the 'role' of the Swiss owner (Krause-Bösel, a pun on the German word for 'evil'), explained. The house had become a site of spatial practices that were not unlike the specific anti-capitalist rejection that marked Tacheles. Spontaneous concerts were organized at the windows in order to 'surprise passers-by'; other residents played the roles of noisy neighbours (a full description of the activities in the house can be found at www.ozwei.net/daheim/index.html). In other words, the house is not just an image of disruption, but a spatial image, in that it is a site of practices that shape an encounter with the urban environment, not just for passers-by, but also for neighbouring tenants: one tenant next door had also decorated his window. The house itself was decorated with the names of the occupants in the form of 'museum signs'.

From Janet Ward's pragmatic point of view, such resistance would be ultimately futile. Yet, according to the *Tagesspiegel* article, the house was apparently framed as the 'first stage' in the Tour de Kastanie on a pseudo-'estate agent' map of the city that echoes the form of spatial practice conducted by the IBA-Alt in its exhibitions of the 1980s (see Chapter Three). The principle here is movement as spatial practice and the shaping of attention to the built environment that 'resists' the imposition of exchange value upon space, without resorting to 'restorative nostalgia', or 'petrification', as Janet Ward terms it.[8] This itinerary can be juxtaposed with other itineraries of the city that were shaped, for example, at the more highly visible obsolescent site of Potsdamer Platz.

Regulating the museal gaze at Potsdamer Platz

Janet Ward neatly sums up the dilemma the city planners faced at Potsdamer Platz, 'to re-insert physical nodes of relevance and connectivity into its urban center, which was, essentially, a series of wastelands [...]'.[9]

In fact, though Ward puts the emphasis on the imposition of synchronic infrastructures, it is conceptions of the urban past that underpin the reconstruction of Berlin's centre due to the subterranean influence of Halbwachs's theories of collective memory upon architectural design and urban planning. The *Planwerk Innenstadt*, the planning scheme that outlined the plans for developing Berlin's centre post-unifcation, was profoundly influenced by the work of the second IBA in Berlin – discussed in Chapters Two and Three – which set the principles of 'careful renewal' and 'critical reconstruction' in constructing a memory of the urban. These principles were predicated on the work and thought of the Italian architect Aldo Rossi, particularly his idea of the persistent street network as the 'genetic code' of the city.[10] Such a code is, according to Rossi, ideally not part of an explicit sign system, but the *Planwerk Innenstadt* codified it into a fixed image in setting down regulations relating to building height and usage that belonged to a particular moment in the city's historical development – an irony that was not lost on many critics.[11] The spaces and buildings constructed according to these principles (e.g. those at Spittelmarkt or those planned for the Molkenmarkt) are intended to shape a city in the European tradition, a technological construction, after the fact, of the conditions under which place memory can apparently evolve.

The *Planwerk Innenstadt* is a prescription for the spatio-temporal forms within which urban life is played out, after the disappearance of a conventional place memory. The spatio-temporal conditions in which it is realized are unavoidably those of the contemporary post-urban city. The encounter with the built environment is organized in these spaces to form not just an official narrative, but a regulated form of spatio-temporal encounter with the urban past that relies upon the elision of cultural and communicative memory.

This is explicit in the city's official self-presentation as museum, *Berlin: Open City. The City as Exhibition*, which ran from 1999 to 2000 (although, in the nature of the undertaking, it effectively continues to exist).[12] The 'exhibition guide' argued that the ten routes it outlines are 'to be mastered in around four hours of walking', and are 'not tourist trails following the famous landmarks. Street crossings and eyesores are as much part of reality as harmony and idyll' (*BOS*, 7). The routes engage explicitly with the everyday spatial practice of the city, but always in the form of a guided itinerary that constructs the tourist as 'individual urban explorer' (*individueller Stadterkunder*) (*BOS*, 8), working with the rhetorical distinction of the 'true traveller' who also travels *by foot*, in search of the 'authentic' experience of the urban environment, compared to the 'mere' tourist. The itineraries are not exclusively related to the past, but seamlessly interweave past and present in their trajectories. Route 3, moving 'between myth and future', integrates tarrying (*verweilen*) at Potsdamer Platz with the contemplation of three forms of post-war urban planning: the planned cityscape of the 1950s and 1960s, as illustrated by the *Kulturforum*, the results of the 1987 IBA-Neu in Kreuzberg, and Mehringplatz as an example of 1960s planning for the 'car-friendly city' with its ubiquitous urban freeways.

While this itinerary focuses mainly on still-functional parts of the built environment, it does take in material remnants of the past, such as the 'Topography of the Terror', but subordinates their material opacity to, in this case, the discussion and illustration of Peter Zumthor's (at that time) planned structure at the site (*BOS*, 78–9). In the case of the Hochbunker near the Anhalter Bahnhof, or the remains of the Berlin Wall at the Niederkirchnerstrasse, the guide merely provides historical information that situates the remnants firmly in the past – there is no sense of their current function, other than as illustrations of the unique cultural memory of this non-generic city. These remnants are imbued with memory value as isolated *lieux de mémoire* within the framework of cultural memory that, in Aleida Assmann's terms, translates an object from the 'storehouse repository' into the 'functional memory' of cultural memory. Yet this experience of cultural memory is still dependent on a particular mode of encounter with the built environment: the guide implies that the tourist (or visitor to the 'exhibition') is travelling on foot and frequently refers back pejoratively to the obsessive focus on automobility of an earlier generation, which was responsible for the demolition of place memory (*BOS*, 77, 88). This pedestrian mode of encounter is a key dynamic of place memory, predicated on the immediate, spontaneous and reciprocal relationship between citizen and built environment. The encounters with the remnants in this city on display are, however, inevitably shaped by their framing in the guide, which, as Boyer suggests of the city of collective memory in general, undercuts 'a more spontaneous reaction [...] [these are] theatrical stage sets that have little to say about the memory of place.'[13] They do, however, have something to say about *how* this form of urban memory is produced.

Each of the objects listed in the guide is delimited, albeit in different ways, by the frame which documents its past and makes a case for its historical significance. This strategy can then be seen at work in other 'antique' material remnants to be found on display at Potsdamer Platz: fragments of the Berlin Wall, the former Kaisersaal in the Hotel Esplanade within the Sony Center, the façade of the Esplanade itself, the façade of Haus Huth, the reconstructed traffic lights and the former S-Bahn sign for Potsdamer Platz encased within the Sony Center.

The former S-Bahn sign for Potsdamer Platz is incorporated within 'Bahn Tower', the name which had been given to the tower that had originally been intended for the Sony corporation headquarters, and was then leased to the German railway corporation, the Deutsche Bahn.

Encased in its glass vitrine, the object is intended to be encountered as if in a museum, a form of encounter that is enhanced by the framing in glass of the façade of the Hotel Esplanade round the corner, and the 'Kaisersaal' of the former Hotel, which had been moved, in an example of technological virtuosity, from its original site to be incorporated into the structure of the Sony Center. The encounter with the palimpsestic quality of urban space reinforced its paradigmatic status after 1989, but, following the pattern described by De Certeau for Paris in 'Ghosts in the City', it was largely reincorporated within the synchronic urban gaze in the construction of narratives of cultural memory. The museal urban gaze is instrumentalized here to create a sense of narrative coherence, of a past seamlessly incorporated into the present. These objects are not obstacles to movement, to the circulatory rhythms of the city. The glass is of course not the only element in the framing, as there is also the use of signs.

An analysis of the textual component of the framing of many objects at the Potsdamer Platz reveals the 'official' narrative of cultural memory as one which privileges the Wilhelmine and Weimar periods, fundamentally disregards the Third Reich, and presents the GDR as a period that has been 'overcome'. From this point of view, it would be easy to suggest that these framings represent an example of remembering 'badly', in that they do not value the 'correct' version of history that demands an engagement with the Third Reich. The informational content of the frame is, however, only one element in the encounter with the object; there is also the materiality of the object itself, its 'subterranean attractions' (Boyer), which can be further glossed in terms of Riegl's identification of the 'age value' of the unintended monument, or, as Baudrillard puts it, '[the antique] is there to conjure up time as part of the atmosphere.'[14] Yet the form of the frame, which at Potsdamer Platz includes the use of display glass and signage, gives the objects the particular status of the antique, 'to the extent that is [also] experienced as a sign.'[15]

It might nevertheless be claimed, with Baudrillard, that these objects, in their exhibition setting in a 'new' city centre at Potsdamer Platz that is predicated on consumerist display, are 'not on a par with other objects' and falsely manifest themselves as 'total, as an authentic presence.'[16] Beyond the semantic content of the framing that places them within a certain historical urban and national narrative, these remnants are also framed as material that direct an encounter with Berlin as a city replete with urban memory.

A further example elucidates what is at stake in the production of urban memory at Potsdamer Platz. Burgin suggests that 'if the past is really to touch us then it is more likely to be when we least expect it, as when some of its litter blows across our path',[17] but who are we and what is our path? Moving through Potsdamer Platz is, in principle, a timetabled experience of consumption.[18] If we doubt this, then let's take a wander down Bellevuestrasse, along the rear side of the Sony Center – though, why would we, given that there are no more shops in this direction? But let's assume we do so anyway. We might well miss a plaque, for it is 'only' a sign. This plaque is, moreover, not displayed in upright and thus more visible fashion, like the Wall fragments, or the S-Bahn sign. Rather it is embedded in the ground, not the pavement (as with the Stolpersteine), but rather in the margin between the pavement and the Bellevuestrasse.

This is a plaque to mark *not* the original place where the Volksgerichtshof – the National Socialist court of 'justice' – stood, but rather where the entrance to the court stood. Yet, for all that it is only a sign, its location also frames a particular form of encounter. (One assumes that the entrance was much larger than the size of the plaque, hence its positioning must be deliberate). This encounter with the place is thus multiply marginalized: not in the original location of the building – which would be at the heart of the Sony Center – and thus separated off from the punctual circulation of tourists and consumers; not on the pavement – where it might interrupt the punctual passage of the passers-by; and it is not particularly visible. Yet it also bears the hallmark of the traditional framing of the official monument of mourning – it is rendered in bronze, like the plaques which frame the ruin of the Kaiser William Memorial Church in the west of the city, or even that which is attached to the artificial reconstruction of the traffic lights on Potsdamer Platz and the S-Bahn just discussed above.

In terms of the construction of an official narrative, it seems clear that while the celebration of a narrative of pre- and post-1933 Germany is displayed explicitly in the main thoroughfares of the new Potsdamer Platz, the period of National Socialism is marginalized. It is not just the content that matters here, but the spatio-temporal framework within which a museal site is constructed. Whereas the monuments in the main thoroughfares of Potsdamer Platz are organized to be encountered (and explained) as in a museum, this is clearly not the case with the plaque marking the threshold to the Volksgerichtshof. While it could be argued that it is theoretically 'present' as a specific location in the urban space, we see that presence in urban space is not a neutral affair. As we saw elsewhere at Potsdamer Platz, the narrative elaboration that is cultural memory is preceded by an encounter with the mnemic trace. Here, materiality is performed by the marginalized brass plaque. The Volksgerichtshof has been reconsigned to the storehouse repository of urban memory. The plaque commemorating the Volksgerichthof unintentionally uncovers some of the key dynamics of urban memory and allows us to reinforce what we have understood to constitute place memory. It is not only derived from the age value of 'antique' objects, but also from the form of attentiveness that is required even to perceive the object in the first place.[19]

Deregulating the museal gaze at Potsdamer Platz

Curators and collectors were drawn to the Potsdamer Platz as a site of urban transformation where the production of spatial images was taking place. Andreas Huyssen's essay, 'The Voids of Berlin' is fundamentally a valorization of Daniel Libeskind's construction of a form of place memory through the maintenance of the 'void' at the newly founded Jewish Museum. Less frequently recalled is that Libeskind conceived two highly complex plans for the allegorical incorporation of the past with the city, 'Über den Linden', and his design for Potsdamer Platz, 'Out of Line', which approached the site as a puzzle derived from a series of fragments of the urban past.[20] There was a collective dimension to this conception, one that transcended the local, and offers our first version of the collective that contemporary urban memory might address:

> This space is based on the simple principle that people from around the world form the shareholder's association, thus owning a share of Potsdamer Platz. Soil from the world on the roof, wilderness from Berlin on the ground. Everyone now has the right to a space in the wilderness, the possibility of cultivation, streams of seeds powered by wind and sail, the eye-I-cure, thunderstorms, sky-books, artificial sun-rain, sparkwriting, plantation in the clouds, the waterfall, inspiration ... all necessities in the Berlin of tomorrow.

Libeskind's highly theoretical conception of a 'globally connected' Berlin is central to the argument of this final chapter, a Berlin not just for Berliners. Whereas Libeskind's ideas remained on the drawing table, a 'practical' engagement with the materiality of Potsdamer Platz is demonstrated by

Wenn man aus dem Gebäude des Ring- und Vorortbahnhofes auf den Vorplatz tritt,
fällt einem immer als erstes die Werbung der Telegraphenfabrik Töpffer & Sohn auf der
rückseitigen Brandmauer eines Hauses in der Köthener Straße ins Auge.

17. Arwed Messmer/Annett Gröschner, 'Potsdamer Platz: Anno Zero #11', 1995. 50 x 64 C-print
from the series *Potsdamer Platz Anno Zero 1994/95*. Courtesy of the artists. 'If one comes out of the
suburban station building on to the forecourt, the first thing that always strikes one's eye is the
advertisement for the telegraph factory Töpffer & Son on the back side of a firewall of a house in
the Köthener Strasse.'

Arwed Messmer and Annett Gröschner's series, 'Potsdamer Platz Anno
Zero' (1994/5). This is a series of 25 captioned photographs showing the Platz
at the beginning of construction, dating from between January 1994 and
February 1995. The work won Messmer the Otto-Steinert-Preis of the German Photographic Society in 1995, and was most recently to be seen in the
'89/09 – Art between Traces and Utopia' exhibition in 2009 at the Berlinische
Galerie. In their fixation on the marginal traces of building development,
and the decision to set these traces against the surrounding cityscape,
Messmer's photographs diverge from the celebratory vision of the iconic
city centre that was offered at the Info Box. Messmer's work documents the
encounter with the urban environment as an act of collection and curation.

In the example chosen here (Fig. 17), an extended exposure time is revealed through the blurred bushes on the left-hand side of the photograph,
indicating the act of collection as one of static contemplation (in Czaplicka's

sense). The movement of the bushes reveals the photograph as an indexical record of passing time, while also capturing obsolescence (the car wreck, for example). The act of collection is staged within the encounter of the viewer with the photograph. It is not simply a photograph, however, for the illusion of unmediated visual access is broken through the use of the textual supplement. This sign, unlike Boltanski's signs at *Missing House*, is not a plaque – though it is an integral part of the image – but it does similarly highlight the sparse image's need for supplementary explanation. Gröschner's text, however, does not supplement the image in a straightforward way. Rather, it foregrounds the spatial encounter with the site in an unspecified historical context: the visitor is departing from one of the nodal transport infrastructure points in the city and the text highlights the form of visual attention that is generated by the built environment. In that sense, it alludes to the formation of communicative memory in the built environment, while the photograph points to the way that that communicative memory has been rendered impossible through the building's contemporary absence. Our encounter with the 'spatial image' of photograph and caption is fractured temporally while we apparently remain in a state of spatial contemplation (if we consider the work's conventional display within an exhibition setting). Through its interplay of text and image, the work undercuts both the illusion of the visual immediacy of material traces and the illusion of a separate and definitive supplementarity which text can supply, while also reminding us of the layers of a past (if not of a clear history) that are present, if not always immediately visible in the city.[21]

Film after the synchronic city

The uncertainty of the present also opened up the potential for forms of 'cultural resistance', as Evelyn Preuss describes the critical positions assumed by many films of the 1990s that both revisited the past and reimagined the present in Berlin.[22] Film is another medium in which the layers of the past can be made visible, and this is certainly the case with Thomas Schadt's *Berlin. Sinfonie einer Großstadt*, a documentary film made over the course of 2001 that generates the presence of the past within the capital of the united German nation. Schadt's film would not exist without the presence of a Weimar predecessor, Walther Ruttmann's 1927 film *Berlin. Die Sinfonie der Großstadt*. As has been well-documented, Ruttmann's film, ostensibly a documentary of city life, is a celebration of the machine-city constructed through the five acts of a day in the life of *the* metropolis: Berlin, in 1927, embodies the archetypal traces of modern metropolitan life. Through its double refusal of the definite article, Schadt's title is immediately more modest, denying the archetypal and emphasizing the idea that Berlin could be 'any' city. In his introduction to the book version of his work, Schadt observes that he maintained 'a fundamental distance' to Ruttmann's film, since the latter's 'futuristic vision of the city was not fulfilled.'[23] For Schadt, this is down to the course of German history after 1945, for Schadt claims that he cannot 'look at Berlin without thinking about what took place between 1927 and 2002 in Germany and elsewhere.'[24] One notes that Schadt talks of 'looking' at Berlin, and not, for example, 'thinking of it'. In other words, it is the visual impact of the city that gives it its anamnestic dimension and triggers remembrance of the complex relationship between the 1920s and the present. Let us begin by considering how this anamnestic dimension is generated in two ways in the film.

First, there is the remembrance of images from preceding films, predominantly Ruttmann's film, and the way in which those are reworked for a reading of the present. Second, there is the use of images of the past to evoke memories of Berlin's history, pointing towards a sense of historical awareness absent in Ruttmann's film. Schadt's film, and its gaze, are located both 'beyond' the synchronic city and within a counter-narrative founded on a way of seeing that he recalls from Henri Alekan's camerawork in Wenders's *Wings of Desire* and the photography of August Sander.[25] Wenders's work with Alekan was very much an homage to the cinematography on *La Belle et La Bête* (1946). Implicit in both Wenders's and Schadt's references to these image-makers is a 'way of seeing' that is rooted in a response to urban modernity in the 1920s. In Sander's remarks on his exhibition at the Cologne Art Union in November 1927, he argued that 'nothing seems better suited than photography to give an absolutely faithful historical picture of our time.' In his work, Sander sought to avoid 'sugar-glazed photography, gimmicks, poses and fancy effects.'[26] Schadt renounces the possibility of special effects in his film, although we will go on to examine the 'effect' of the still image within the film itself.[27] The ethical integrity of Sander's project is described by Schadt as a complex aesthetically constructed authenticity.[28] Schadt's documentary film is a complex aesthetic engagement with authentic material, showing how a way of seeing developed in the 1920s is re-invoked by visual culture in post-unification Berlin.[29]

Legitimized through reference back to Sander, Schadt establishes a similarly complex and reflective way of seeing the city in his film. It could indeed be argued that, for Schadt, August Sander is a more significant reference point from the Weimar period than the apparently self-evident

Walther Ruttmann. Whereas Wenders gains historical legitimation for
his project through reference to his antecedents, Schadt does not use his
obvious Weimar prototype (Ruttmann) as a way of legitimizing his own
procedures. Rather Schadt's use of imagery from earlier films, principally
but not only Ruttmann's, establishes a dialectic between the repetition
and reworking of imagery. Underpinning Schadt's reworking of Ruttmann's
imagery is an implicitly critical dialogue. The way in which the remembrance of images is staged in Schadt's film virtually repeats the original.
The most obvious example is the film's conclusion, where the shot of light
upon water is a direct repetition of the opening image of Ruttmann's 1927
film. The shots of office elevators moving up and down on the outside of
the Ludwig-Erhard Haus[30] seem to repeat directly the office elevators from
Fritz Lang's *Metropolis* (1927). The irony here, of course, is that in *Metropolis*
they were the studio set of an imagined city that had not yet come into
realization.[31] This neatly illustrates one form of the interplay of the visual
culture of the 1920s with that of contemporary Berlin: the studio set as city
has become the city as studio set.

There are a number of shots in Schadt's film that seem to recall Wim
Wenders's *Der Himmel über Berlin*, such as those of the Siegessäule (23), or
of a cloud-laden sky pierced with sunlight, or that of an *Imbiß* on Potsdamer
Platz (55). The *Imbiß* is a key location for the interaction of the angels and
Peter Falk in Wenders's film as an invocation of the 'life-world' within the
anonymous city. With this latter image, it becomes clear that every repetition is already a reworking, as the *Imbiß* in Schadt's film is framed against
the striking new steel and glass entrance to the Potsdamer Platz railway and
underground station, thus implying a 'life-world' at the mercy of the forces
of homogenization, a concern with which again Schadt's film engages, but
which is of little interest to Ruttmann's celebration of urban technology.

These images from Schadt's film fundamentally repeat the aesthetic and
thematic concerns of the earlier images that they recall, but a refracted
memory of images is present in a more 'critical' form in other sequences.
This is most noticeable in his presentation of the synchronized industrial
modernity that Ruttmann's film sought to celebrate. Like Ruttmann, Schadt
seems to be fascinated with the symmetrical 'poetry' of 'machinery', such
as in the cigarette factory (34) or the newspaper printing house (29). Where
Ruttmann sought to present the dynamic speed of wheels, Schadt focuses
on the slow, laborious duration of the production process, as in the frequent
sequences of bread or tablets being propelled along conveyor belts before in-
eluctably tipping off the edge onto another conveyor belt, something which
the spectator is invited to anticipate due to the angle of the shot. Due to the

slow-moving conveyor belt, this becomes a painful anticipation. Schadt also focuses more obviously on the production of commodities (cigarettes, beer bottles), whose consumption he illustrates throughout the film, rather than industrial production *per se*, which is the principal concern for Ruttmann. Schadt's film is informed by a contemporary ecological consciousness, in that he shows detritus being sorted on conveyor belts at one point. Scenes such as the sorting of the rubbish also embed the labourer more thoroughly within industrial processes than is the case in Ruttmann's film, where the worker's hand, in close-up, is necessary to start the wheels, which, however, once in motion, run of their own accord.

Schadt revisits many of the key *topoi* of Ruttmann's film to offer a vision of the fate of modernity. This refracted perspective on the industrialized modern metropolis is also underlined by the way in which Schadt reworks one central *topos* of Ruttmann's view of the city: industrialized time. Georg Simmel had observed in his essay on the metropolis and mental life that 'the relationships [...] of the typical metropolitan [...] are so complex that without the strictest punctuality in promises and services the whole structure would break down into an inextricable chaos',[32] and with his recurring shots of clocks precisely 'on the hour' Ruttmann's film illustrates this rather literally. Schadt too uses the clock motif, but the difference is that his clocks are rarely 'on the hour', suggesting a more subjective sense of time and its regulation in the city, rather than the mechanical dominance at work in both Ruttmann's film and Fritz Lang's *Metropolis*. This ironic repetition and refraction of motifs can also be seen in the use of display windows, which, again in line with Simmel's analysis of commodification in the metropolis, Ruttmann showed as being sites of voyeuristic desire, most obviously in the scene where a man and a prostitute exchange glances through a shop window. Schadt shows a *Hundesalon* on Maybachufer in Neukölln in front of which stroll a large hound and its owner, both gazing into the display window. Such a relaxed and ironic repetition of one of the central themes of the visual culture of urban modernity (highlighted, for example, in the paintings of Ernst Ludwig Kirchner and Fritz Lang's 1931 film *M*, where Peter Lorre's character espies his victim in a mirrored reflection in a shop display of knives) could be said to playfully renounce one of the key neuroses of that modernity. Ruttmann's film, through its focus on the grand picture palaces and the audiences flocking to see Chaplin, celebrated the fact that the Berlin of the 1920s was a 'cinematic city' in the double sense, as observed by Janet Ward, that 'beyond the projected images of early German cinema [was] a three-dimensional, socioeconomic dimension manifest in the architecture of the Weimar film industry.'[33] Schadt, by contrast, may show us the celebrities arriving on the red carpet to attend film premieres, as well as an open-air cinema on the Museumsinsel, but his camera also presents us with an erstwhile *Kino Sojus*, now obviously a supermarket, on an empty Allee der Kosmonauten in Marzahn.[34]

What clearly distinguishes Schadt's film from its predecessor is its awareness of the presence of the past in the urban environment. Schadt's film catalogues the city's wounds, for example showing both the Soviet *Ehrenmal* in Treptower Park and the Olympic Stadium in Charlottenburg, entering a former air-raid bunker in Wedding, as well as displaying fragments of the former Wall and the Jewish Cemetery in Prenzlauer Berg. Beyond this, he also, however, reflects upon the fact that, as we saw in our discussion of Potsdamer Platz, these 'sights' of memory also constitute a key element in the visual encounter with the city. This is most evident in the representation of Checkpoint Charlie, where Frank Thiel's iconic images of the border guards (at the centre of Friedrichstrasse) are contrapunctually set in the context both of the new city architecture and the giant billboards which adorn the urban landscape (40-41). A similar counterpoint is achieved in his image of the (at that time) future 'Memorial to the Murdered Jews of Europe', which is advertised through a giant sign that Schadt carefully composes against the background of the new architecture of Potsdamer Platz and alongside a similarly large billboard advertising a SAT 1 reality programme *Girls Camp* (44). Such involuntarily crass juxtapositions, which the city itself offers and which Schadt's gaze frame, point to an obvious tension between the 'memory value' and 'exchange value' of the urban environment. This was evident in debates about the role of the completed Holocaust monument within public space.[35] Schadt's mise-en-scènes seek to do justice to the complexity of the image of the past in its current context and the complexity of 'narrativizing' objects of the past in the present.

The complexity of the image of the past is taken up at five specific points in the film, where it projects images from the past. At each point, a still camera is focused, from within, on the cupola of the Reichstag, the ostensible embodiment of transparent democracy. The focus then resolves, like an extended exposure, to reveal a photographic image from the past, in each case of the Reichstag. The first is of the Wilhelmine Reichstag, but this is immediately juxtaposed with a rack of postcards of Berlin, 'wie es war', with archaic images of archetypal representative urban architecture (railway stations etc.), alongside which, out of focus, are postcards of the interior of the new cupola. Schadt thus highlights the commodification of images of the past, something in which, of course, he is also engaged. This still image of the Wilhelmine Reichstag then triggers a montage of military monuments (e.g. Bismarck) and a recollection of German imperial ambition (a statue holding a globe), before moving into a series of images related to the remembrance, in Berlin, of the 9/11 attacks on iconic buildings in the United States. From this montage of images it would be possible to construct a critique of imperialist ambition that reaches to the present, but the absence of commentary leaves it very much to the spectator to make these links.

Just as with the first image of the Reichstag, the next four still images curate the viewer's 'beam of attention' for a further montage of images related to the city's memory landscape: the next still is of the Reichstag fire and this is linked directly to Werner March's Olympic Stadium (76). The third follows on from the preserved graffiti and shows the Reichstag in ruins in 1945 (72), an image which is then connected to the Soviet monument in Treptower Park (80). The fourth image then shows the gathering at the Reichstag on 1 May 1962, with the giant sign declaring 'Freiheit kennt keine Mauer', and this is then linked to a series of images related to the Wall (90-91) and the repressive GDR state (Hohenschönhausen).

As discussed in the introduction, James Elkins has argued that 'images, in visual studies, are too often either immediately self-interpreting or stand-ins for information that is non-visual.'[36] The documentary film, which works with and relies on the medium's indexical quality, brings such questions to the fore, as we saw with *Die Mauer*. That Schadt chooses a *photographic* image is significant in that, theoretically, he could have montaged cinematic footage of the past in the manner of Joachim Fest's 1977 historical documentary *Hitler. Eine Karriere*.[37] The still image, within a cinematic production, produces a very different effect, especially when used, as here by Schadt, to suspend time in a manner completely different from the way in which Ruttmann's film celebrated movement and the rhythm of empty homogeneous time passing, both in the city and in film. This aesthetic effect – the disruption of the flow of time – is as important as the content of the image, for the images Schadt shows might be taken to be immediately self-interpreting or to stand in for information that is non-visual. The visual information communicated is the freezing of synchronic, cinematic time.

Schadt's renunciation of any explication of these images that would clarify the critical memory value of the fragment, is complicated, as that renunciation might generate a kind of nostalgia, in that the auratic sense of the past that is transmitted by the 'age value' of the still photograph simply gives the viewer precisely that: an image *of* the past, with its monumental memory value. The images in Schadt's film are produced in monochrome – he used colour negative that was then developed in black-and-white – which could be argued to produce a certain timeless dimension. It is important, however, to note that Schadt does not seek to bridge the gap between the aesthetic effect and critical knowledge through textual commentary, other than perhaps when he focuses on a *sign* in the Jewish Cemetery that explains that what is beneath the surface are the bodies of *Kriegsgegner* who were discovered by the SS, hung and interred on that spot (79).

This refusal, by and large, to explain and clarify the images is an important decision. Much memory work that is (to be) carried out in the visual field relies on the willingness and ability of the spectators to do that work. It is this refusal that Evelyn Preuss criticizes in her reading of Schadt's film. She accuses him of 'dissolving unproblematically [from the past] into the contemporary', something our analysis has already addressed, but her major concern revolves around his 'abstracting and aestheticising impetus' which neither 'contextualises nor even clearly names' locations, thus rendering them 'undecipherable'.[38]

Often the verbal is required as a supplement to the image to ensure the critical perspective of the museal gaze. The verbal is practically absent from Schadt's film, as Preuss notes. For Preuss, the 'reliance on the audience's knowledge' is a questionable strategy, as 'historical images are left without dates, rendering them as ghostly apparitions outside of time.'[39] In essence, Preuss wishes to abolish the ambiguity of the 'monumental' image and demands that the audience be able 'to recognize and connect the places to historical narrative', in other words be able to make the images make sense (although it is difficult to see how the mere supplementary provision of the date actually resolves this problem).[40] Schadt's refusal to supply the supplement, effectively leaving the 'image' as a 'secret about a secret',[41] is condemned as an aestheticizing strategy that undermines the potential for critical history on the part of the spectator.[42] Yet Preuss herself illustrates all too well the contingency of images when she takes Schadt to task for his presentation of the Prenzlauer Berg Jewish Cemetery, with 'shots of the sunlight dancing on the stones. [...] In the context of German history, these images [...] trigger associations with the fire of Nazi crematoria [...].'[43] Such an association is made (subjectively) by Preuss, thus ironically demonstrating the potential 'critical memory value' of such an *image* to awaken historical associations. Schadt's refusal to offer an interpretative framework other than the one offered by his selection of images can be read positively as forcing the viewer into an active encounter rather than simply passively consuming a particular interpretation. While Preuss argues that the 'shots of historical and memorial sites tend to be devoid of people, they present no agent to carry on the remembrance',[44] such an argument erases the critical potential of the presence of the film's audience, something which she actually demonstrates herself in the example cited above.

This 'montage' of the past within the present mirrors the paradigm for embedding the past within the present that can be seen elsewhere in the new Berlin Republic.[45] In its perpetual return to Foster's Reichstag, Schadt's film is very much a product of contemporary Berlin's engagement with the visual culture of the past, but is highly subtle in terms of the way it remembers images and interrogates images of remembrance. In composing a mode of encounter that imagines its antecedents in the likes of the Weimar photographer, August Sander, it poses, but does not answer, questions of how images can carry the potential for a critical engagement with the past. Through its reference back to Ruttmann's film, it recalls Berlin as the 1920s as the apogee of urban modernity and points, through its own historical awareness, to that decade's apparent lack of a historical awareness. In so doing it reflects, and reflects upon, an uncertainty about the status of the contemporary city, while at the same time constituting that urban environment through its representation of the lived experience of the city, and the cinematic encounter with urban memory, in a moment of inducing the audience to see beyond the synchronic rhythm of the city/cinematic image.

The memory event in the global tourist city

In the city's official self-presentation as museum discussed earlier, *Berlin: Open City. The City as Exhibition*, which ran from 1999 to 2000, experience is framed as an event (*Erlebnis*). While the implicit tourist collective shaped by the guided walks remains precisely that – implicit – the collective urban event had established as a paradigmatic form of urban experience by the mid-2000s in Berlin. This has its roots in the Love Parade, the electronic dance festival that ran, intermittently, in the city in the summer between 1989 and 2010.

This event culture also manifested itself in the encounter with the past, as for example in Christo's 'Wrapped Reichstag' project, realized in 1995 after decades of planning, and despite its local, specific historical resonances, it was, as Beatrice Hanssen described it, an example of 'globalized art in a national context' and presents 'the first truly global media art event.'[46] And while images of this event did indeed circulate around the world, it also needs to be understood as a specific spatial image, a material intervention in the Berlin cityscape, which, as Andreas Huyssen suggests in his essay on 'Monumental Seduction', 'did function as a strategy to make visible, to unveil, to reveal what was hidden when it [the Reichstag] was visible.[47]

'Wrapped Reichstag' was a striking reversal of the otherwise dominant palimpsest paradigm, as it involved adding layers to a structure, rather than digging to get a view of the 'depths' of past time. For Huyssen, the project became 'a monument to democratic culture', opening up 'a space for reflection and contemplation as well as for memory', for 'a fleeting and transitory epiphany.[48] The elision of contemplation, memory and epiphany here by Huyssen suggests an emphasis on the temporality of the encounter rather than the narratives elaborated. Yet for Huyssen, the wrapping 'muted [...] the memory of speeches from its windows, of the raising of German or Soviet flags on its roof.' In other words, Huyssen remembered what was not present as remembrance in Christo's framing of the site, which constructed an encounter with place. Huyssen used his own photograph of citizens and visitors staring up at the structure to illustrate the encounter with the wrapping of the building, but what this photograph also shows is the fence which separates a public from the structure, a 'ground-level' photograph that contrasts with his employment of the 'official' Columbia University photograph in the same essay, which presents a distanced overview with no 'human grounding' of the image. Each photograph tells a different story of a mode of encounter, of a particular 'beam of attention'.

The power of the visual and the temporal and spatial location of the spectator, are important factors in the encounter with any monument in public space. Henri Lefebvre suggests that a monument 'does not have a "signified" (or "signifieds"); rather it has a *horizon of meaning*: a specific or indefinite multiplicity of meanings.[49] To return to the categories we introduced in Chapter Two, the 'monumental memory value' of the urban environment is produced by reducing the contextualization of the image, implying an unmediated access to the past and emphasizing its poetic qualities. There is nothing either within or outside the frame to mediate its meaning, thus the *horizon of meaning* is shaped by the codifications of the aesthetic technologies. This is also at stake in Hoheisel's 'Gate of the Germans' (see the introduction), Christo's 'Wrapped Reichstag', and also at another intervention in the city's centre, an installation, temporarily located at the Brandenburg Gate by the artist Marcel Backhaus working for the architectural association 'Gruppe 180' and with the backing of the Berlin Senate in 2005, to mark the sixtieth anniversary of the end of the Second World War.[50]

A photograph of the installation was taken by Miguel Parra Jimenez and posted on the Trekearthers site.[51] This is a photograph of a constructed image of the ruins of central Berlin at the end of the Second World War. The installation demonstrates how, like Christo's project, the palimpsest paradigm for the display of urban memory had become institutionalized by the mid-2000s (as notably celebrated by Andreas Huyssen in his essay 'After the War: Berlin as Palimpsest'). The problem with Huyssen's position is that it privileges the verbal sign, the notion of Berlin as 'disparate city-text that is being re-written while previous text is preserved', while underplaying the centrality of the visual encounter with the city.[52]

While Backhaus's installation could be said to 'fracture' the monumental space of the city centre that is framed by the Brandenburg Gate, the Reichstag, Albert Speer's East-West axis that leads to it, and the Pariser Platz on the far side of the gate, the aesthetic technologies it employs in fact heighten the poetic effects of the image: the gothic rubble and the predominance of stone produce a ruin aesthetic, while the use of a monochrome image heightens the sense of historical distance: the past does not coexist with the present, but is coded as distinct, while also being directly accessible in visual terms. The absence of the actual ruined material is compensated for by the material photographic image of the material. The photograph of the ruin operates as a surface on to which memory value can be projected, depending on the perspective.

According to Paul Virilio, the 'overexposed city' is entered not through a gate or through an *arc de triomphe* but rather through an electronic audience system. 'If the metropolis is still a place, a geographic site, it no longer has anything to do with the classical oppositions of city/country nor centre/periphery.'[53] Yet, what Berlin seeks to offer is precisely an experience of the 'centre' through the encounter with the defunctionalized remnant of a 'gate' that has been imbued with 'memory value', not so much in terms of the memory of cultural narrative, but in terms of an encounter with a specific, material city. The Brandenburg Gate may have no function in terms of organizing urban experience as a gateway, but it is however, an integral part of the tourist infrastructure of Berlin,[54] and, as with Hoheisel and Backhaus, it can reassert the significance of the city as **centre**.[55]

Urban memory at/of the city centre: Palace of the Republic

The Daimler-Benz development at Potsdamer Platz was officially opened by the Federal President of Germany, Roman Herzog, on 2 October 1998, in a ceremony with large-scale celebrations and musical performances. If this marked the 'closure' of the former 'wasteland', attention now shifted east towards the 'Mitte', the district which housed the Museum Island, and above all, the obsolete Palace of the Republic.

The question that the Palace of the Republic poses to memory in post-unification Berlin has generally been understood in terms of the cultural memory of the GDR. The Palace of the Republic was built between 1973 and 1976 as a multifunctional building. It was the site of the infrequent meetings of the East German parliament, the *Volkskammer*, but precisely for that reason it can barely be considered to have been the seat of power in the GDR, which was located in the Central Committee of the leading Socialist Unity Party. It was a place for state occasions, such as the party conferences of the SED, but also a place for cultural and entertainment activities. Its communal functions are neatly captured in the 1977 DEFA film, *Du und Icke und Berlin*, where it is the location for the social interaction of many of the characters.[56] In other words, as well as being a space of state representation, it was also a site of spatial practices, with the ensuing place memories that might be connected with that.

Those place memories expressed themselves in response to the threat posed to the structure after unification. Although other major and minor modernist building projects of the GDR era, such as the Foreign Ministry and the Ahornblatt, soon fell to the wrecking ball, this was not the fate of the Palace, which was closed by the GDR government on 19 September 1990, before unification took place, on health and safety grounds. The use of asbestos in its construction meant that the building apparently needed a programme of renovation before it could be safely used.

Given the general tendency towards demolition, the threat towards the building generated local resistance in the form of a museal gaze that remembered the spatial practices associated with the site. As a building that no longer fulfilled its previous function, its meaning was debatable. For many, after the fall of the Wall, the Palace was not a symbol of the SED dictatorship, 'the true meaning of the building is too civic, too uncertain and palimpsestic.'[57] Those demanding the maintenance of the Palace asserted the value of the memories they associated with the space in a series of publications. As a prominent marker of the shift in the GDR towards a more consumer-oriented socialism, the Palace was also designed as a place for a wide variety of cultural and leisure activities. The building provides the focus for those memories (and thus for an ambivalent relationship to the GDR state).[58] This form of memory value offers clear parallels to the defence of the Kaiser William Memorial Church in the immediate post-war era: a (renovated) Palace should remain as a spatial image of a previous order. Those resisting, however, were not in a position to create powerful spatial images, unlike those who wanted the return of the City Palace (see below). The West Berlin newspaper *Tagesspiegel* pointed towards the difference between spatial interaction with the building and a remnant that has been reduced to a distant image: 'The "House of the People" generated a tangled set of relations for those in the East, those from the West merely see the dead-eyed building and wonder what all the fuss is about.'[59]

The question that the Palace poses is, however, not simply how one deals with the place memories, but is also shaped by the fact that it inhabits a 'loaded' historical space at the former 'city centre' around the Museum Island. In addition, the Palace was a prominent architectural structure, which, in the eyes of its defenders, represented a piece of 'world-standard' construction.[60] In other words, it raised the question of how a 'city centre' should be envisaged. For that reason, the installation on the front of the Palace of a large-scale façade representing the former Stadtschloss by William Boddien and the *Förderverein Berliner Schloss e.V.* in 1993 is significant not so much in terms of the 'monarchist' cultural narrative which it might imply, but as the urban museal gaze which it shapes upon a putatively coherent city centre.

This is the construction of 'place' in the city centre, but it is certainly not the palimpsest principle at work here, rather it is the masking of layers of the past in the production of a 'monumental memory value' which implies seamless historical continuity through its framing of the encounter with the historical façade of the Stadtschloss. Indeed, for Dieter Hoffmann-Axthelm, it would represent the triumph of *Stadtbildpflege* over both critical and antiquarian historical work.[61]

Boddien's intervention was part of the public debate and academic discussion about the Palacee that ran almost without end since unification.[62] The variety of perspectives demonstrate that the Palace, as a building which has lost its function, becomes the projection site for different forms of memory value. These forms of cultural memory are undercut by the position of the building in the centre of a tourist city. In 1991 Otto Merk observed that tourists could have no idea what this building means: 'Explanatory plaques [...] which say something about the building, which is visually not to be missed, are presumably too expensive.' In the next ten years, in line with the production of the city as museal space, signs appeared. From 2003, sixty-eight signs were erected (for five years) close to the Palace of the Republic: posted on to the wooden fence surrounding the building, they told the history of the space now occupied by the Palace and the Schlossplatz through images and text (the history of the Palace of the Republic was presented on two of these). Official excavations carried out on the Schlossplatz allowed the display of foundations whose visual effect was reminiscent of those previously exhibited along the Topography of the Terror, reminding visitors and tourists of the presence of a material past.

In 1996, Federal President Roman Herzog indicated how far the material trace as a palimpsest of the historical process had become institutionally paradigmatic when he envisaged a solution that combined both the Palace of the Republic and a rebuilt Schloss.[63] At this stage, though, the building was not beyond renovation, nor did it *appear* to be a ruin, except for those who saw it as a ruin of a debased form of modernist architecture. Time, that most perennial of the processes of ruination, worked away on the structure over this period. Like the Gestapo-terrain, the period of time the site spent as an unintended monument is important in the evolution of its meaning as a palace of ruin.

After wranglings that went on for a decade, the Palace of the Republic was condemned to demolition. The asbestos removal work which, although not quite the final act in the process of ruination, meant the removal of all signs of the previous uses which the building had. By 2003, the interior of the Palace now had the archetypal visual attraction of the ruin for a museal gaze. The ruin now offered the possibilities of a different kind of memory value, through a return to the paradigm of the Mythos Berlin exhibition, its *Zwischennutzung* – the interstitial reappropriation of the site for cultural activities.

This was initiated in November 2001 before the removal of the asbestos and the final decision on the building's fate, and took place between 4 July and 26 July 2003. The projects that were staged in the building were expressly art projects that stressed the sensory encounter with the site. While the projects for the most part enabled a collective experience of the dynamics of place for its visitors, it would not be wrong to suggest they were as 'apolitical' as the games of beach volleyball that were organized under the commercial auspices of Jever Pilsner and the like at this time on the appropriated 'empty space' in front of the Palace.

One project from this interstitial phase that might be said to address the political history of the site did so in an indirect fashion that also addressed the politics of the museal gaze. Lars Ramberg's 'Doubt' (*Zweifel*), was, like Boltanski's 'Missing House', a material (and verbal) intervention in the urban site, installing a series of letters facing west and spelling out 'ZWEIFEL' on the top of the now defunct Palast.

As a form of integrated caption, 'Zweifel' can be read as a commentary on the uncertain political and cultural status of the Palace in post-unification Berlin. The installed letters suggest the need for a supplement to the unintended monument, just as they themselves are a commentary on the supplementary meanings that had been applied to the Palast since the end of the GDR – as well as to the (now detached) emblem that sought to define the building's function between 1976 and 1990. What 'Zweifel' underlines is uncertainty: an intellectual uncertainty about what the building signifies. Moreover, it highlights this referential uncertainty not by refusing referentiality but by foregrounding its work. In other words, while 'Zweifel' may highlight indeterminacy, it does not deny meaning as a whole, but merely the definitive imposition of meaning. It is an investigation of the technologies of transmission, creating the preconditions for the generation of meaning-effects through a museal gaze and a spatial image.

Beyond its playful engagement with the meaning of the building, like many of the other *Zwischennutzung* projects that took place within the Palast, 'Zweifel' invited a material encounter with the installation itself. Lifted out of the conventional tourist itinerary, visitors could stand on the Palace's roof and move amongst the letters (whose meaning, if they were non-German speakers, would remain a mystery to them), simultaneously gaining a high-level perspective on the city centre normally only afforded to those in the café of the Television tower. 'Zweifel' was temporally limited; it came to an end in 2005 (with the end of the *Zwischennutzung* initiative).

Another project from this period in the history of remembrance at the Palace site similarly illustrates the dynamics of place memory. Both in its subject matter and in its material, Tacita Dean's 2004 film, *Palast*, reflected on the question of obsolescence. Dean wrote about the decaying building:

> When the Palast der Republik was first opened in 1976, it was clad in white marble with 180 metres of windowed façade, triumphant in its transparent splendour. [...] There is now no trace of the white marble; the structure is raw wood and the windows are tarnished like dirty metal. It is as if the state is letting time make up its mind – letting entropy do the job and make the decision it is loathe to make. But the sore in the centre of the city is too public, and so a month ago, the wedding cake won and the Palast der Republik was condemned. The revivalists were triumphant. Soon Museum Island will be homogenized into stone white fakery and will no longer twinkle with a thousand setting suns.[64]

Dean's project, a ten-minute film, is an 'unintended monument' to film as a medium of preserving threatened objects at the time of celluloid's own growing obsolescence and in doing so it offers a haptic experience of historical material (both film and the building). It is a work which effectively induces a 'slow, reflective analogue state', as opposed to 'instantaneous, vacuous digital image technologies', in the rhetoric of synchronicity and contemplation invoked by Sean Rainbird, writing about Dean's Berlin works.[65] Any attempt to describe in words Dean's film will inevitably fall back onto a rhetoric of contemplation, intense attention and the apprehension of passing time: we experience the film's use of ambient urban sound, the exclusive use of close-ups of the structure, only ever showing a section of the windowed walls and giving no sense of its scale, while referring to the fracturing of the image in the series of celluloid frames; the lingering on the baroque outlines and green domes of the Dom standing next to the palace. Dean's work, though itself an act of musealization, is, unlike Ramberg's, not site-specific, being designed for the sensory-motor scheme of the gallery/ museum, with its inscribed expectations of contemplation and reflection.

In her commentary, Dean makes it clear that knowledge of the building's history was irrelevant to her approach to the object. Rather than simply an affirmation of Bazin's ontology of the photographic image (something evident in Sophie Calle's verbal-photographic work 'The Detachment'), Dean's project is founded on a complex engagement with indexical materiality that implies the index of time as temporal experience, the passing of time, rather than historical experience. Film is still ultimately conceived as an index, however, and the spectator still situated in a conventional exhibition context in Dean's work, for all the evocation of a reflective, slow experience of an architectural structure. It was also dissectible into a series of plates for separate exhibition, ensuring an afterlife for the still image, if not the film, which is now archived in the vaults of Tate London. Dean's target is not synchronicity, but the absence of time, per se.

The decline of the Palace was, of course, a highly visible phenomenon in the centre of the city, and as such attracted interest from artist-curators, such as Thomas Florschuetz, with his photographs of the 'Museumsinsel', views of the Palace's interior, and its environs, as glimpsed through milky, distorting (window) frames.

Our focus up to now has been on how the museal urban gaze develops in relation to material or photographic remnants. How does that gaze relate to the process of demolition, the emergence of an 'any-space-whatever' and its dissociated spatial rhythms.

One answer was provided by a project exhibited in 2009 at the Temporary Art Hall, another interstitial use of this 'empty' urban space, located in the close vicinity of where the Palace had stood. In Allora & Calzadilla's 'How to Appear Invisible', which ran from 11 July to 6 September 2009, the demolition was captured on film. The film was part of a two-piece exhibition and shown in a darkened room that recreated a conventional cinematic experience.

It opens with what appears to be a fairly straightforward, if disturbing documentation of the images and sounds of the demolition of the Palace of the Republic. After about five minutes, an Alsatian wanders, as if by chance, across the shot. The Alsatian is wearing a Kentucky Fried Chicken bucket around its neck that frames and blinkers its gaze, concentrating its attention. The camera, as if now seized by curiosity, tracks the dog's movements through the empty interiors and wasteland exteriors of the site, following its rhythms through the any-space-whatever. The camera's attention moves then between the dog, the demolition activities, and the larger cityscape. Occasionally we have a close-up of the dog, apparently looking intently in search of the thing to attract its attention. The film concludes with the dog settling down at the foot of the rubble of one of the semi-demolished remnants.

The leaflet accompanying the installation suggests that the piece ad-dresses the 'historically significant grounds where the Kunsthalle has been temporarily erected: the Schlossplatz with its remaining traces and signs.' The film itself does not communicate any historical facts relating to the site's significance; its communication is primarily through a gaze, the visual immediacy of the fragmented built environment. This visual immediacy is interrogated through the foregrounding of mediated gazes: the dog's gaze is framed by the KFC-cone collar, ours by the camera lens.

This, then, is one post-unification formulation of the museal urban gaze, a hybrid of inhabitant and visitor engaged in Benjaminian rag-picking amongst the rubble. What emerges is the mode of encounter. The postcard that advertised the exhibition, creates an image of contemplation within contemplation, the still image framing the dog in the foreground, in the middle ground, a fragment of the Palace remains that juts out beyond the frame, while in the background the Dom is placed more neatly within the frame of the photograph. In that sense, here, the photograph performs its own act of narrativization, the encounter produces a narrative hierarchy that however remains complex and unresolved.

The local and the global

An exhibition held in the Rotes Rathaus in Berlin-Mitte at the same time in July 2009 illustrated that the visible obsolescence of the GDR cityscape had had an afterlife in the new regime of representation that has developed in the reconstruction of the new German capital, one which had much in common with the presentation of obsolescent ruins in the 1950s in both West and East Berlin, as discussed in Chapter One. The poster outside the

Rathaus announcing the exhibition: juxtaposed two photographs, showing (presumably) the same courtyard in its condition in 1993 and in 2008. The textual captions 'Die Gerettete Mitte' and 'Die Sanierung der Spandauer Vorstadt 1993-2008 und der Rosenthaler Vorstadt 1994-2009' frame how one is to meant to 'read' the images, in case one were tempted to value the dilapidated façades of the past over the whitewashed present.

The exhibition took place in an upper room in the Rathaus and began with the photographer, Klaus Bädicker's, biography alongside four boards, titled 'Impressions of the Rosenthaler Vorstadt from the 1980s' which displayed the condition of certain *Hinterhöfe* in that decade through a series of large-format monochrome photographs. It was striking that the 'captioning' was set to one side of the photographs, heightening the impression that the pictures communicate self-evidently their 'message'. For those who had lived there at the time, there might be a moment of visual anamnesis of their former spatial practices. For visitors, like myself, the generic 'age value' qualities of decay in the images might well be the prime element communicated. So, as with the first set of images on the exhibition poster, these are potentially ambiguous images, whose meaning is primarily generated by their juxtaposition with the images of the renewed district in the rest of the exhibition. Interestingly, these photographs were not directly juxtaposed with the images of the renovated buildings, and in their large format, approach the status of independent aesthetic objects, rather than a 'mere' documentation of the built environment.

The absence of further information relating to these photographs can be contrasted with the abundance of textual and visual information contained on the other boards in the exhibition. The initial board, 'Die Gerettete Mitte', followed the exhibition poster in juxtaposing the before and now condition of six spaces in the district. The rest of the boards were titled thematically and comprised a compendium of the important aspects of contemporary urban renewal, from a reflective and meticulous planning culture to a documentation of the history of the district.

It is interesting to observe the ambiguity of the display of 'age value' in Bädicker's photographs, removed from the original East Berlin context in which they were taken.[66] They no longer function as a critical evocation of an otherwise disregarded life-world, but are subsumed within the logic that previously informed the GDR state's triumphalist instrumentalization of the visual signs of physical but also moral obsolescence. That logic has now been appropriated by the champions of urban renewal in the 'new' Berlin, rendering the 'old' GDR cityscape redundant and the 'new'/renewed Berlin as functional, not in terms of a utopian vision of the future (the logic in both post-war West and East Berlin), but as the mastering and incorporation of the former cityscape.

Anonymous asynchronous centre

The official exhibition incorporated and presented the contemporary hegemonic visualization of the city with the visual media at its disposal. The logic of that visualization is subtly undermined in a collection of photographs by Arwed Messmer, entitled *Anonyme Mitte* (2009). Messmer's photographs of Berlin-Mitte in its post-unification state of demolition/ transition are juxtaposed with images discovered by Mesmmer in his archival work. These had been taken by Fritz Tiedemann under contract by the GDR state in 1951. Rather than working with a conventional old/new juxtaposition, Messmer's volume, which made use of pages that folded out to reveal panoramas, quite literally opens out our awareness of the desire for new states (the GDR in 1951, the Federal Republic in the present) to establish their own legitimacy through the moulding of the cityscape, seemingly unaware that their cityscape will itself be 'the past' one day.

Messmer engages with the curation, production, and exhibition of an archive, recording moments of encounter that then reproduce themselves. Artistic engagement in the encounter with empty sites in this part of the city has been relentless, as if the 'closure' of the Potsdamer Platz had forced the search for 'wounds' in the cityscape to alight on this remaining site of an uncertain past, present, and future.

Barbara Pousstichi's 2010 project, 'Echo', cloaked the Temporary Art Hall in a mock-up of the Palace structure, perhaps as a comment on the perpetual reformulations of the structure, while creating the uncanny effect of the presence of the disappeared structure in an unfamiliar, yet familiar location in the cityscape. Pousstichi replaced the insignia of the hammer and sickle with a clock, suggesting again the replacement of explicit ideology with the invisible ideology of synchronic urban activity. As Diederich Diederichsen observed of the project, invoking, in the De Certeauian term of the 'obstacle', the encounter with the past and the ambiguities of the museal gaze:

> It [...] places an obstacle in the path of those who would like to take renewed command of history as an interplay of constant and variable in which only those who are currently in power determine what the constant is and what it represents, and what the variable is.[67]

Time frames in the digital city

The Temporary Art Hall is no more, as the location is at time of writing (January 2016) almost wholly occupied by the new structure of the Humboldt Forum. The Palace survived for a number of years, however, in the digital form of Lars Ramberg's photographic archive, at www.palastdeszweifels. de.[68] It could be argued that the material dimensions of the encounter with the installation are now reduced to the visual spectacle of the photographs that document the installation's presence in the cityscape. Yet the visual is not necessarily a reduction; it poses instead a different set of problems, offering the opportunity to focus on the mechanisms by which the visual form of the cityscape becomes a projection surface for historical narra- tives through the work of the encounter. It is here that Ramberg explicitly reimagines his project as a form of place memory after the fact, while posing questions about the hyperspatial navigation of the (im)material city centre in the 'posturban' twenty-first century.

The website presented us with little information for navigation, other than the navigation menu which contains a series of dates (1940, 1978, 2005, 2007 and 'now') as well as an alternating series of images (which it later becomes clear come from the 2005 series).[69] If you click on 2007, for example, you see images from the period of the building's dismantling. Only the datelink and the related URL related function as supplements to these images, in this case: www.palastdeszweifels.de/index2007.html.[70]

If one clicks on '1978' things are less straightforward. There is a postcard with a caption celebrating the exhibition of paintings in the Grosse Foyer, but this is followed by images of a march from 1 May 1959 (conveniently the date is marked on the photograph), then a couple crossing a road, and then another colour framing of the Palast. If the ostensibly firm link between the historical date (1978) and the indexical quality of the photograph (as physical trace of the cityscape) are placed 'in doubt', then such pseudo- indexicality becomes part of a playful interaction with HTML (HyperText Markup Language) when we click on 1940, for which the URL is www. palastdeszweifels.de/index1930.html.[71]

The series of images here are, it would seem, not all from the same year, though it is impossible to make a definitive judgment (again here the non-chronological ordering of the images seems important). We have standard images of the Schloss façade, but interspersed with a photograph of the Schloss in a ruinous state, and another, presumably of the demolition, followed again by an intact Schloss, seen from above set in snow, followed by a painting of the Schloss from a much earlier era; the sequence then starts again.

Ramberg's online exhibition can be seen simply as a cynical comment on the vanishing material presence of the GDR cityscape; perhaps it is a contemporary form of the *Kaiserpanorama*. The Imperial Panorama was the means of determining the 'selectivity and rhythm of attentive response' of the urban audience at the turn of the previous century – Ramberg's is thus an ironic version of the urban training implicit in this panorama for the 'internet age'.[72] Ramberg's online exhibition exploited the possibilities and limitations of such a form of exhibiting 'the past', exploring questions and raising doubts about narrative linearity, legibility, and visibility, and as such is a welcome commentary on the flood of Palast images that (over)populate the internet.[73] In such images, the past is fixed, apparently, in a series of figures that represent states of the past but Ramberg's online exhibition demonstrates the seductive but fallible self-evidence of documentary images of material remnants. The final date, in a permanent state of becoming, is 'now' (*jetzt*). On 11 February 2011, when I first accessed it, the view from the webcam was of the Deutsches Historisches Museum which showed Berlin's ever-ongoing antithesis to the value of the past: the circulation of traffic through the city centre, the timeless and time-coded, the punctual city as seen from a historical museum.

These visual cultural engagements with the urban past interrogate the contemporary dynamics of urban memory, viewing acts of evocation, and reminiscence as technologies in themselves. It is not primarily the (historical) meaning of the sites that is to be recovered, but the mode of encounter with these sites that is to be produced. Through an investigation of those technologies they undermine touristic itineraries that are predicated on the same model of regulation as conventional engagements with urban space and time. They enable us to experience place in the city in a way that resonates not only with Halbwachs's conception of how urban transformation provokes the resistance of local traditions, but also with how the conceived collective memory relates to the experience of place. These international artists reframe our understanding of urban memory as something distinct from the Assmann's conception of cultural memory, which is all too often focused around a national identity. They bring out the complex interplay between the encounter and its narrativization in the museal urban gaze.

Conclusion

The Collectives of Contemporary Urban Memory

In the conclusion of her 2005 book, *The New Berlin*, Karen Till reproduces her 2002 fieldnotes about her return to the Topography of Terror (a place to which she is drawn whenever she is in the city). At that time, it remained 'incomplete', the provisional cement walls of the proposed Zumthor building concealed behind a wooden fence. The fence was the site of an exhibition addressing questions of racism and prejudice in contemporary Germany. Till concludes her reflections on this exhibition, and its location on the margins of the 'spectacle advertised by city marketers', with the following remarks which, on the one hand, unintentionally echo Wim Wenders while self-consciously invoking Walter Benjamin:

> Walking through this space, citizens *and* visitors were asked to look critically at their performances in the staging of a *Weltstadt*, to relate their everyday urban experiences to those of others living in the past, present and future. In doing so, some individuals may have experienced a momentary shock of recognition, an awakening to the not yet conscious knowledge of the 'what has been' in the now. [my italics - SW][1]

Given the Benjaminian inflection of her concluding words, perhaps the most striking aspect of Till's imagined scenario is the absence of a collective. The order in which this 'shock' works, according to Till, is also interesting: conscious critical reflection generates the as yet unconscious awareness of asynchronicity. For Wim Wenders, by contrast, Berlin's wounds were able to generate the experience of asynchronicity themselves for 'the visitor *and* the people of Berlin'. [again my italics - SW]

The 'and' of Wenders and Till ostensibly frames the citizens of Berlin and its tourists as a collective. This is why we have needed this term, 'urban memory', to describe the difference to place memory.[2] If place memory, in Connerton's and Halbwachs's models, was always collective, then in order to describe a place memory that is always and already 'artificial' because it is not (necessarily) rooted in local experience, what are the collective coordinates of an urban memory? As the leaflet to 'The Original Walking Tours in English' puts it: 'We all know it happened in Berlin, but WHERE?' This is not only an invocation of a collective, but it also demonstrates, as does Connerton's work, that there is an undeniable contemporary thirst for the experience of place, which Berlin promises to assuage. Hence the ongoing collection, curation, and exhibition of the any-space-whatevers of Berlin, and the production of spatial images.

Paul Connerton's assertion that 'modernity forgets', with which we began this study, needs to be revised. It fails to recognize that modernity, in spite of its forces of erasure, does not create a space 'wiped [entirely] clean'. Instead, the remnants and empty space left behind represent a potential. The material remnants at Potsdamer Platz, such as these fragments of Wall incorporated within the new Ministry for the Environment are manifold – and this does not begin to count the fragments of imitation or real wall on display in the most unlikely places in Berlin, be it in Shoe City at Alexanderplatz, the Europa Center close to the Kaiser William Memorial Church or those cocoa-solid slabs of pseudo-Wall on sale in the upmarket chocolatier Fassbender & Rausch at the Gendarmenmarkt. Yet, as this book has argued throughout, the material remnant has been a central element in an encounter with the past that has been a trigger to remembering. The fragment, however, is not self-sufficient; its critical potential can only unfold if the dynamics of place memory are put in place. Here the Wall fragment fulfils precisely what Janet Ward criticizes as the 'petrification' of remains.

This collective of consumers of the past must be read alongside the collective that is formed by the encounter with the past, and in conclusion I want to compare two particular spatial images of the urban past that date from the end date in this book's title, 2012 – also the year in which Ramberg's immaterial archive of the Palace of the Republic vanished into cyberspace.

The first of these is a marginal form of commemoration created for the celebrations of the 775th anniversary of Berlin's founding in 2012. The anniversary was an event that incorporated many of the strategies of 'memory value' that we have seen develop throughout this book. In 2008, Dieter Hoffmann-Axthelm edited a collection of essays for the journal *Ästhetik und Kommunikation* under the title, 'Amoklauf des Gedenkens', which bemoaned the omnipresence of an unreflective memory culture in the city of Berlin and beyond. This celebration of 2012 could be read as a symptom of the normative dominance of 'cultural memory' in the reaffirmation of a (relatively simplistic) narrative of continuity about the city. As one might expect, the 'event' was a key form of collective urban experience during the celebrations, following on from our discussion of this in Chapter Four, in relation to Christo's 'Wrapped Reichstag'.

The slogan for the commemorations was 'Grund zum Feiern?' ('A Reason to Celebrate?'), whose question mark indicated perhaps an uncertainty about having another city anniversary only 25 years after the previous one. One

18. Installation on the Breite Strasse for the 2012 city anniversary, 'Grund zum Feiern'. Photograph: Simon Ward.

less obvious form of commemoration of place spoke quite specifically to this slogan that plays on the double meaning of Grund as both 'reason', i.e. a reason to celebrate, but also 'ground' as something quite material, i.e. the material city as the source, root, and origin of the commemoration. In the summer of 2012, I came out of the Stadtbibliothek in the Breite Strasse and encountered this (Fig. 18) printed on the pavement:

While this might seem like a form of official, legitimized graffiti, a 'defacing' of the cityscape that can of course be found throughout Berlin, it is actually, also, a further application of the palimpsest principle. It is an example of how official practices have adapted artistic strategies – in this case the *Stolpersteine* (stumble-stones) which are mini-plaques to be found on the pavements of Berlin, recalling former residents who were victims of the National Socialist regime's policies. In the 2012 version, the 'ground' is made to 'speak', here, not through a plaque, or stumble stone, but through a self-consciously provisional micro-narrative of the spatial practices of the past. It is a cultural memory for the location, predicated, as we have argued throughout this book, on the dynamics of place memory.

This disruption of urban spatial practice has now become a codified means of framing cultural memory. There were a large number of this kind of short sentence printed on the streets of 'Old Berlin' for the commemoration, some of which appeared as fragments from 'old-style' chronicles, others more explicitly naming dates and activities for which this site was the particular grounds. What is at stake here? While it is tempting to decode a narrative of cultural memory that leaps back over the centuries to reassert a 'normal' urban continuity, something that was arguably at stake in both East and West in 1987, what actually connects the activities of the practices of 1987 and 2012, for example, is their use of the dynamics of place memory in the city.

The museal urban gaze and its modulation of attention is now paradigmatic and embedded into the structure of the city and its display of urban continuity, founded on a narrative of a natural urban history which rather undoes the paradigm of 'critical memory value', which, as we can recall from Chapter Two, involves making the historical process visible. The printed words on the street will gradually fade and become invisible, and will not remain as an obstacle, as the material remnant might. The seamless musealization of the city, and its natural philosophy of urban history, its framing of the urban past as a directed visual consumption – '**See** what is left of the 1000 year Reich [...] **See** the exact position of Hitler's bunker', as the Walking Tours leaflet promises – might lead one to a rather pessimistic conclusion.

In the spirit of optimism, let me offer a counter-example with which to conclude. It might seem that with the establishment of the Humboldt-Forum on Schlossplatz, initially in the form of a corner fragment that echoed the fragment of Schinkel's Bauakademie on the far side of that same Platz, the potential for urban memory in the encounter with fragmented, incomplete urban spaces might be vanishing in Berlin.

In the summer of 2012, however, the Spanish artist, Juan Garaizabal, found yet one more overlooked place in the east of the city centre, on the corner of Mauerstrasse/Krausenstrasse, just round the corner from Friedrichstrasse. As the exhibition leaflet described it, Garaizabal's sculpture 'brought the Bethlehem Church, destroyed in the Second World War, back to its proper place.' He did, not, however, reconstruct the church, but constructed the frame of the building out of metal, so that it stood, as a fragile skeleton on its former location (Fig. 19). Not far from the sculpture, in the Museum for Communication on the Leipziger Strasse, an accompanying exhibition, not unlike the model used by Boltanski's 'Missing House' project, gathered together some of the artist's research, drafts, models, and sketches, as well as historical photographs which, again according to the leaflet, 'make this lost monument's history feel tangible.' While it seems a little unfair to

19. Juan Garazaibal, 'Memoria Urbana', Bethlehemkirchplatz, Berlin, 2012. Photograph: Simon Ward.

take the verbal explication of the work to task, it is important to note how the photograph is accorded the potential of evoking place memory. The installation is more interesting than its textual supplement. For while the leaflet again suggested that the sculpture 'remembers the friendly relations between Prussia and the Bohemian refugees, for whom the church was built in 1737', nothing at the site actually makes this connection explicit. What instead the installation enables (it is still standing) is an encounter with place: the city as museum, but in the form of an urban museum, in which the modes of encountering the city are also incorporated. It is not a *Stolperstein*, but permanently incomplete, composed not only out of the immateriality of light and air, by the trigger of the outline of the structure which is not only visible in the metal forms, but also, importantly, on the ground, which traces the ground plan of the former church, in an ironic echo of the *Planwerk Innenstadt's* insistence on recreating solid, material structures on the basis of the former city's street structures.[3] With Garazaibal's work, we are back with Halbwachs, in the sacred structures of collective place memory that we discussed in the introduction. Garazaibal's work not only invokes a narrative of cultural memory that brings us back to the globally inclusive community envisaged by Libeskind at the start of this chapter, but it also forms a collective for that narrative, a transient, migratory collective that might stop and wo/ander in this curious gap in the cityscape. We might recuperate the word 'denizens' in its historical sense to denote those who are accorded rights without belonging to a place, to describe this collective.

'Memoria Urbana' is predicated on the dynamics of place memory. The installation provides an encounter with place, indeed a remembrance of place memory's dynamics. 'Memoria Urbana', an encounter framed in Berlin beyond monocultural language, an urban place not to dwell, but to pass through. Garazaibal's installation also offers one solution to the question of what constitutes memory for an urban collective. In 'Memoria Urbana', the figures of the inhabitant and the visitor are also combined in the migrant artist who participates in the curation of the cityscape and whose work is welcomed into the city archive.[4]

We have seen a constant interaction between unofficial and official cultures of memory production, and more experimental forms of visual cultural engagement with the city, most notably in the paradigm of the urban palimpsest, understood as a visual encounter with material, rather than a simple decoding of verbal traces. The work of Garazaibal, and its incorporation into the city's official archive, demonstrates the crucial role of critical visual practice in the shaping of the city's memory culture. In tracing that culture's emergence over the past fifty years, we have observed the role which artists and photographers have played in shaping the museal urban gaze since it was initially formulated by Wolf Jobst Siedler and Elisabeth Niggemeyer in explicit response to the impositions of the synchronic urban gaze on post-war Berlin. The cultural practices of collectors, curators, and exhibitors of the city's repository have often been initiated and reflected upon by cultural producers, who take on and define the task of producing the spatial images, which then become part of the institutional framework of urban memory. These playful cultural producers are of course not to be thought in opposition to the dealers in the exchange value of space, but their relationship is also not an easy collaboration, as they produce a frame of attention that has to be produced at odds with the prevailing conditions of the contemporary city.

In his 1985 film essay *As One Sees* (*Wie man sieht*), Harun Farocki reflects on how a city emerges out of an encounter that is different from the instrumentalizing military and economic gaze. 'A beautiful notion: the traveller pauses at the crossroads in order to think through in the present moment the possible origins and destinations. The city emerges as a result of this pausing for thought and reflection.'[5]

If urban culture emerges in spatial interstices, then its temporal locus is the moment of reflection around which a collective might form, a moment of reflection put in place by artists and architects who come to Berlin to shape its urban memory culture from all over the globe, as a brief list of those discussed here illustrates: Garazaibal (Spain), Boltanski (Switzerland), Attie and Libeskind (USA).[6] The critical practice of urban memory has to keep open the possibility of a collective resistance or some kind of obstacle to the process of synchronization. Divested of a nostalgic longing for authentic place, it can be a tool for continuing to generate vigilance towards the cityscape that is encountered (*begegnet*) as an indirect object, and towards the discontinuities and asynchronicities of urban time and space.

Epilogue

'Genuine memory must therefore reveal an image
of the person who remembers'[1]

One final spatial image, to reflect on the repository, the archive, display, curation, and the role of the academic as a collector, curator, and interpreter of urban remnants in a foreign city.

In 2009, after I had been working on this project for a number of years, and following my visit to the Rathaus, to see the Bädicker exhibition, and to the Kunsthalle to see Allora & Calzadilla's film discussed in Chapter Four, I indulged in a little field work before returning to the library in the Breite Strasse. I wandered on to the grass which had been laid over the now empty site of the former Palace of the Republic, in what might be read as the unintended literalization of the metaphor of 'letting grass grow over the past'. Fascinated by the ageing of concrete, that foundational material of post-war Berlin, I could not help strolling across the grass towards the remaining fragments of the Palace structure, its concrete foundations rooted in the ground. I could not help noticing a piece of paper that was poking out of a crevice in the concrete. Nor could I help approaching the piece of paper, removing it from its resting place, and inspecting it. I read it, and 'completely controlled' by my Fujipix camera, appropriated it with a snapshot:[2]

The note, written in German, read (my translation):

> The ex-'GDR' is a disturbance... But why?
> Now the Palace of the Republic is gone. OK, and?
> The ex-'GDR' is still always there whatever happens.
> The DDR-Museum, T-Shirt, souvenir [illegible]
> ... Everything that makes money. I find that a shame.
> The GDR is not worse than the Nazi era
> And it is also German history
>
> [MARGINAL ASIDE] I enjoyed coming here for 30 years.

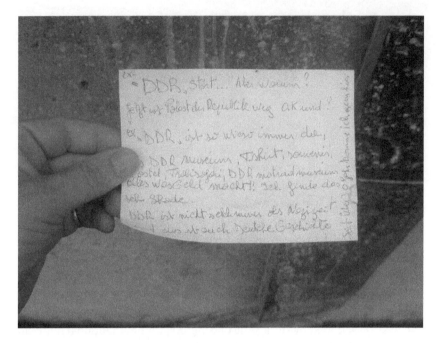

20. Note discovered at the site of the former Palace of the Republic, with the hand of the book's author (2009). Photograph: Simon Ward.

There it was, the habit of spatial practice, place memory, invoked on the margin of a narrative of nations, in the margins of a vanishing building in the centre of a city.

I put the memory back where it cleaved to the crevice, and returned to my pile of books in the library.

Notes

Introduction

1. Assmann, 2006b, p. 339.
2. Staiger and Steiner, p. 11. Janet Ward makes a forceful and repeated case for the moral role of 'public history' in *Post-Wall Berlin*.
3. Nora, 1989, p. 13.
4. Connerton, p. 5.
5. Connerton, p. 121.
6. Lefebvre, 1974, p. 307.
7. My discussion of the dynamics of 'urban memory' here expands upon and, hopefully, unpacks somewhat Janet Ward's assertion that 'we' 'need' both communicative and cultural memory. Ward, 2011, p. 98.
8. One of the aims of this book is to open out the horizons as well as clarify what is specific about 'urban memory'. The term is used explicitly in, for example, Mark Crinson, *Urban Memory: History and Amnesia in the Modern City,* but also two uses of the term, in specific reference to Daniel Libeskind, in Janet Ward's *Post-Wall Berlin*, p. 329 and p. 330.
9. Halbwachs, p. 133
10. Halbwachs, p. 134.
11. Lefebvre, 1974, p. 307
12. Janet Ward uses the term 'metropolitan memory' to describe this phenomenon, referring to the work of Aldo Rossi; Ward, 2011, p. 224. See Chapter 3 for a discussion of Rossi's particular influence on this specific form of urban memory in Berlin.
13. Halbwachs, p. 134.
14. Halbwachs, p. 135.
15. Halbwachs, p. 135.
16. The production of the 'spatial image' generates a combined form of communicative and cultural memory (see also footnote 8).
17. Connerton, p. 34 [my italics].
18. Halbwachs, p. 136 [my italics].
19. Halbwachs, p. 135.
20. Walter Benjamin, 1973, p. 243.
21. Ibid.
22. De Certeau, 1984, p. 89.
23. Assmann, 2006b, p. 300 [my translation].
24. Walter Benjamin, 1972, p. 216.
25. Koepnick, 2006, p. 13.
26. Bennett, p. 263.
27. Frisby, p, 312.

28. Ladd, 1997, p. 1. Jennifer Jordan, in *Structures of Memory*, discusses the role of what, perhaps unfortunately given the neo-liberal logic implied, she terms 'memorial entrepreneurs', but again the only ghosts her book is interested in are 'those generated by [...] persecution by and resistance to the Nazi regime.' P. 19.
29. Wenders, 1977, pp. 98-99.
30. Till, 2005, p. 101.
31. Huyssen, 1994, p. 35.
32. Bennett, p. 264.
33. Huyssen, 1994, p. 255.
34. Huyssen, 1994, p. 255.
35. Huyssen, 1994, p. 34.
36. Huyssen, 1994, p. 30.
37. Huyssen, 1994, p. 31.
38. Huyssen, 1994, p. 31.
39. Nora, p. 19.
40. Huyssen, 1994, p. 33.
41. Bennett, p. 273.
42. Huyssen, 1994, p. 34.
43. Huyssen, 1994, p. 34.
44. Riegl, 1996, p. 145.
45. Huyssen, 1994, p. 255.
46. Huyssen, 1994, p. 58.
47. Hein, p. 118.
48. Pile, p. 217.
49. Till, pp. 100-101.
50. De Certeau, 2002, p. 133.
51. De Certeau, 2002, p. 138.
52. De Certeau, 2002, p. 134.
53. De Certeau, 2002, p. 135.
54. De Certeau, 2002, p. 136.
55. Nora, p. 9.
56. Cf. Till, p. 102, for a Benjamin-influenced account of this reworking of perception through the 'shock' effect of 'age value'.
57. By contrast, Janet Ward would insist on the 'public history' functionalization of the remnant to give it validity. Ward, p. 127, p. 271.
58. Riegl, 1994, p. 145.
59. Burgin, p. 20.
60. Sheringham, p. 7.
61. Sheringham, p. 9.
62. Sheringham, p. 16.
63. Assmann, 2006b, p. 309.
64. Assmann, 2006b, p. 309.
65. Hayden, p. 227.

66. Koepnick, 2001, p. 352. See also, more recently, Long, p. 25.
67. There is a fascinating footnote in Karen Till's book that opens up the question of the 'insider'/'outsider's 'sense of place': Till, p. 252, footnote 1. By contrast, Janet Ward constantly shifts between the positions of 'we' (scholars?) and 'tourists/visitors' and 'Berliners' in her book. The question of the collective address of the 'spatial image' is one that I address specifically in the conclusion.
68. Lefebvre, 2004, p. 27.
69. Dehio, p. 143.
70. There is a curious consonance between Dehio's position and that of Janet Ward in *Post-Wall Berlin*, in their denigration of the 'obsolescent', and the need for 'public history' to play a didactic role. Ward assigns obsolescent spaces a very particular role in the history of the city that has effectively been overcome in the post-unification period.
71. It is this focus on visual culture and its practices that distinguishes this book from Andrew Webber's Benjaminian archaeology of Berlin in the twentieth century, which is focused predominantly through the lens of national identity.
72. Assmann, 2006a, p. 12 [my translation].
73. Crang, p. 195.
74. Assmann, 2006a, p. 13 [my translation].
75. Long, p. 25.
76. Elkins, p. 99.
77. Koepnick, 2006, p. 14.
78. Koepnick, 2006, p. 266.
79. Assmann, 2006a, p. 216.
80. Assmann, 2007, p. 168.
81. Compare Rudy Koshar's rather abrupt dismissal of a related artistic practice of the countermonument in Neukölln in the 1980s. The discussion of aesthetic practice is explained by the 'fact' that 'the very notion of a disappearing monument, a celebration of absence, had much to do with the special anxiety of how it felt to imagine being German.' Koshar, pp. 266-67.
82. For a reading of these functions of 'rubble photography' see, for example, Steven Hoelscher, '"Dresden, a Camera Accuses": Rubble Photography and the Politics of Memory in a Divided Germany', *History of Photography* 36, no. 3 (2012): 288-305.
83. Gronert, p. 20.
84. Wilson, 2005, p. 108.
85. Bennett, p. 276. Indeed the opening dialogue between the two principal characters of the film (Elle and Lui) expresses the conventional critique of musealization, summarized by Andreas Huyssen as a process that is 'freezing, sterilizing, dehistoricizing and decontextualizing'; the reduction of the past to a framed image, 'drained of life'. Huyssen, 1994, p. 30
86. Ng, p. 146.

87. Deleuze, p. 8.
88. Kleihues, 1993b, p. 33
89. Cf. Colomb, 2007, for a comprehensive summary of this period. Colomb's argument that this case study shows the need to move beyond identity debates to consider the renegotiation of the social uses and public nature of a strategic inner-city site in a market economy is one that overlaps with my own. Her emphasis on the 'interim use' is one that I expand on by treating the artistic works in detail in themselves. Lars Ramberg's *Zweifel*, for example, is mentioned briefly in footnote 82.

1.   Remembering the 'Murdered City'

1. Schwedler, p. 3 [my translation, as are all following citations from Schwedler]
2. Schwedler, p. 11.
3. *Interbau*, p. 12.
4. Bodenschatz, p. 71.
5. Hagemann, p. 4.
6. Hagemann, p. 10.
7. Bodenschatz, p. 74.
8. To apply such a hermeneutics of suspicion to these photo books and view every demolition as evidence not of the operations of the synchronic gaze, but of national amnesia, is plausible. It however not only lacks evidential basis, but any lack of evidence can simply be used as evidence of amnesia.
9. Schwedler, 1957, p. 1.
10. See, for example, Professor Paul Clemens's article in the *Tagesspiegel* of 4 May 1957 on the tasks of monument preservation today and tomorrow, which illustrates neatly the problems of formulating the role of preservation at a time when it is merely one voice of (at least) three – the others (including Hans Scharoun) argued that 'urban planning has become the "symbol' of a new age"'. Clemens is reduced to reiterating the role of a marginalized voice warning against the transgression of the laws and foundations of the 'Gewordenen'.
11. If nothing else, this should remind us that there is nothing particularly new or surprising about the municipal display of building projects. Cf. Janet Ward, 2011, pp. 305-307.
12. For extensive discussions of this case, see Simon Ward, 2006a, pp. 250-255, and Warnke, pp. 220-231.
13. Gremmels, p. 31.
14. Assmann, 2006b, p. 309.
15. Nora, p. 19.
16. Posener, p. 52 [my translation, as are all following citations from Posener].
17. Posener, p. 53.
18. Siedler, p. 4.

19.   Siedler, p. 80.

20.   Siedler, p. 9.

21.   Siedler, p. 13.

22.   Siedler, p. 1.

23.   Siedler, p. 74.

24.   Siedler, p. 79.

25.   Siedler, pp. 26-27.

26.   This formal celebration of automobilized perception is exemplified in one final photo book from this era: Horst Cornelsen's *Gebaut in 25 Jahren* (1973), which functions as an apposite summary of the outcome of the plans for Berlin's reconstruction first formulated by Hans Scharoun in 1946, to which Cornelsen also refers.

27.   The camera elsewhere records remnants of collective spatial practice: shop fronts, pubs with billiard tables.

28.   This process is reinforced by captions which elaborate the stories that would have been part of the oral memory of the local collective if it had not required the preservation in this form of memorialization that not only records, but also shapes a visual encounter. For example, in the section on 'shops', on p. 137, we have the story of the second-hand shop in a cellar in Kreuzberg. On the following page, a portrait of the fishmongers Margarethe and Max Kuhn, is amplified through a narrative about the practices in their shop. Similarly the pub of Gerhard and Luci Leydicke not only records the history of the building in Schöneberg, and with it the collective spatial practice of the neighbourhood, but also includes the letters received in May and July 1963 by the Leydickes from a real estate firm regarding the future demolition of their pub as part of the urban regeneration in that part of the city.

29.   Bartetzko, p. 55. One further example: 'In the case of Germany after 1945, it is the swift extension of the industrial production bases and not the working-through of the responsibility for the senseless murder of millions, and for the destruction of one own's homeland, which caused something to be started – if that has indeed happened at all.' Mitscherlich, p. 68.

30.   Bartetzko, p. 55.

31.   Mitscherlich, p. 16.

32.   Mitscherlich, p. 66.

33.   Mitscherlich, p. 70.

34.   Siedler, p. 199.

35.   Maether, p. 72.

36.   Maether, p. 36.

37.   Maether, p. 62.

38.   Maether, p. 62.

39.   Maether, p. 62.

40.   Maether, p. 62.

41. Walter Ulbricht, 'Rede auf dem III. Parteitag der SED', in *Zur Geschichte der deutschen Arbeiterbewegung,* III, Berlin 1983, pp. 750-752. [My translation]

42. Maether, p. 152, 276, 280, 281.

43. Maether, p. 257.

44. Maether, p. 326.

45. Strauss's film was not made. From a Western perspective, Leo de Laforgue did make a film, *Berlin wie es war* (1951), which instrumentalized still images of the Schloss demolition to make a propaganda point about the 'cultural philistinism' of the GDR regime.

46. Demps, p. 64. For a similar, if less grounded conclusion, see Ladd, 1997, p. 57.

47. These principles are reproduced in von Beyme and Durth, pp. 30-31.

48. Hain, pp. 44-48.

49. Hain, p. 49.

50. Kaiser, p. 17.

51. Hagemann, 1956.

52. E.g. Hermann Exner, *Berlin Heute und Morgen,* Berlin 1953.

53. For such a reading of urban planning in Berlin in the twentieth century, see Sonne.

54. Pöschk, p. 605.

55. Pöschk, p. 605.

56. Pöschk, p. 608.

57. Zache, p. 356.

58. Zache's article also used a photograph of a 'typische[n] Fassade' as illustration, but this did not so overtly serve the same function of displaying 'physical obsolescence', although it was juxtaposed with a scaffold-filled streetscape on the same page.

59. Mitscherlich, p. 66.

60. The information for this section was taken from a *Spiegel* article about the Bauwochen and the anti-Bauwochen events. This article is also interesting due to its visual presentation of obsolescence and the blankness of the modern urban environment. 'Slums verschoben', *Der Spiegel,* 9 September 1968.

61. All the office could offer however was advice; there would be no financial support to owners once they had been notified.

62. This is Emil Fahrenkamp's modernist Shell House (from 1930).

63. Emmerich, pp. 239-395.

64. Kuehne, 1971.

65. Kuehne, 1974.

66. Janet Ward, 2011.

2. 'Place Memory Work' in Berlin 1975-1989

1. Kleihues, 1993a, p. 14.

2. Aldo Rossi, p. 87. See also Boyer, 187-88.

3.   Kleihues, 1993a.
4.   Kleihues, 1993a, p. 14.
5.   Kleihues, 1993a, p. 18.
6.   Kleihues, 1993a, p. 24.
7.   Kleihues, 1993a, p. 25.
8.   Kleihues, 1977a.
9.   Kleihues, 1993b, p. 33.
10.   Klotz, n.p.
11.   Kleihues, 1977b.
12.   Hoffmann-Axthelm, 1978.
13.   Hoffmann-Axthelm, 1978, p. 14.
14.   Hoffmann-Axthelm, 1978, p. 15.
15.   Hoffmann-Axthelm, 1978, p. 14.
16.   Hoffmann-Axthelm, 1978, p. 18.
17.   Hoffmann-Axthelm, 1978, p. 20.
18.   According to Hoffmann-Axthelm, the synchronic urban gaze's production
       of a lack of connection for the new inhabitants of the southern Friedrich-
       stadt is doubled here, as it is related not only to the built environment
       as it was (the source of place memory), but also to contemporary spatial
       practices. As a space it is not recognizable, as the site is covered by the
       'Autodrom' – ironically, something with which most Kreuzberg citizens at
       that time would have been familiar.
19.   Hoffmann-Axthelm, 1978, p. 19.
20.   Hoffmann-Axthelm, 1978, p. 19.
21.   Another way of describing this would be through Svetlana Boym's concepts
       of 'restorative' and 'reflective' nostalgia. Boym, 2002.
22.   Nietzsche, 1972, pp. 230-237. Nietzsche's third category, antiquarian history,
       is more obviously applicable to the heritage and conservation practices of
       institutional monument preservation.
23.   Hoffmann-Axthelm, 1978, p. 36.
24.   Hoffmann-Axthelm's use of Otto Borutta's Mehringplatz photograph at the
       start of his essay is interesting as much for its unspoken reliance on the self-
       evidence of the image, and the non-interrogation of Otto Borutta's image
       as itself the product of a synchronic urban gaze, as for what it ostensibly
       illustrates ('ruin fields') and what is required as a textual supplement.
25.   This can be seen in the photographic collection, *Im Abriss* (discussed be-
       low), which does not just archive photographs, but also city plans in its vast
       repository of materials relating to Potsdamer Platz. On pages 217-219 it re-
       produces a map of the Grundriss of the area from the Neue Nationalgalerie
       in the West to the Askanischer Platz in the East (although marked on this
       are former buildings/squares, such as the site of the Volksgerichtshof, the
       Potsdamer Bahnhof, the Haus Vaterland. Marked on these maps are, first,
       the road plans of the 1960s and 1970s, second the actual state of develop-
       ment in 1982, and finally Speer's plans for the space where it was crossed by

his intended North-South axis. The map has an interesting gap. In the far-right centre of the plan, where the Berlin Wall runs in a straight east-west direction, on the Niederkirchnerstrasse, there are two 'former' buildings, neither of which are named. This space, as the map indicates, was due to be 'filled in' by the urban motorway. The space was, however, later not seen as 'empty'.

26. Young, p. 85.
27. Kraus, p. 36.
28. Rurup, p. 212.
29. Rurup, p. 205.
30. Rurup, p. 212.
31. Conrads, p. 39.
32. Hämer, p. 32.
33. Friedrich, p. 81.
34. Hoffmann-Axthelm, 1995a, p. 68.
35. Hoffmann-Axthelm, 1995a, p. 98.
36. Burgin, p. 29.
37. Young, p. 85.
38. On the history of the Anhalter Bahnhof, see Maier, 1984. Maier's use of archive photographs, in particular of the demolition of the station in 1962, would be worthy of interrogation.
39. Karasek, p. 258.
40. Mülhaupt, p. 25.
41. Huyssen, 2003b, p. 40.
42. Engert, n.p.
43. Rheinsberg, 1982, p. 15.
44. Bischoff, p. 8.
45. Bischoff, pp. 8-9.
46. Frecot, 1982a, p. 253.
47. Frecot, 1982b, p. 7.
48. Frecot, 1982b, p. 7.
49. Frecot, 1982b, p. 14.
50. Ullmann, p. 12.
51. Ullmann, p. 13.
52. Frecot, 1982b, p. 7.
53. Ullmann, p. 13.
54. Frecot, 1981, p. 5.
55. Frecot, 1981, p. 6.
56. On 'media archaeology' and indexicality, see Parikka, pp. 62-64.
57. Frecot, 1981, p. 6.
58. Parikka, p. 64.
59. Frecot, 1990, p. 7.
60. Seidenstücker, pp. 503-11.

61. The distinction to be foregrounded primarily here is to the nostalgic, melancholic practice of Siedler and Niggemeyer, who share Frecot's rejection of post-war urban reconstruction, but are fatalistically bound to a conservative, pessimistic view of historical agency.
62. Schmidt, 1973, n.p.
63. The Schmidt archive does not have digital copies of Schmidt's early collections, which is interesting in itself. Schmidt's 2005 collection, *Berlin nach 45*, includes many of his photographs from the early 1980s and in its use of blank pages echoes Wenders's reading of Berlin's cityscape after 1945. I choose the illustration here because it reinforces (more subtly!) the strategy of 'old and new' from 1973, while also 'representing' the Anhalter Bahnhof, a location which runs throughout this book, at the centre of its broad panorama.
64. Köster, p. 46.
65. The German here is *begegnen*, a verb that does not take a direct, but rather an indirect object. I discuss the resonances of this indirectness in the conclusion.
66. Kil, p. 1.
67. Kil, p. 2.
68. Kil, p. 2.
69. Wüst, p. 6.
70. It was published by Stapp, who also published *Young, Old Berlin*, for example.
71. Schmidt, n.p.
72. The fact that the name of a former inhabitant's girlfriend, 'Rita', is inscribed within a heart on a door in Sunny's boyfriend's apartment is a direct citation of the Paul/a inscribed within a heart on Paula's door in the earlier film.
73. See, for example, the installation at the Wall: http://www.frauenstudien-muenchen.de/wp-content/gallery/redupers/H_S_Redupers_Wall_300.jpg (Accessed 31 August 2015).

3. The Remembered City On Display, 1984-1993

1. Peterek, p. 4.
2. Peterek, p. 6.
3. Knödler-Bunte, p. 10
4. Knödler-Bunte, p. 10.
5. Knödler-Bunte, p. 12.
6. Vostell, p. 104.
7. Vostell, p. 104
8. Lichtenstern, pp. 129-130.
9. Wenders, 1997, pp. 98-99.
10. Wenders, 1997, pp. 96-97.
11. Janet Ward, 2001, p. 237.

12.   Bennett, p. 264.
13.   Wenders, 1997, p. 96.
14.   Kreuder, p. 36.
15.   Huyssen, 1994, p. 235.
16.   Janet Ward discusses this sequence in *Post-Wall Berlin*, pp. 3-4.
17.   In this context, we are looking at some of the effects of the Honecker-era attempt to create a more comfortable living experience for the GDR citizens, on the self-proclaimed basis of a 'real existing Socialism', which was, however, more an admission of the limits of the progress which the state could hope to make.
18.   This overlap between the 'real' visual culture scene in East Berlin and that of the film is also evident in the posters for the work of Frank Seidel and Christian Brachwitz that decorate Brenner's apartment (until he moves out), and in the appearance of Seidel in a non-speaking role as the sculptor of the ultimately rejected monument that should form a provocative adornment to Brenner's development.
19.   This echoes the economic rationale for renovation applied to earlier GDR projects.
20.   The film also shares with *Good Bye, Lenin* a common GDR joke about the quality of the Trabant.
21.   Byg, p. 60.
22.   Webber, p. 264.
23.   For details of the projects, see Glasmeier, pp. 43-228.
24.   On the relation between these two categories, see the distinction Christine Boyer makes between the antiquarian curator and the collector as historical materialist in a Benjaminian sense. What she does not account for is the shift in the meaning of 'curation' in the context of urban memory and artistic practice, as demonstrated by Boltanksi and other artists discussed in Chapters Two, Three and Four of this book. See Boyer, p. 191.
25.   Czaplicka, p. 156.
26.   Czaplicka, p. 187.
27.   Czaplicka, p. 171.
28.   Solomon-Godeau, p. 17.
29.   Ladd, 2000, p. 21.
30.   Endlich, pp. 213-14. For an extended discussion, see Simon Ward, 2015, pp. 100-101.
31.   Attie, p. 75. Accessible, including Attie's photographs of the project, at: http://www.jstor.org/view/00043249/sp060003/06x0045s/0
32.   The arrival of 'Western' art practice in the East did meet with resistance, for example, at the attempt to say 'farewell' to Lenin by the exile Polish artist, Krzystof Wodiczko at Leninplatz, or Via Lewandowsky's intervention at the former House of the Ministries, which was destroyed by anti-unification protesters on 7 October 1989.

4. In Search of a City?

1. Janet Ward, 2011, p. 213.
2. Janet Ward's approach in *Post-Wall Berlin* is framed by prescriptions of how 'the city' should function. Berlin's specific qualities are measured against the logic of an economic model in which the calculations of 'world city ranking' go hand in hand with the calculations as to the economic cost-benefit analysis of the transformations in Berlin. Ward privileges the synchronic organization of the urban infrastructure, and by implication accepts the principle that the 'denizens' (her term) of Berlin should be better trained in how to see and function within that synchronic city.
3. In *Post-Wall Berlin*, Janet Ward is consistently scathing of those who suffer from a 'melancholic nostalgia over the demise of Berlin's voids' (p. 320), and of those would wish to 'petrify' the wounds and empty spaces of the city. As I have consistently argued throughout this book, the point of the encounter with the wound is that it eludes such petrification as a fixed image.
4. Virilio, p. 442.
5. For a sociological reading of this process, see Colomb, 2010.
6. Cf. Stewart, p. 61.
7. Jenner, p. 12.
8. Janet Ward, p. 320.
9. Janet Ward, 2011, p. 197.
10. Rossi, p. 87. See also Boyer, 187-88.
11. Cf. Kähler, pp. 386-87. That the point of origin is '1940' is demonstrated by the use of this date as the first point of reference in those maps that show the development of Berlin's street networks.
12. *Berlin: offene Stadt. Die Stadt als Ausstellung*, hereafter *BOS*.
13. Boyer, p. 373.
14. Baudrillard, p. 74.
15. Baudrillard, p. 74.
16. Baudrillard, p. 75.
17. Burgin, p. 28.
18. Janet Ward suggests that the Wall's presence at Potsdamer Platz would not be very 'satisfying' for tourists. Ward, 2011, p. 96.
19. The mutability of the memory landscape is neatly demonstrated by the fact that since I wrote these particular paragraphs, the city (clearly aware of this 'failing') has placed another sign, indicating the presence of the Volksgerichtshof, this time on the sidewalk beside the main thoroughfare of the Potsdamer Strasse. A photograph of this sign can be seen on the Chapter Four section of the website associated with this book.
20. See Janet Ward, 2011, pp. 260-273 for a more detailed description of what she terms Libeskind's 'subversive urban memory'.
21. An interesting comparison to this artistic work at the 'city centre' is that carried out in gentrifying East Berlin districts, such as Prenzlauer Berg

and Friedrichshain, by the artist Joachim Seinfeld from the 1990s onwards. Seinfeld removed the 'old' wallpaper from hallways about to be renovated, and then developed projections of 'old' photographs on the material surface of the wallpaper. These works were then named after the address where the wallpaper had hung. These works also play with the illusion of the visual immediacy and indexicality of material traces, and the illusion of a separate and definitive supplementarity which text can supply, while also reminding us of the *layers* of a past that are threatened and soon to become invisible. Seinfeld's work can be seen at http://www.lichtundsilber.de/js-berlin0.html (Accessed 10 July 2015)

22.   . Preuss, pp. 123-124. See also Janet Ward's discussion of *Berlin Babylon* in 2011, p. 307-308.

23.   Schadt, 2002a, p. 13.

24.   Schadt, 2002a, p. 13.

25.   Schadt, 2002a, p. 14. Wenders also engages with Sander's photography in *Wings of Desire*.

26.   Sander, p. 646.

27.   Schadt, 2002a, p. 14.

28.   Schadt, 2002b, p. 76.

29.   This strategy of invoking earlier ways of seeing is also evident in Wenders's *Faraway, So Close*. Here, a key scene shows Cassiel (Otto Sander) entering the Altes Museum, in which, upon seeing Tony Baker (Horst Buchholz), he suddenly falls into a reverie and finds himself looking at the 1937 Entartete Kunst exhibition from a strangely canted angle. Wenders deliberately reproduces the skewed modernist perspective so detested by those with traditional understandings of art. As in *Wings of Desire*, where he had carefully constructed a mise-en-scène of Otto Dix's portrait of Sylvia von Harden in the climactic Esplanade scene, Wenders once more invokes, in that film's sequel, a painterly perspective as a historical model for a complex and reflective 'way of seeing' that counteracts conventional patterns of perception.

30.   Schadt, 2002a, p. 46. I refer, as far as possible, to stills from the film reproduced in Schadt's volume, cited earlier, for the reader's cross-reference. Page numbers will appear in brackets in the text. The aesthetic resonance of these stills is a clear indication that Schadt's film aspires to the condition of the photographic still image, for which observation I am indebted to Andrew Webber and his paper on Schadt and Ruttmann given at the CUTG in Leeds in April 2006.

31.   Neumann, p. 144.

32.   Simmel, p. 177.

33.   Janet Ward, 2001a, p. 21.

34.   A fascination with dilapidated cinemas as evidence of former urban spatial practices is evident in Steven Barber's *Projected Cities*.

35.   Cf. Simon Ward, 2006b, pp. 85-86.

36. Elkins, p. 99.
37. Wenders, 1997.
38. Preuss, p. 128.
39. Preuss, p. 125.
40. Preuss, p. 138.
41. Schadt, 2002b, p. 99, citing the photographer Diane Arbus.
42. Janet Ward discusses the same problem from the position of the account-ability of 'public history' in relation to Peter Eisenman's Memorial to the Murdered Jews of Europe in *Post-Wall Berlin*, pp. 249-253.
43. Preuss, p. 135.
44. Preuss, p. 128.
45. Simon Ward, 2006a.
46. Hansen, pp. 350-368.
47. Huyssen, 2003b, p. 36.
48. Huyssen, 2003b, p. 36.
49. Lefebvre, 1974, p. 222.
50. N.N., 'Künstler und der Senat erinnern an den 2. Mai 1945'.
51. At http://www.trekearth.com/gallery/Europe/Germany/East/Berlin/Berlin/photo178645.htm
52. Huyssen, 2003a, p. 81.
53. Virilio, p. 441.
54. Other spaces, such as the Holocaust Memorial, have been *constructed* to address a global audience. These sites offer an aesthetic and possibly monu-mental experience, but critical memory work is intended to be enabled by the accompanying documentation centre.
55. In the case of Michael Majerus's 2002 installation of an image of the Palast-bunker it can also be reutilized to play radically with questions of centre and periphery.
56. This film could have formed part of the analysis of GDR film in the 1970s in Chapter Two, given that its plot concerns a builder coming from the prov-inces to the city, and many of his early adventures involve him adapting to the synchronic rhythms of the urban environment. It shows, however, no critical interest in obsolescent structures.
57. Kuppinger, p. 23.
58. For example, Hans Jacobus, 'Erinnerungen.' Indeed many of the contribu-tions to *Kampf um den Palast* and *Der Palast muß weg weg weg* invoke this kind of memory value.
59. N.N., 'Palast der Gefühle'.
60. Kuppinger, 'Friede den Palästen'.
61. Hoffmann-Axthelm, 1995b.
62. Much of this is collated in Schlug.
63. Letter from the Bundespräsidialamt, 25 April 1996, reproduced in *Der Palast muß weg weg weg*. For more of the many examples of official use of the

palimpsest paradigm in the reuse of administrative buildings, see Simon
Ward, 2006a.

64.   Dean, p. 95.

65.   Rainbird, p. 7.

66.   Bädicker's photography is on display at www.baedicker.de (accessed
       1 March 2015). It is a remarkable archive that, probably unintentionally,
       plays with the referentiality of the photographs Bädicker took between 1984
       and 1994.

67.   Diederichsen, p. 31.

68.   Accessed 11 February 2011.

69.   This form of presentation parodies the presentation of the historical lineage
       that justifies the *Planwerk Innenstadt*. See: http://www.stadtentwicklung.
       berlin.de/planen/planwerke/de/planwerk_innenstadt/planwerkstaetten/
       spittelmarkt/entwicklung.shtml (accessed 22 May 2014). 1940 is also, ironi-
       cally, the first point of reference in Hans Stimmann's collection of maps
       that show the development of Berlin's street networks. Stimmann, 2002.

70.   Accessed 22 May 2012. The site is no longer accessible.

71.   Accessed 22 May 2012. The site is no longer accessible.

72.   Crary, p. 147.

73.   Berlin's memory cityscape appears in more refined virtual form, for exam-
       ple, in Rimini Protokoll's 2011 mobile 'radio play' about the Stasi ('50 Kilo-
       meters of Files'), or the Hypercities thick mapping of historical Berlin maps
       at http://www.berlin.ucla.edu/research/ (Accessed 10 July 2015).

Conclusion

1.   Till, p. 228.

2.   Janet Ward's invocations of 'most tourists', 'denizens of Berlin', 'we', and a
       'public' addressed by 'public history' in Berlin form, for me, a rather uneasy
       collective.

3.   The square had indeed been an abandoned location since the end of the
       Second World War. The mosaic was installed in the 1990s, before the square
       was officially named Bethlehemkirchplatz in 1999. See: http://www.kkbs.de/
       page/214/bethlehemskirche (Accessed 10 July 2015)

4.   It needs to be observed (and my attentive reader may have already observed
       it in the illustration) that 'Memoria Urbana' shares the Bethlehemkirchplatz
       with an earlier installation, the sculpture 'Houseball', which was created by
       Claes Oldenburg and Coosje van Bruggen in 1993, and ultimately located on
       this site, after a rather peripatetic career. It is striking that this installation
       also connects to the question of refugees, even if 'Houseball' works more
       with material shock value of incongruity than the subtle play with visibility
       and invisibility of 'Memoria Urbana'. For more information, and images,
       of 'Houseball', see: http://oldenburgvanbruggen.com/largescaleprojects/
       houseball.htm (Accessed 1 June 2015)

5.   Farocki, p. 25.
6.   Not to mention the international academics who have come to study its memory culture (e.g. Ladd, Till, Webber, Jordan, Ward – and Ward).

Epilogue

1.   Benjamin, 2005, p. 576.
2.   Smithson, p. 70.

Bibliography

Assmann, Aleida. *Der lange Schatten der Vergangenheit: Erinnerungskultur und Geschichtspolitik.* Munich: Beck, 2006a.

—. *Erinnerungsräume: Formen und Wandlungen des kulturellen Gedächtnisses.* Munich: Beck, 2006b.

—. *Geschichte im Gedächtnis.* Munich: Beck, 2007.

Attie, Shimon.'The Writing on the Wall, Berlin, 1992-93: Projections in Berlin's Jewish Quarter.' *Art Journal* 62/3 (2003): 74-83.

Bartetzko, Dieter. *Verbaute Geschichte.* Darmstadt: Luchterhand, 1986.

Baudrillard, Jean. *The System of Objects.* London: Verso, 1996.

Behnert, Heinz G. *Palast/Palazzo 1973/1998. Das Denkmalbuch zum Palast der Republik.* Berlin: edition bodoni, 1997.

Benjamin, Andrew. 'Eisenman and the Housing of Tradition.' In *Rethinking Architecture*, edited by Neil Leach, 286-301. London: Routledge, 1997.

Benjamin, Walter. 'Erfahrung und Armut.' In *Gesammelte Schriften*, edited by Rolf Tiedemann and Hermann Schweppenhäuser. Vol. 2, 213-218.. Frankfurt am Main: Suhrkamp, 1972-1999. 7 vols.

—. 'The Work of Art in the Age of its Mechanical Reproduction.' In *Illuminations*, edited by Hannah Arendt, translated by Harry Zohn, 219-254. London: Jonathan Cape, 1973.

—. 'Excavation and Memory'. In *Walter Benjamin: Selected Writings, Vol 2.2, 1931-1934*, edited by Howard Eiland and Matthew W. Jennings, 57. Cambridge, MA: Belknap Press, 2005.

Bennett, Tony. 'Civic Seeing: Museums and the Organization of Vision.' In *A Companion to Museum Studies,* edited by Sharon MacDonald, 263-281 Oxford: Blackwell, 2006.

Berlin, Berliner Festspiele und Architektenkammer, ed. *Berlin: offene Stadt. Die Stadt als Ausstellung.* Berlin: Nicolai, 1999.

Beyme, Klaus von, and Durth, Werner. *Neue Städte aus Ruinen: Deutscher Städtebau in der Nachkriegszeit.* Munich: Prestel, 1992.

Bischoff, Ulrich. 'Eine begehbare Plastik.' In *Botschaften*, edited by Raffael Rheinsberg, 11. Berlin: Frölich und Kaufmann, 1982.

Bodenschatz, Harald. *Schluss mit der Zerstörung: Stadterneuerung und städtische Opposition in West-Berlin, Amsterdam und London.* Giessen: Anabas, 1983.

Boyer, Christine. *The City of Collective Memory: Its Historical Imagery and Architectural Entertainments.* Cambridge: MIT, 1994.

Boym, Svetlana. *The Future of Nostalgia.* New York: Basic Books, 2002.

Buck-Morss, Susan. *Dreamworld and Catastrophe: The Passing of Mass Utopia in East and West.* Cambridge: MIT, 2000.

Burgin, Victor. 'Monument and Melancholia.' In *Memory Culture and the Contemporary City*, edited by Henriette Steiner, Uta Steiger and Andrew Webber, 17-31. Basingstoke: Palgrave Macmillan, 2009.

Byg, Barton. 'Parameters for institutional and thematic integration of filmmakers from the former GDR.' In *What Remains? East German Culture and the Postwar Public*, edited by Marc Silberman, 64-74. Washington, DC: AICGS, 1991.

Certeau, Michel de. 'Ghosts in the City.' In *The Practice of Everyday Life, vol. 2*, edited by Luce
    Giard and Pierre Mayol, translated by Timothy J. Tomasik, 133-144. Berkeley: University of
    California Press, 2002.
—. 'Walking in the City.' In *The Practice of Everyday Life vol. 1*, edited by Luce Giard, translated
    Steven Rendall, 91-110. Berkeley: University of California Press, 1984.
Colomb, Claire. *Staging the New Berlin: Place Marketing and the Politics of Urban Reinvention
    post-1989*. London: Routledge, 2012.
—. 'Requiem for a Lost *Palast*. "Revanchist Urban Planning" and "Burdened Landscapes" of the
    German Democratic Republic in the New Berlin.' *Planning Perspectives* 22 (2007): 283–323.
—. 'Pushing the Urban Frontier: Temporary Uses of Space, City Marketing and the Creative City
    Discourse in 2000s Berlin.' *Journal of Urban Affairs* 34/2 (2010): 131–152.
Connerton, Paul. *How Modernity Forgets*. Cambridge: Cambridge University Press, 2009.
Conrads, Ulrich. 'Schorf aus Eisen.' In *Dokumentation. Offener Wettbewerb: Berlin - Südliche
    Friedrichstadt. Gestaltung des Geländes des ehemaligen Prinz-Albrecht-Palais*, 39-42. Berlin:
    IBA, 1985.
Crang, Mike. 'Rhythms of the City: Temporalised Space and Motion.' In *Timespace: Geographies
    of Temporalities*, edited by Nigel Thrift and Jon May, 187-207. London: Routledge, 2001.
Crary, Jonathan. *Suspensions of Perception: Attention, Spectacle and Modern Culture*. Cambridge,
    MA, and London: MIT Press, 1999.
Crinson, Mark. *Urban Memory: History and Amnesia in the Modern City*. London: Routledge, 2005.
Czaplicka, John. 'History, Aesthetics, and Contemporary Commemorative Practice in Berlin.'
    New German Critique 65 (1995): 155-187.

Dean, Tacita. 'Palast.' In *Film Works*, edited by Briony Fer, Rina Carvajal and Tacita Dean, 95.
    New York: Edizioni Charta Srl, 2007.
Dehio, Georg. 'Denkmalpflege und Denkmalschutz im neunzehnten Jahrhundert [Rede von
    1905].' In *Denkmalpflege: Deutsche Texte aus drei Jahrhunderten*, edited by Norbert Huse,
    139-146. Munich, 1984.
Deleuze, Gilles. *Cinema 2: The Time-Image*. Translated by H. Tomlinson and R. Galeta. Min-
    neapolis: University of Minnesota Press, 1989.
Demps, Laurenz. 'Schloß versus sozialistische Stadtmitte.' In *Schloss und Schlossbezirk in der
    Mitte Berlins: Das Zentrum der Stadt als politischer und gesellschaftlicher Ort,* edited by
    Wolfgang Ribbe, 159-167. Publikationen der Historische Kommission zu Berlin, 2005.
Diederichsen, Diedrich. 'What Time is Germany?' In *Bettina Pousttchi: Echo Berlin*. Cologne:
    Walter König, 2010.

Elkins, James. 'Preface to the book *A Skeptical Introduction to Visual Culture*', *Journal of Visual
    Culture*, 1/1 (2002), 93-99.
Eisentraut, Wolf-Rüdiger. 'Kontrapunkte.' In *Kampf um den Palast*, edited by Horst Wellner and
    Rudolf Ellereit, 73-75. Berlin: Spotless, 1994.
Emmerich, Wolfgang. *Kleine Literaturgeschichte der DDR*. Leipzig: Kiepenhauer, 1996.
Endlich, Stefanie. *Wege zur Erinnerung: Gedenkstätten und -orte für die Opfer des Nationalsozi-
    alismus in Berlin und Brandenburg*. Berlin: Metropol, 1996.
Engert, Gabrielle. 'Versunkene Pracht.' *Die Zeit* 11 June 1982.
Exner, Hermann. *Berlin Heute und Morgen*, Berlin: Das Neue Berlin, 1953.

Farocki, Harun. 'Wie man sieht.' *Die Republik* 76 (1986): 32-104.

Frecot, Janos. 'Nähe und Distanz.' In *Fritz Eschen: Photographien Berlin 1945-1950*, edited by Janos Frecot, 7-9. Berlin: Nicolai, 1990.

—. *Berlin fotografisch: Fotografie in Berlin 1860-1982*. Berlin: Berlinische Galerie, 1982a.

—. *Berlin im Abriss*. Berlin: Berlinische Galerie, 1981.

—. 'Tiergartenviertel, 1965.' In *Botschaften*, edited by Raffael Rheinsberg, 251-254. Berlin: Frölich und Kaufmann, 1982b.

Friedrich, Thomas. 'Das Gestapo- und SS-Gelände im Jahre 1987.' In *Der umschwiegene Ort*, edited by Leonie Baumann, 81-82. Berlin: Neue Gesellschaft für Bildende Kunst, 1987.

Frisby, David. *Cityscapes of Modernity*. London: Polity, 2001.

Geist, Johann Friedrich. 'Der Palast der Republik aus westlicher Sicht.' In *Der Palast muß weg weg weg* by Günter Görlich et al., 23-30. Berlin: Spotless, 1994.

Glasmeier, Michael. *Die Endlichkeit der Freiheit Berlin 1990*. Berlin: Edition Hentrich, 1990.

Gremmels, Heinrich. 'Kultur und Planung.' In *Stadt und Städtebau: Vorträge und Gespräche während der Berliner Bauwochen 1962*, edited by Hermann Wegner, 21-50. Berlin: Staneck, 1963.

Gronert, Stefan. *The Düsseldorf School of Photography*. New York: Aperture Foundation, 2010.

Hagemann, Otto. *Das neue Gesicht Berlins: ein Bildbuch*. Berlin: Arani, 1957.

Hain, Simone. 'Berlin Ost: "Im Westen wird man sich wundern".' In *Neue Städte aus Ruinen: Deutscher Städtebau in der Nachkriegszeit*, edited by Klaus von Beyme and Werner Durth, 32-57. Munich: Prestel, 1992.

Halbwachs, Maurice. 'Space and the Collective Memory.' In *The Collective Memory*, translated by Francis J. Ditter, Jr., and Vida Yazdi Ditter, 128-156. New York: Harper & Row, 1980.

Hämer, Hardt-Waltherr. 'Prinz-Albrecht Palais.' *Dokumentation. Offener Wettbewerb: Berlin - Südliche Friedrichstadt. Gestaltung des Geländes des ehemaligen Prinz-Albrecht-Palais*, 32. Berlin: IBA, 1985.

Hansen, Beatrice. 'Christo's *Wrapped Reichstag*: Globalized Art in a National Context.' *Germanic Review* 73 (1998): 350-368.

Hayden, Dolores. *The Power of Place: Urban Landscapes as Public History*. Cambridge, MA: MIT, 1995.

Hein, Hilde. *Public Art: Thinking Museums Differently*. Lanham, MD: Mira Press, 2006.

Hoffmann-Axthelm, Dieter. 'Der stadtgeschichtliche Bestand.' In *Dokumentation zum Gelände des ehemaligen Prinz-Albrecht-Palais und seine Umgebung*, 32-45. Berlin: Bauaustellung Berlin, 1983.

—. 'Vom Umgang mit zerstörter Stadtgeschichte.' *ARCH+* 40/41 (1978): 14-20.

—. 'Wie lesbar ist die Geschichte?' In *Rettung der Architektur vor sich selbst*, 92-99. Braunschweig: Vieweg, 1995a.

—. 'Zumutung Berliner Schloß – und wie man ihr begegnen könnte.' In *Die Rettung der Architektur vor sich selbst*, 100-114. Berlin: Vieweg, 1995b.

Huyssen, Andreas. 'After the War: Berlin as Palimpsest.' In *Present Pasts. Urban Palimpsests and the Politics of Memory*, 72-84. Stanford, CA: Stanford University Press, 2003a.

—. 'Monumental Seduction.' In *Present Pasts: Urban Palimpsests and the Politics of Memory*, 30-48. Stanford, CA: Stanford University Press, 2003b.

—. 'The Voids of Berlin.' *Present Pasts: Urban Palimpsests and the Politics of Memory*, 49-71. Stanford, CA: Stanford University Press, 2003c.

—. *Twilight Memories: Marking Time in a Culture of Amnesia*. London: Routledge, 1994.

Jacobus, Hans. 'Erinnerungen.' In *Kampf um den Palast*, edited by Rudolf Ellereit and Horst
   Wellner, 81-82. Berlin: Spotless, 1994.
Jenner, Judith. 'Die Poesie der Besetzung.' *Der Tagesspiegel* 15 October 2005.
Jordan, Jennifer. *Structures of Memory: Understanding Urban Change in Berlin and Beyond*.
   Stanford, CA: Stanford University Press, 2006.

Kähler, Gert. 'Als der Dampf sich nun erhob.' In *Stadt der Architektur der Stadt*. edited by Josef
   Paul Kleihues, Paul Kahlfeldt, and Thorsten Scheer, 381-387. Berlin: Nicolai, 2000.
Kaiser, Josef. 'Die Fortsetzung der Stalinallee vom Starnberger Platz bis zum Alexanderplatz',
   in *Neues Deutschland* 1 January 1960, p. 5
Karasek, Hellmuth. 'Hölderlin im Olympia-Stadion.' *Der Spiegel* 5 December 1977.
Kil, Wolfgang. 'Untitled Introduction.' In *Friedrichshain*, edited by Ulrich Wüst. Berlin: Foto-
   galerie Berlin-Friedrichshain, 1985.
Kleihues, Josef P. 'Modelle für eine Stadt.' *Berliner Morgenpost* 18 January 1977a.
—. 'Programmvorschläge für eine internationale Bauausstellung zur Wiederbelebung des alten
   Berlins.' *Berliner Morgenpost* 18 January 1977b.
—. 'Städtebau als Erinnerung.' In *Internationale Bauausstellung Berlin 1984/87: die Neubauge-
   biete*, edited by Josef P. Kleihues, 14-29. Stuttgart: Hatje Cantz, 1993a.
—. 'Südliche Friedrichstadt.' In *Internationale Bauausstellung Berlin 1984/87*, edited by Josef P.
   Kleihues, 31-34. Stuttgart: Hatje Cantz, 1993b.
Klotz, Heinrich. 'Aus den sinnlosen Fragmenten muss eine Umwelt werden.' *Berliner Morgenpost*
   18 January 1977.
Knödler-Bunte, Eberhard. 'Mythos Berlin – Wahrnehmungsgeschichte einer industriellen
   Metropole. Zum Konzept einer räumlich-inszenierten Ausstellung zur 750-Jahresfeier
   in Berlin.' In *Mythos Berlin Concepte*, edited by Freya Mülhaupt et al., 8-21. Berlin: Verlag
   Ästhetik und Kommunikation, 1986.
Koepnick, Lutz. 'Forget Berlin.' *The German Quarterly* 74/4 (2001): 343-354.
—. *Framing Attention: Windows on Modern German Culture*. Baltimore: Johns Hopkins University
   Press, 2006.
Koshar, Rudy. *From Monuments to Traces: Artifacts of German Memory, 1870-1990*. Berkeley:
   University of California Press, 2000.
Köster, Hein. 'Strukturen.' *form + zweck* 4 (1980): 46-49.
Kraus, Michael. 'Kein Ort für Strassen.' In *Der umschwiegene Ort*, edited by Sabine Weissler,
   35-36. Berlin: Neue Gesellschaft für Bildende Kunst, 1986.
Kreuder, Friedemann. 'Hotel Esplanade: The Cultural History of a Berlin Location.' *PAJ* 22/2
   (2000): 22-38.
Kuehne, Gunter. 'Nicht im Verzeichnis der Berliner Baudenkmale: Kurfürstendamm 37.' *Der
   Tagesspiegel* 27 June 1971.
—. 'Verliert Berlin sein Gesicht? Stadtbild in Gefahr.' *Der Tagesspiegel* 28 April 1974.
Kuppinger, Thomas. 'Friede den Palästen.' *Zitty* 25 (1991): 23.

Ladd, Brian. 'Center and Periphery in the New Berlin: Architecture, Public Art, and the Search
   for Identity.' *PAJ: A Journal of Performance and Art* 22 (2000): 7-21.
—. *The Ghosts of Berlin: Confronting German History in the Urban Landscape*. Chicago: University
   of Chicago Press, 1997.
Laudenbach, Peter. 'Dirigent auf Montage.' *tip* 15(2003): 56-57.
Lefebvre, Henri. 'Seen from the Window.' *Rhythmanalysis*, 17-27. London: Continuum International, 2004.

—. *The Production of Space*. Translated by Donald Nicholson Smith. Oxford: Blackwells, 1991 [1974].

Lichtenstern, Christa. 'Berlin (1985-1987): Werkentwicklung und Symbolgehalt.' In *Kunst im öffentlichen Raum. Berlin 1987* (Katalog der Ausstellung Skulpturenboulevard Kurfürstendamm Tauentzien Berlin 1987), edited by Neuer Berliner Kunstverein, 129-130. Berlin: Neuer Berliner Kunstverei, 1987.

Long, J.J. 'Photography/Topography: Viewing Berlin 1880/2000.' *New German Critique* 116 (2012): 25-45.

Maether, Bernhard. *Die Vernichtung des Berliner Stadtschlosses*. Berlin: Arno Spitz, 2000.

Maier, Helmut. *Berlin: Anhalter Bahnhof*. Berlin: Ästhetik und Kommunikation, 1984.

Mennel, Barbara, and Jaimey Fisher. *Space, Place and Mobility in German Literary and Visual Culture*. Amsterdam: Rodopi, 2011.

Merk, Otto. 'Schandfleck der Republik.' *Berliner Zeitung* 29 July 1992.

Mitscherlich, Alexander. *Die Unwirtlichkeit unserer Städte*. Frankfurt am Main: Suhrkamp, 1965.

Mülhaupt, Freya. 'Der Anhalter Bahnhof – Versionen. Eine Text-Bild Collage.' In *Mythos Berlin Concepte*, edited by Freya Mülhaupt et al., 22-27. Berlin: Verlag Ästhetik und Kommunikation, 1986.

N.N. *Interbau Berlin 1957: Internationale Bauausstellung im Berliner Hansaviertel*. Berlin: Internationale Bauausstellung, 1958.

—. 'Künstler und der Senat erinnern an den 2. Mai 1945.' *Der Tagesspiegel* 3 May 2005.

—. 'Palast der Gefühle.' *Der Tagesspiegel* 27 March 1993.

—. 'Slums verschoben.' *Der Spiegel*. 9 September 1968.

Neumann, Dietrich. 'The Urbanistic Vision in Fritz Lang's Metropolis.' In *Dancing on the Volcano*, edited by Thomas Kniesche and Stephen Brockmann, 143-161. Columbia: Camden House, 1994.

Ng, Julia. 'The Virtual Landscape of Berlin.' In *Urban Space and Cityscapes*, edited by Christoph Linder, 137-154. London: Routledge, 2006.

Nietzsche, Friedrich. 'Unzeitgemässe Betrachtungen, Zweites Stück: Vom Nutzen und Nachtheil der Historie für das Leben.' In *Kritische Gesamtausgabe*, edited by Giorgio Colli and Mazzino Montinari, 243-334. Berlin: De Gruyter, 1972.

Nora, Pierre. 'Between History and Memory: Les lieux de memoire.' *Representations* 26 (1989): 7-24.

Parikka, Jussi. 'Operative Media Archaeology: Wolfgang Ernst's Materialist Media Diagrammatics.' *Theory, Culture & Society* 28/5 (2011): 52-74.

Peterek, Michael. 'IBA Berichtsherbst 1984: Weihrauch, Ausstellungsmarathon, Wende?' *ARCH+* 77 (1984): 4-22.

Pile, Steve. 'Ghosts and the City of Hope.' In *The Emancipatory City?*, edited by Loretta Lees, 210-228. London: Sage, 2004.

Pöschk, Klaus. 'Städtebauliche Umgestaltung und Rekonstruktion des Wohngebietes "Arkonaplatz" in Berlin-Mitte.' *Deutsche Architektur* 20/10 (1971): 602-609.

Posener, Julius. 'Stadtbild und Geschichte'. In *Berliner Bauwochen*, edited by Hermann Wegner, 51-71.

Preuss, Evelyn. 'The Collapse of Time: German History and Identity in Hubertus Siegert's *Berlin Babylon* (2001) and Thomas Schadt's *Berlin: Sinfonie einer Großstadt*.' In *Berlin: The Symphony Continues*, edited by Rachel J. Halverson, Kristie A. Foell and Carol Anne Costabile-Heming, 120-142. Berlin: Walter de Gruyter, 2004.

Rainbird, Sean. 'Berlin Works.' In *Tacita Dean. Berlin Works*, edited by Mark Godfrey and Tacita Dean, 6-11. St Ives: Tate, 2005.

Rheinsberg, Raffael. *Botschaften: Archäologie eines Krieges*. Berlin: Frölich & Kaufmann, 1982.

—. *Anhalter Bahnhof*. Berlin: Galerie Gianozzo, 1980.

Riegl, Alois. 'Der moderne Denkmalkultus: Sein Wesen und seine Entstehung.' In *Gesammelte Aufsätze*, 139-184. Vienna: WUV-Universitätsverlag, 1996 [1903].

Rossi, Aldo. *Architecture of the City*. Cambridge, MA: MIT Press, 1984.

Rurup, Reinhard. *Topography of Terror: Gestapo, SS and Reichssicherheithauptamt on the 'Prinz-Albrecht-Terrain'. A Documentation*. Translated by Werner T. Angress. Berlin: Verlag Wilmuth Arenhövel, 1989.

Sander, August. 'Remarks on my Exhibition at the Cologne Art Union." In *The Weimar Republic Sourcebook*, edited by Martin Jay, Edward Dimendberg and Anton Kaes, 645-646. Berkeley: University of California Press, 1994.

Schadt, Thomas. *Berlin: Sinfonie einer Großstadt*. Berlin: Nicolai, 2002.

—. *Das Gefühl des Augenblicks*. Bergisch-Gladbach: Lubbe, 2002.

Schlug, Alexander, *Palast der Republik: Politischer Diskurs und private Erinnerung*. Berlin: BWV Verlag 2007.

Schmidt, Michael. *Berlin: Stadtlandschaften und Menschen*. Berlin: Stapp, 1978.

—. *Berlin-Kreuzberg*. Berlin: Bezirksamt Kreuzberg, 1973.

—. *Berlin nach 45*. Berlin: Nicolai, 2005.

Schwedler, Rolf. *Die Hauptstadt im Aufbau*. Köln: Dt. Verband für Wohnungswesen, Städtebau und Raumplanung, 1957.

Schweitzer, Eva. 'Palast der Republik droht jetzt doch die Abrißbirne.' *Der Tagesspiegel* 4 October 1992.

Seidenstücker, Friedrich. *Von Weimar bis zum Ende: Fotografien aus bewegter Zeit*, edited by Ann and Jürgen Wilde. Berlin: DBT im Bertelsmann, 1999.

Sheringham, Michael. 'Archiving.' In *Restless Cities*, edited by Matthew Beaumon and Gregory Dart, 1-18. London: Verso, 2010.

Siedler, Wolf Jobst. *Die Gemordete Stadt*. Berlin: Siedler, 1993 [1961].

Simmel, Georg. 'The Metropolis and Mental Life.' In *Simmel on Culture*, edited by David Frisby, translated by David Frisby, 174-185. London: Sage, 1997.

Smithson, Robert. 'A Tour of the Monuments of Passaic.' In *The Collected Writings*, 68-74. Berkeley: University of California Press, 1996.

Solomon-Godeau, Abigail. 'Mourning or Melancholia: Christian Boltanski's "Missing House".' *Oxford Art Journal* 21/2 (1998): 3-20.

Sonne, Wolfgang. 'Specific Intentions – General Realities: On the Relation between Urban Forms and Political Aspirations in Berlin during the 20th Century.' *Planning Perspectives* 7 (2004): 283-310.

Steiner, Henriette and Steiger, Uta. 'Introduction.' In *Memory Culture and the Contemporary City*, edited by Henriette Steiner, Uta Steiger and Andrew Webber, 1-15. Basingstoke: Palgrave Macmillan, 2009.

Stewart, Janet. 'Das Kunsthaus Tacheles: The Berlin Architectural Debate of the 1990s in Micro-Historical Context.' In *Recasting German Identity: Culture, Politics and Literature in the Berlin Republic*, edited by Frank Finlay and Stuart Taberner, 50-66. Rochester: Camden House, 2002.

Stimmann, Hans. *Die gezeichnete Stadt. Die Physiognomie der Berliner Innenstadt in Schwarz- und Parzellenplänen*, Berlin: Nicolai, 2002

Till, Karen. *The New Berlin. Memory, Politics. Place*. Minneapolis: University of Minnesota Press, 2005.

Ullmann, Gerhard. '10 Fragen an Janos Frecot.' *Berliner Kunstblatt* 64 (1989): 13.

Virilio, Paul. 'The Overexposed City.' In *The Blackwell City Reader*, edited by Gary Bridge and Sophie Watson, 441-444. Oxford: Blackwell, 2002.
Vostell, Wolf. 'Die Schildkröte.' In *Mythos Berlin Concepte*, edited by Eberhard Knödler-Bunte, 104-105. Berlin: Verlag Ästhetik und Kommunikation, 1986.

Ward, Janet. 'Berlin, the Virtual, Global City.' *Journal of Visual Culture* 3/2 (2004): 239-256.
—. 'Kracauer versus the Weimar film-city.' In *Peripheral Visions: The Hidden Stages of Weimar Cinema*, edited by Kenneth S. Calhoon, 21-37. Detroit: Wayne State University Press, 2001a.
—. *Post-Wall Berlin. Borders, Space and Identity*. London: Routledge, 2011.
—. *Weimar Surfaces*. Berkeley: University of Califonia Press, 2001b.
Ward, Simon. 'Encountering Lateness in Postunification Berlin.' *New German Critique* 42/2 (2015): 115-135.
—. 'Representing "Normality": Architecture in Berlin.' In *German Culture, Politics, and Literature into the Twenty-First Century: Beyond Normalization*, edited by Stuart Taberner and Paul Cooke, 75-88. Rochester: Camden House, 2006a.
—. 'Sites of Memory, Sites of the Imagination: Monumental and Urban Space.' In *Imagining the City, volume 2*, edited by Christian Emden, Catherine Keen and David Midgley, 241-262. Oxford: Peter Lang, 2006b.
Warnke, Stephanie. *Stein gegen Stein: Architektur und Medien im geteilten Berlin 1950-1970*. Frankfurt am Main: Campus, 2009.
Webber, Andrew. *Berlin in the Twentieth Century*. Cambridge: Cambridge University Press, 2007.
Wenders, Wim. 'That's Entertainment.' In *Emotion Pictures: Reflections on the Cinema*, 93-99. London: Faber & Faber, 1989.
—. 'The Urban Landscape from the Point of View of Images.' In *The Act of Seeing: Essays and Conversations*, 93-101. London: Faber and Faber, 1997.
Wilson, Emma. *Alain Resnais*. Manchester: Manchester University Press, 2006.
—. 'Material Remains: Night and Fog.' *October* 112 (2005): 89-110.
Wohnungswesen, Senatsverwaltung Bau- und. *Berliner Bauwochen 1960*. Berlin: Internationaler Industriespiegel, 1960.
Wüst, Ulrich. *Fotografien*. Berlin: Fotogalerie Berlin-Friedrichshain, 1986.

Young, James. *The Texture of Memory*. London: Yale University Press, 1993.

Zache, Manfred. 'Modernisierung im Stadtgebiet Prenzlauer Berg.' *Deutsche Architektur* 23/6 (1973): 354-357.

Filmography

Carow, Heiner, *The Legend of Paul and Paula* (East Germany, 1973, 105 mins).
Kahane, Peter, *The Architects* (East Germany, 1990, 110 mins).
Sander, Helke, *The All-Round Reduced Personality* (West Germany, 1978, 98 mins).
Schadt, Thomas, *Berlin. Symphony of a Great City* (Germany, 2002, 77 mins).
Thome, Rudolf, *Chamissoplatz* (West Germany, 1980, 112 mins).
Wenders, Wim, *Far Away, So Close* (Germany, 1993, 140 mins).
Wenders, Wim, *Summer in the City* (West Germany, 1970, 116 mins).
Wenders, Wim, *Wings of Desire* (West Germany, 1987, 128 mins).
Wolf, Konrad, *Solo Sunny* (East Germany, 1980, 100 mins).

List of Illustrations

on to the forecourt, the first thing that always strikes one's eye is the advertisement for the telegraph factory Töpffer & Son on the back side of a firewall of a house in the Köthener Strasse.'

18. Installation on the Breite Strasse for the 2012 city anniversary, 'Grund zum Feiern'. Photograph: Simon Ward.

19. Juan Garazaibal, 'Memoria Urbana', Bethlehemkirchplatz, Berlin, 2012. Photograph: Simon Ward.

20. Note discovered at the site of the former Palace of the Republic, with the hand of the book's author (2009) Photograph: Simon Ward.

Index